FORCED OUT

Kevin Maxwell

Forced Out

A Detective's Story of Prejudice and Resilience

GRANTA

Granta Publications, 12 Addison Avenue, London W11 4QR

First published in Great Britain by Granta Books in 2020

References to websites were correct at the time of writing.

A CIP catalogue record for this book is available from the British Library.

9 8 7 6 5 4 3 2 1

ISBN 978 1 84627 680 4
eISBN 978 1 84627 682 8

www.granta.com

Typeset in Bembo by Avon DataSet Ltd, 4 Arden Court, Arden Road, Alcester, Warwickshire B49 6HN
Printed and bound by CPI Group (UK) Ltd, Croydon CR0 4YY

Abraham Lincoln said: 'All that I am, or hope to be, I owe to my angel mother.' I owe everything, including my life, to my beautiful, beloved mother, Annie Maxwell (née Johnson). I dedicate this book to her and all those like her who 'keep on keepin' on' in the face of adversity.

Change will not come if we wait for some other person or if we wait for some other time. We are the ones we've been waiting for. We are the change that we seek.

Barack Obama

Contents

Author's Note

On a summer's afternoon, I fell ill and collapsed at Heathrow Airport. At the time I was working as a detective in the counter terrorism command at London's Metropolitan Police, having transferred as a detective from the criminal investigation department at Greater Manchester Police. Afterwards, my life and how I saw the world around me changed. I began to think about how the culture in policing impacted communities when it came to crime and terrorism, and the effect prejudice and discrimination had on staff. I was forced to speak out, but it came with devastating consequences.

Forced Out is my account of what happened in the years leading up to my illness, as well as during and after it. It is about making sense of my eleven years on the Force, and finding closure so that I can embrace the present. We consider America to have a terrible record for racism in the police, without acknowledging what is going on closer to home, in Britain. Brutality, racism and the denial of civil liberties in the UK simply don't receive the same sort of scrutiny.

I hope this book will contribute to changing that.

PART ONE

1

Against All Odds

In July 1981, three months after my third birthday, riots broke out in my neighbourhood, Toxteth, one of Britain's most deprived urban areas. A former royal chase, it is now an inner-city part of Liverpool, within walking distance of the city centre and the banks of the River Mersey.

Like my parents – a white Liverpool Irish mother and a black West Indian father – immigrants from all over the world had flocked to Liverpool for a better life. Some came to Britain after it had colonised their countries. Others came after defending the country during the Second World War, to help rebuild the nation. For so many tired feet, 'home' was my city. Liverpool's Chinese community is the oldest in Europe and its black community the oldest in the UK. Liverpool, Britain's biggest former slave port and birthplace of the Beatles, was a multicultural melting pot, a hub of people who looked different, spoke differently and even smelt different.

Many settled in Toxteth because of its proximity to the city centre and the seafront. But over the years the culturally diverse communities in and around Toxteth had faced prejudice, hostility and misdirected anger. By the time of the Toxteth riots, the hundreds of mainly black, brown, and poor white people had

had enough of being over-policed, criminalised and forgotten by the British establishment.

I was only a young child, but I have some vivid memories of the riots. I watched as smoke billowed and cops jumped out of Black Marias (the big police vans used to transport prisoners) dressed in traditional helmets and tunics, carrying thick wooden truncheons and plastic riot shields. Rioters were chased around my estate and, when they were caught, retribution was swift and brutal.

The riots were some of the worst urban riots anywhere in the world during the twentieth century, and the first time British police used incapacitant spray on the mainland to control civil unrest.

You would have thought that witnessing this so early on in my life would have turned me against the police, like so many other young men – especially young black and brown men – growing up in deprived areas. But it didn't.

I was born in 1978, two months before my mum's forty-second birthday. I was her eleventh and last child – she had her own football team – and a surprise pregnancy for her and my family. Mum was pregnant at the same time as one of my elder sisters, and my nephew was born a couple of months after I was. Like all of my siblings, I was mixed-race. My mother was white, with long brown hair and piercing blue eyes flecked with green. I was a brown-skinned, brown-eyed boy, but I remember being proud when I spotted that we had exactly the same ears.

A week after my arrival in this world, I was taken to the family home at 11 Falkner Place. The house was one of the biggest on the housing estate. It had four bedrooms with bunk beds, and a garden with two swings and a see-saw, which stood in the shadows of two enormous trees that rose high above a black wooden fence. We even had a free-standing fruit machine in the kitchen for all the kids to play on, though it didn't swallow the money Mum gave us to slot in as there was no lock on the cash box. We weren't allowed to gamble!

There was a real community spirit on the Falkner housing estate, with regular street parties to celebrate national occasions. Adults kept an eye on one another's children. The estate was the backdrop to a very happy, fulfilled childhood. I loved life. I loved my family, I loved my house. I loved my friends. I loved my school. I loved my teachers. I loved church. I even loved my goldfish. I adored my mum. I just never felt a lack of love. There's hardly a childhood photo where I'm not smiling.

My love of the iconic blue uniform was evident very early on. I insisted that any toys bought for me for birthdays, Christmas and Easter were police-themed Lego. For my fifth birthday, my mum bought me my first bike. It was decorated in police stickers and accompanied by a *CHiPs*-style motorcycle helmet, from the famous American cop show. I was elated. I was obsessed with, seduced by, the police force; I was a little boy who wanted nothing so much as to 'protect and serve'.

Every spare moment I had as a child was spent at home, building my Lego police stations or watching American cop shows. My favourites were *Cagney & Lacey*, *T. J. Hooker*, and *Hill Street Blues* with Sergeant Esterhaus's 'Hey, let's be careful out there'. I named every Lego officer I had after characters from *The Bill*.

I drew the ranks of the police onto an A4 sheet of paper to cut out and glue to my Lego people, so that everyone knew the chain of command – because of course I had the structure of the police figured out, even in the days before Wikipedia. I knew how many ranks a constable had to climb before becoming a chief constable: nine (constable, sergeant, inspector, chief inspector, superintendent, chief superintendent, assistant chief constable, deputy chief constable and chief constable). I knew that if you were a detective, that title went in front of your rank up to chief superintendent only. I knew that in London the ranks differed in name after chief superintendent (the sixth rank) and that there were two more in the capital than in other UK forces, making it eleven: commander, deputy assistant commissioner, assistant commissioner, deputy commissioner and, at the very top of the Force, commissioner.

My brother had taught me the phonetic alphabet from A to Z, Alpha to Zulu (so I finally worked out what the British cop show *Juliet Bravo* was all about). With my new-found knowledge, I read the number plates of the cars I saw on my estate and pretended I was undercover, the only person privy to a secret one-man operation, keeping an eye on my neighbourhood.

To me, fed on pop culture, kept safe and happy by a loving mother and never running into any trouble, the police were the bastion of justice and equality. I so desperately wanted to be *one of them* and couldn't wait to grow up to fulfil my dream of working for the Force.

Three months after getting my first bike, the man I knew as my father died, aged forty-seven. He was a big man with skin much darker than my own. He didn't live with us, but instead lived around the corner in his own home. He liked to dip his toast in tea and got as much pleasure out of feeding me Fox's Golden Crunch cream biscuits as I got from eating them. My mum never cohabited with anyone again, opting to raise her young children on her own. She dedicated her life to her family and her Roman Catholic faith.

Mum liked to remind my older brothers that there was one man in the house, and it was her. She was the boss. She had to be, if she was going to keep so many young people in check. She was a disciplinarian, but a loving and warm woman. I know she did her utmost with what she had, which wasn't much. Our faces were always clean and our stomachs always full. She went out of her way to help others too. Sometimes she'd cook enough food, like Irish stew and West African dishes, to share with neighbours on the estate who couldn't afford to eat properly.

In 1985, the on-off riots that had caused such unrest on the estate finally came to an end. I'd spent four years watching my estate burn. Though I didn't understand the full implications at the time, I knew many people were saying that the police were wrong in how they had dealt with the community. Whilst at my local church, where I served as an altar boy, I became aware that the Roman Catholic Archbishop of Liverpool, Derek Worlock, criticised the police for their 'overzealous and provocative tactics',[1] which included drumming batons on riot shields. Community leaders claimed that the Force regarded anyone who was black as a criminal, and acted accordingly.

But anger begets anger. In October 1985, for example, Constable Keith Blakelock became isolated from his colleagues during the Broadwater Farm Riots in London and was hacked to death. It was a horrific murder that left much hate in the air.

The working classes of Toxteth felt divided and desperate. There were barely any jobs and there was very little hope. Those who were lucky enough to be employed did manual work like cleaning, as my mum did at World Friendship House, a hostel for overseas students in Liverpool. Those who weren't so lucky were left with scant options. Poor, bored and disillusioned, these communities demanded action. The police were a symbol of the state they felt had abandoned them, so they were an easy target. But the police were also the state's enforcers, and mistrust towards them was often justified. Young black men in particular felt the brunt of the 'sus laws', which were aimed at 'suspected' persons 'loitering' with intent to commit an indictable offence, contrary to Section 4 of the Vagrancy Act 1824. 'Loitering' and 'suspected' were defined by the police, and there was no need for a victim or witness.

In the wake of the riots, the British Conservative Cabinet recommended that Prime Minister Margaret Thatcher abandon Liverpool altogether as a lost cause, a 'managed decline'.[2] The prime minister placed the blame firmly on the shoulders of the parents of Liverpool, saying: 'Parents, and all citizens, have a duty both to teach the principle of law and order and to see that it is upheld.'[3] She even ordered an official investigation into allegations that youngsters in my area were being trained in 'anti-police methods' at a youth training centre run by the Workers Revolutionary Party. Mistrust and fear crackled through the community, sparking the riots, and it took four years before the flames were dampened.

The year following the riots, my friends and I explored our housing estate. Many buildings were still burnt out and empty. People were starting to leave the estate, but those deserted buildings just made me, as a young boy, more fond of it. They were places to explore.

Abandoned and derelict houses were my favourites. 'Bombdies', we called them, from the bombed-out houses of the past war. With the boarding ripped off so many of the houses and no running water or electricity, only a glimmer of sunlight would shine through on the broken detritus of former happy homes. I felt keenly that each one had its own story, and I wanted to know them all. I think these cast-off shells from the riots were where my investigative skills were born!

As a young explorer, I was intrigued by everything. When my friends and I got stung by nettles as we played, I'd watch the older kids use dock leaves to get rid of the swelling caused by their stings. It was fascinating. We could be stung one minute and medicated the next, without needing to go to a hospital for once. I wasn't clumsy, but my explorations did often have consequences and I had my fair share of tetanus shots at Myrtle Street Children's Hospital. If I wasn't falling off a wall or being bitten by an unleashed dog my friends had provoked, I was falling down a manhole someone had uncovered to sell for scrap, sitting in the sewer, and waiting to be rescued by the local fire brigade.

Once, when I was walking along Myrtle Street to my house behind a much older white couple, I heard them describe Toxteth as 'Niggerland'. I had no idea how terrible a slur this was. As kids on the estate, we often repeated words we'd heard adults say in the city without really knowing what they meant. 'Nigger' and 'Nig-Nog' came up a lot. I once overheard a joke, which I repeated to my mixed-race friends in the corner of the school playground: 'Why are black people so tall? Because their knee grows!' They found it hilarious. We took on racist nicknames without understanding that they were racist. One of my brothers was small, so he was 'the Chink'. One of my sisters had frizzy hair, so she was 'the Golliwog'. One of my brothers had curly hair instead of Afro hair, a bit like a Sri Lankan, so he was 'the Paki'. (Despite the fact that Sri Lanka, India and Pakistan are all different countries, we applied 'Paki' to all of them.) And me? I was 'the Bajan'.

When I was eight years old – old enough to understand – Mum sat me down on the bench in our back room and told me why the other kids called me 'the Bajan'.

I had a different father to my siblings. My father was from Barbados, where the people are known as Bajans as well as Barbadians. Mum was separated and my father's wife had died from cancer some years before my birth, so when they fell in love, they weren't hurting anyone. My father had wanted Mum and me to live with him. He had four children – three boys and a girl – from his previous marriage. But going off with my father and me was never an option for my mother. I was to stay with her and the only family I knew and loved, my older five brothers and five sisters.

My father subsequently met another woman and had a child with his new wife a year after I was born, so he had six children altogether. I never felt the lack of a father. I had male role models in my five older brothers, who I looked up to and who looked out for me. I knew my siblings also lived fatherless lives, so it didn't feel like a stigma. And my mother loved me as much as two parents would.

My older brothers shaped my understanding of masculinity, but I also knew I was different to them. I was keener on playing 'doctors and doctors' than 'doctors and nurses'. I saw my brothers and their friends with girls, but I was more interested in the boys on my estate. I sensed that Mum knew I was different too, but she never made a fuss about it. I was encouraged to be myself and experiment, even trying on my sisters' make-up! I was never told to stop acting in a certain way nor forced to play with boys' toys. I was the second of Mum's children to be gay. One of my older sisters had come out as a lesbian, and her sexuality caused her much pain and suffering. Mum was determined that I shouldn't feel the same anguish, and so I grew up knowing only acceptance of my sexuality.

In 1989, when I was in my last year of primary school at St Saviours, there was a major football game in the Hillsborough Stadium in Sheffield. Liverpool were playing Nottingham Forest as part of the FA Cup semi-final. What happened on that day in April is now infamous. There was a crush in the pens where Liverpool fans were standing; 96 football supporters died and 766 were injured, the worst sporting disaster in British history. It's only recently that we have the full story of what happened, following the report from the Hillsborough Independent Panel chaired by the Church of England Bishop of Liverpool, James Jones.[4] Shortly before kick-off, in an attempt to ease overcrowding outside the entrance turnstiles, the police match commander had ordered an exit gate to be opened. This decision led to an influx of more supporters into already overcrowded pens, and the crush became fatal.

Following the deaths and injuries, the police fed false stories to the press, claiming that hooliganism on the part of drunk Liverpool supporters was the root cause of the disaster. The *Sun* newspaper, under the headline 'The Truth', reported that Liverpool fans urinated on officers, pickpocketed the dead victims and prevented the brave cops from giving the kiss of life to some of the victims. This was the information they'd been given by the police, and it was a total lie.

It was a turning point for my city's attitude towards the press and police, and to this day you can't buy a copy of *The Sun* in Liverpool. Only in 2012 did the Hillsborough Independent Panel discover that any notes from the investigation that reflected badly on the South Yorkshire Police had been deleted from more than a hundred statements. The bodies of those killed had even been tested for alcohol, to find a reason to blame them. The panel concluded that 41 of the 96 who died could have been saved. Hillsborough remains one of the most jarring tragedies in Liverpool's recent history. It led my aunt to ask me why I wanted to join the police. What could I say?

I didn't want to be one of those people who hated the police. I didn't want to give up on my dream. I wanted to help people who couldn't help themselves, and believed that joining the Force was the best way to do this. No matter what I saw, no matter what I heard, something inside me made me feel compelled to serve. I wanted to be one of those good guys.

Just after the Hillsborough disaster, Liverpool City Council issued a compulsory relocation order, informing the residents of my estate that all the houses would be demolished to make way for the new Liverpool Women's Hospital. Despite the riots, my neighbourhood was still a close-knit community, and now people were to be displaced to areas unfamiliar and often hostile to them. Many argued that the riots were the true reason for this – the establishment wanting to spread all the black people out, disperse the ghetto. But the relocations took time, and families were left in perilous conditions.

As my friends and their families moved out one by one, those who remained on the estate made a 'video nasty' of life on the Falkner, detailing how they had been forgotten by the establishment.[5] The *Liverpool Echo* published a feature on it, with four pictures: one showing a 'warning' to the police: 'Enter at own risk'; another of overgrown trees and gardens; one of rats feeding on rubbish; and the last was of me, sitting happily on a wall (beaming and without a care in the world) with my niece and two friends, above the caption 'Playtime peril: kids out on the streets where manhole covers are missing and rubbish covers the pavements.' The newspaper called us the 'forgotten' residents of 'Stalag Falkner', in reference to German prison camps from the Second World War. The video was organised by staff of the Liverpool 8 Law Centre to help improve conditions for the remaining families. Though my house and others were spotless (my mum was a proud woman), Liverpool's chief of community health, Dr John Ashton, told the paper: 'This estate is really appalling. The residents who remain are living in the most incredible squalor. It is by far the worst I have ever seen.'

My family was the last to go – there were so many of us that they needed to find us a big enough place to live. For a long time, our house on Toxteth was the only occupied building, brightly lit in a field of darkness in the evenings. It was like Hallowe'en every night. When we were finally relocated, we moved to Wavertree, a predominantly white and working-class area.

In spite of this upheaval, my mum continued to be an immensely loving and strong woman. Mum's determination to give her children the attention and room for growth they needed was reflected in one of my early passions – performing. I loved singing, acting and dancing, and would often ask Mum if I could put on a show for her and her friends, or the family members who visited our house, like my aunt Mary, my godmother Alice, or black elders like Uncle Billy. When I performed, I was insistent that my audience sat quietly on the long wooden benches we owned. There would be an interval for them to talk – and refreshments provided! It was a lot of fun, but I also turned out to be pretty good at it, and on 1 December 1991, when I was thirteen, I sang at the Liverpool Philharmonic Hall as part of the annual 'Stars of Tomorrow' talent show. I was dressed in full Stevie Wonder style – false braids and dark sunglasses. 'Stars of Tomorrow' was an opportunity for talented children from the estates to gain confidence in front of a large audience. The county dignitaries, including the lord mayor, mayors of Merseyside and the chief constable of police, were among the audience in the packed hall. The lord mayor, Councillor Trevor Smith, wrote at the front of the show's programme: 'Liverpool has all too frequently been the subject of misleading publicity and I hope that the national media will see the show and will then appreciate the verve and talent that exists amongst the young people of our great city.' It seemed as if we were finally moving on from the riots and the horrors of Hillsborough.

At the very back of the programme for 'Stars of Tomorrow' I noticed an advert for Merseyside Police, with four pictures of ethnic minority officers: a black man, an East Asian woman, a South Asian man and a woman who looked mixed-race. It read: 'They all belong to one race . . . the race against crime[!]'

It went on:

> The men and women of the Merseyside Police Service form an essential part of community life. In order to tackle crime and racism effectively, policing requires proper representation from all sectors of the community. That's why in the race against crime the Merseyside Police Service is actively looking to recruit Black, Asian and Chinese officers, who are currently under represented [sic] within the service.

I was so hooked on the advert, that I scribbled down the number for police recruitment – although I was of course much too young to join, I decided that I would call them as soon as I was old enough – and nearly missed my call to perform 'I Just Called to Say I Love You'; which would have been embarrassing with an audience of nearly two thousand people. I liked singing, but it just didn't match my desire to become a policeman.

In July 1993, I signed with a television agency in London, Cheryl Standford, and my first paid role, in April 1994, was in *The Bill*, the television programme I had watched and obsessed over all those years before. It was fate, I thought. In the 5 December 1993 programme for the Philharmonic, I saw three of the same police officers again (joined by two others, also of colour) under the headline 'Uniformly we're all blue[!]' I too wanted to be blue.

At Childwall Comprehensive School, the boys I played with were all white. My friends of colour from my old housing estate had gone to other secondary schools in Toxteth, like Shorefields. There was a relative of my nephew's at Childwall and one or two other mixed-race boys, but they were in different classes to me. The year I joined the seniors, one of my classmates was the daughter of Liverpool's so-called militant Labour leader, Derek Hatton, who intrigued my mum. Derek became well known at my school, because of the police raids on his home just a few hundred yards away.

After arriving at Childwall from Toxteth, I was put in the 'library' class until assessed. Unlike the kids from my new school's local catchment area, who went straight into their classes, as an 'outsider' I had to take English and maths tests in the school library before being placed with my peers. After my assessments, I was placed mostly in the top sets for all my subjects. I was never going to be an academic, but I was a smart boy.

By the time I joined Childwall, I'd been part of the St John Ambulance cadets – the national first aid organisation – for a few years. The brigade dressed very similarly to the police and used the same British army rank structure, so naturally it appealed to me. In fact, the chief constable of Merseyside Police, James Sharples, was the St John county director. Every Monday, I attended the local cadet division, Edge Hill. I was a committed cadet and received a Special Service Shield, awarded to cadets who completed a minimum of 200 hours' voluntary service in the community.

I biked home late one Saturday afternoon after volunteering at Goodison, home to Everton's football club, and was just pausing outside my new house. I was looking up at my bedroom window, which was on the top floor. As the youngest child, I had inherited the room from my older sister, who had inherited it from another older sister, and so on. It had gone from pink to, eventually, floral blue for me, courtesy of my lesbian sister and her partner. It was a treasure trove for my nieces and nephews who visited – I had a basketball net, an old-school green text screen computer, films on VHS tapes, music cassettes, CDs, remote-controlled cars and other thrilling spoils. I even had a pub-sized snooker table and a weight bench, although I used neither (the snooker table was eventually put away to make room for a great big wooden double bed my mum bought me). So naturally I was feeling smug.

I was looking up in this smug state of mind when a police car pulled up alongside me, in the same green-and-blue striped Merseyside Police vehicle that sat amongst my many Corgi cars. There were two officers in it, a man and a woman, and the woman aggressively asked me what I was doing. I explained that I lived at the house and was just looking up at my bedroom. As the officers were about to question me further, Mum came to the front door. They looked from me to her, back to me, and just drove off down the street. I was baffled (though not frightened) by the interaction, but Mum knew what had happened.

At the same time that I was with St John, I was also in the Royal Air Force cadets, known as the Air Training Corps. This organisation prepared young people for life in the military and other services. This meant a second uniform – a light blue-grey, instead of St John's black-and-white.

So now I would go to the air cadet unit, 1966 Wavertree

Squadron, every Tuesday and Friday evening, and not long after some of my friends from school joined. It was even more fun when my friends joined, but the cadets were a disciplined force. Once, when on parade, I laughed at a friend's joke. One of our adult leaders heard me and immediately barked, 'Maxwell, stop laughing or I'll rip your head off and shit down your neck!' Charming, I thought, but I did stop laughing.

One night after air training, still in my uniform (which we wore to and from the cadet unit), I was walking home with Mum up Smithdown Road, a well-known street in Liverpool where a lot of the city's students live. We had just got our chicken burger and chips from Jean's chip shop, a treat we'd eat whilst watching television. We were walking arm in arm, as we often did. I was her youngest child, her baby, and we were very affectionate towards each other.

As we were walking past the cemetery where my siblings' father is buried, a police car drove past us, stopped, then reversed, its bright brake lights momentarily blinding us. One of the officers, without acknowledging me, asked Mum: 'Are you okay?' Clearly annoyed, she immediately fired back, 'What do you mean, am I okay? He's my son.' Mum saw what the police were getting at. She had, after all, raised ten mixed-race children before me.

I was too young and naive to understand the nuances of what had happened, or why seeing a brown teenage boy on a bike outside a house, or with a much older white woman in the street, would give the police officers cause for concern. I never thought about the impact of these interactions until adulthood. One of the reasons for that was my mum. She had encouraged me to have a heart as open and generous as hers. I never succumbed to suspicion, fear or hate.

It never occurred to me that I'd be judged by the colour of my skin, with Mum putting such emphasis on the content of my character.

I thrived in my two cadetships, especially at St John Ambulance, where I held the most senior cadet rank as cadet leader (the staff sergeant). I received the Grand Prior award from the Duke of Gloucester, the highest award a cadet can achieve, and on 3 May 1994 I attended the Cadet Reception at Buckingham Palace. I spoke at and compèred the youth presentations at the annual national conferences in Harrogate and Bournemouth, and undertook duties at Arsenal Football Club and Queens Park Rangers alongside the London Paddington division. St John's youth magazine, *The Edge* (run by the St John national headquarters in London), even created an international pen-pal service in my name, 'Maxwell's Pen Pals'.

For the 75th Anniversary of the St John cadets, I was invited to join the planning committee, in order to give everyone the 'benefit of your knowledge and ideas'.[6] I was named Cadet of the Year in 1996, after winning the annual county competition with a presentation entitled 'Drugs, misuse and help', about the things parents can do to help their children. St John's county commissioner Colonel James Egan wrote: 'You have the personality, character, ability and communication skills to convince the panel that you are the only youth capable of representing SJA.'[7]

I'm not listing all these achievements to boast – though, looking back, I am pleased and proud of my adolescent self, especially of becoming one of the Queen's National Young Achievers in 1998; I was pictured in the *Liverpool Echo*, smiling ear to ear, whilst saluting outside Buckingham Palace in my uniform[8] – I'm listing them to give some idea of the astonishment I felt when I went to collect my award and lanyard at the official Cadet of the Year ceremony. The awarding area commander, unprompted, announced to the crowded room: 'By the way, Kevin has won the title on merit and not because of the colour of his skin.'

This was one of those blips. It was like hearing monkey chants and seeing bananas thrown at the black Liverpool football player John Barnes when I was on duty with St John at Anfield.

I learnt to ignore them.

Fundamentally, I was a 'play hard, work hard' kind of youngster. I was never a goody two shoes, not by a long shot, but trouble and me just never hit it off. I had friends who might look to bend rules, but I was the sort of boy who would stand to attention in the living room each night before I went to bed, and salute the television as BBC One played the British national anthem. It was a bit mad, but I didn't care. I was immensely proud. I was doing something different with my life.

In 1993, seventeen days after my fifteenth birthday and the year before I was allowed to officially leave secondary school, a black British teenager named Stephen Lawrence was murdered by a gang of young white men in a racially motivated attack in south-east London.[9] It was horrific, doubly so when details of the police's handling of the case came to light. Again, as with the Hillsborough disaster, we are only now discovering the extent to which the police mishandled this tragic case.

As noted in the 'Macpherson report' – following a public inquiry into matters arising from Stephen's death – officers had committed fundamental errors, like failing to follow obvious leads during the investigation (especially that first 'golden hour' when forensic and other clues are still fresh), but had also failed at the front line of duty: they didn't give Stephen first aid when they reached the scene of the crime (or examine him).[10]

Stephen had received two stab wounds to both sides of his front body, in the right collarbone and left shoulder. The two wounds had severed his axillary arteries, and one also penetrated a lung. It became undeniably obvious that the police had failed the Lawrence family. In a press release, Stephen's parents questioned whether the police 'did not want to get their hands dirty with a black man's blood?'[11] The police denied being racist.

It was as if the universe was telling me: *Don't join the police.*

★

In 1994, having completed mandatory schooling, I started my first job at the Pleasure Island International Festival Park on Liverpool's waterfront. My mum wasn't pleased, as she had wanted me to continue with my education, but I loved working there – the rest of the staff were so much fun and we'd often go out after work, drinking and dancing and generally just enjoying being young. Whilst I worked there, I also set up my own production company and started 'Stars of the Future', Merseyside's biggest variety performance.[12]

After three years the festival park closed, and to my mum's joy I decided to return to education. I started a professional media studies course at Liverpool City College's Faculty of Arts. I had looked to see if there were any police courses I could take before I was eighteen and a half – old enough to officially apply for a job – but there weren't. The closest I came to the police was dressing up as an assistant chief constable for a fancy dress charity night at the Boundary, a local pub where I was now working.

Whilst at college, I applied to study media performance at the University of Salford in Manchester, at the School of Media, Music and Performance, and after an audition was accepted onto the course.

We were encouraged to obtain a theatrical agent, which I wasn't too fussed about, but I didn't want to stand out from my peers. I sent off my performing arts CV to several agencies in London, and ended up being taken on by the renowned Sylvia Young. I soon started to appear in films, on television and on the stage. It was funny, really, because I never considered myself an actor at all. Even after I was cast in an episode of *dinnerladies* and appeared on prime-time television (on 25 November 1999), my ambition never wavered: I just wanted to join the police. Many students at the School of Media, Music and Performance were chasing fame and fortune, but I dreamt of chasing criminals through the back streets of Manchester.

★

That's when my years of dating as a gay man began. I got my heart broken pretty early on; then I went on to date a guy on my course who ended his relationship with his girlfriend to be with me – but he wanted to pretend that we were just friends, and whilst we were on holiday together in Kavos, he said he had to 'go' with girls 'for cover'. I was so devastated that I travelled to Liverpool to see my mum.

Mum was in her bedroom when I arrived, tears running down my face. Immediately concerned, she sat up.

'What's wrong?' she asked.

I froze. I hadn't come out to her yet. Only my university friends knew the truth.

I said I couldn't tell her, because she would disown me. I couldn't risk having the most beautiful person I'd known reject my sexuality and throw me out of her house.

'Don't be silly,' she said. But I couldn't do it. I was too afraid.

Mum got on the phone to one of my sisters in London and told her that something was up with me, but that I wouldn't tell her what. She handed the phone to me. Blunt as usual, my sister said, 'You're upsetting Mum, tell her what's up.'

And so I burst out: 'I'm gay!'

It was out.

'Is that it?' Mum said. She hung up on my sister, wiped my tears and kissed me. She dug around in her purse and pulled out a twenty pound note and a ten pound note.

'I thought you were dying or had killed someone! You're my son. My baby. Now take this and get on the coach to Manchester. Go have a drink on me to celebrate with your gay friends.'

I didn't have to pack my bags. I wasn't being thrown out. With a huge weight lifted off my shoulders, I washed my face in the bathroom and then set out to get the coach to Manchester.

As it sped down the motorway, I cried tears of laughter and joy. I couldn't believe it. I was out. And thirty pounds went a long way back then.

*

The Stephen Lawrence Inquiry was held whilst I was at university. Headed by the former high court judge Sir William Macpherson, it examined Scotland Yard's investigation of Stephen Lawrence's murder, and concluded that the Force was institutionally racist. The Metropolitan Police commissioner, Paul Condon, vehemently denied this.

The BBC reported that senior members of the Black Police Association (BPA) who gave evidence to the Macpherson inquiry said that 'the police should "name and shame" senior officers who are not prepared to act against racism', and that 'the service needs to stamp out what it called a "canteen culture" of racial stereotypes and banter'.[13]

In what was 'an unprecedented admission', and in stark contrast to Condon, David Wilmot, the new chief constable of Greater Manchester Police (GMP), described his Force as 'hav[ing] a problem with internalised racism'.[14] Police chiefs almost never spoke out like this, as it was perceived as undermining public confidence, and I was impressed that he'd dared to do so; it gave me confidence in Manchester. Martin Harding, a chief inspector in Manchester and the most senior black officer in the Force at the time, shared my sentiments, saying he was 'delighted' with Wilmot's comments. Before anything could be done to improve the situation in the police, they first had to admit wrongdoing. A lot of police officers, especially those in London, were furious with Wilmot. In response to their denial of racism, Macpherson said: 'There is a reluctance to accept that it is there, which means that it will probably never be cured.'

At the time that Wilmot spoke out, Manchester's black and Asian communities were suffering high levels of racially motivated hate crimes and harassment.

An estimated 21,000 became victims that year, and each year after. Those were the people I wanted to help, and I was convinced that I could do it as part of Wilmot's fairer, improved Force in Manchester. I believed that the police could and would change. In his report, Macpherson said, 'The need to re-establish trust between minority ethnic communities and the police is paramount . . . seeking to achieve trust and confidence through a demonstration of fairness will not in itself be sufficient. It must be accompanied by a vigorous pursuit of openness and accountability.' I was going to help the police by joining it. I applied to join the Police Service of England and Wales at Greater Manchester. Having studied in Manchester – and still living and working there part-time – it made sense for me to apply to this Force rather than my home one in Liverpool (Merseyside). I also didn't want to put myself in an awkward position in future, if I were called to the home of someone I knew.

My application form, which was received by the Force eighteen days after the Race Relations (Amendment) Act 2000 came into being, asked: 'Why do you wish to join the Police Service?'[15]

Not having to think about the answer, I wrote: 'Since an early age I have always been passionate about the police service and the work officers do in solving crimes and helping others. I am very ambitious[,] knowing I can gain a lot, but equally know I have to give a lot.' I posted it and crossed my fingers. It took around eighteen months to get into the Force; I would have to be patient.

Not long after, I started a job managing one of Manchester's gay super nightclubs, Paradise Factory. My best friend, Dan, and the rest of my friends from university used to joke that I must have been the only manager of a gay nightclub that didn't take drugs. Smoking and drugs never appealed to me. When I was young and curious, my lesbian sister once caught me trying to inhale from a cigarette she'd left on top of a fireplace at her home, and my punishment was being forced to eat the rest of it, which cured me for good (my mum didn't smoke, and smoking wasn't allowed in our house.) Whenever I was at a party in Manchester with my friends and suspected someone was doing drugs, I would simply grab my coat, make my excuses and leave.

My friends never took drugs in front of me or suggested that they were doing any, but I wasn't naive.

I was usually the only one that wasn't taking 'recreational' drugs. It was an unofficial agreement between us. In fact, the Force had no official guidelines for what officers should do when their family or friends took recreational drugs. There was just one reference in the *Blue Book* – an internal 'how to' for incidents and situations in an officer's personal life, which was used by all the country's Forces, though each had its own version; in London's *Blue Book*, Commissioner Kenneth Newman said that in such a situation an officer should leave, and take no further action.

I'd already trained myself to do that.

Despite the drug drawback, I was active on the gay club scene. It was whilst out with Dan at Cruz 101, that I met my first proper boyfriend. I didn't pluck up the courage to talk to him until ten minutes before closing. We had been watching each other all night, as we danced and chatted with our respective friends. It was love at first sight for me. As we all collected our coats from the cloakroom, I found out that he was a medical student. Attractive *and* an intellectual. We started dating, and our steady relationship emboldened him to come out to his parents. My world was changing.

But something else happened that marked a change in the world – mine and everyone else's.

Whilst working in the Paradise Factory office during the day, with the radio on in the background, I heard that a tower had collapsed in New York, at the World Trade Centre. In total disbelief, I turned up the volume to listen to the report. It seemed incomprehensible. I called Dan.

We met in the Slug & Lettuce bar on Canal Street. Here, on a big-screen television, we watched the aftermath of the tower's collapse, horrified. Staring at the screen, trying to take it all in, we then watched a plane fly into a second tower. The bar fell silent. I was numb.

Later, as Dan and I packed up our things and walked home solemnly, I was more determined than ever to get into the police.

I sat some simple tests at GMP, along with the other candidates. To become a police officer in Britain, you didn't have to be very academic, or even provide a secondary school certificate. Applicants only had to pass a very simple literacy and numeracy test. I also had to complete eyesight, hearing and fitness tests. After I got through that, I got a letter back from the police inviting me to an interview. I thought my interview went well, when the all-female interviewing panel asked me if I wanted to be a 'poster boy' for the Force. Black and university educated, I was exactly what they were looking for in their police recruitment campaign to get more ethnic minorities into the service.

I was glad they were impressed by me, but a horrible image of me in uniform plastered on a billboard at Liverpool Lime Street train station flashed before my eyes. I didn't want to be a token, and I certainly didn't want to be instantly recognisable.

After the interview, I received a letter telling me I had been accepted. I was actually going to do the job I'd dreamt of for years. I felt like I had won the lottery. Mum was excited too. She was even more proud of me than before, and didn't stop smiling for several days.

I didn't tell my siblings or any of my extended family, nor did I announce it publicly. I did, however, decide that I would tell some of my closest friends, particularly Dan. I arranged to meet him in a bar in Manchester's gay village, as usual. As he entered Tribeca, I had two beers waiting. As he sat down I said to him, 'I got in.'

'Got in where?' he asked, looking at me strangely.

'The police,' I replied, in a low voice.

'Oh, Kevin.'

Dan wasn't the only person to be worried. The rest of my white liberal friends at university were having none of the police's public statements about changing, and they certainly didn't share my vision of hope. They repeatedly warned me about racism and homophobia still being rife in the Force. But I didn't let any of my friends shake my resolve. I knew what I wanted to do with the rest of my life. All that was left for me to do was to learn how to swim and drive.

At primary school, my idea of swimming was walking across the pool in the shallow end, from one side to the other, as quickly as I could. After hearing of my successful application I only had a few weeks to learn how to swim, so I ended up completing eight lessons in a private swimming pool attached to the instructor's house in Prestwich. It was embarrassing wearing armbands and being surrounded by children, but I was a man on a mission. To my surprise, I enjoyed it and soon became a competent swimmer. The driving also went well, and I bought my first car the day after passing my test, a burgundy Renault Clio.

One day, before I was due to start, I received an unexpected phone call from GMP. The woman from recruitment told me that there was a problem with my application and that it might have to be stalled. I couldn't believe it. I hadn't been in trouble with the police, was fairly well educated, had been in two cadet forces, and had passed the interview and preliminary tests. It didn't make sense that there could be any sort of problem, but the woman said she couldn't give me any more information.

That night, I lay on my bed and cried as I watched my dream go out of the window, unable to understand what had happened. The next day, I telephoned GMP and asked if there was anything I could do to help them, but they said no. The woman on the other end of the phone said it was to do with my brother, but said she couldn't tell me anything else.

A couple of days later I received a further phone call from the Force. The woman from HR at headquarters told me that everything was now okay, and it had just been a misunderstanding, but she still wouldn't tell me anything more. She said I would soon receive my start date in the post.

Not long after, I received my joining letter from the police.[16]
I was to be measured for my uniform and allocated the division
I'd work in. I was required, amongst other things, to have two
current vaccination certificates for hepatitis B and tetanus, as well
as details of my blood group. The letter also reassured me that if I
was a member of the Freemasons I wasn't obliged to disclose that
information. It continued: 'As a professional organisation Greater
Manchester Police is committed to being an effective and fair
employer. You should familiarise yourself with the blue leaflet
outlining our philosophy and professional standards strategy
and our equal opportunities policy,' and concluded: 'On your
employment with Greater Manchester Police and on arrival at
Sedgley Park you will become subject to the police codes of
conduct and discipline. These are governed by the Police Act
1964.'

I went to be measured up for my uniform at the police
clothing stores, in Openshaw in east Manchester. On arrival I
stripped down to my underwear with a group of other hopeful
would-be officers, then set about turning the civilian who had
walked through the door into an officer, ensuring every piece of
kit fitted. The uniform and all the equipment – both operational
and ceremonial, including spares, and riot gear with steel toe-
capped boots – were provided for free. Officers only had to
buy their own patrol footwear. The majority of police bought
Magnum boots. I bought Dr. Martens.

I was issued with a traditional helmet, the kind I'd first seen
during the Toxteth riots, and a flat chequered cap, which other
Forces use only when in a police vehicle, but which formed
part of GMP's everyday operational uniform. We looked more
American, especially with our Chicago police department-style
bomber jackets and the US police's side-handled batons.

Dressed in my uniform, I looked in the long mirror.

Against all odds, I had secured my dream.

2

One of Them

Three months after the 9/11 terrorist attacks in New York, on a cold December morning, I reported for duty at GMP's training school in Bury, a looming brick structure with long iron gates. At twenty-three years old, with my recently issued uniform in bags, I was about to cross the threshold of the Sedgley Park training school and fulfil that dream to become *one of them*.

The British prime minister Sir Robert Peel was born in Bury in 1788. When he founded the Metropolitan Police in 1829 (when he was Home Secretary), he said: 'The police are the public and the public are the police.' The police were there to serve the people and not the state. Scotland Yard, as the Metropolitan Police is also known (after the street on which its headquarters was once situated), was the world's first modern police force. It was the blueprint for others across Britain and around the globe, especially those in the British empire and the US. An institution that old has highly symbolic traditions, starting at training.

After meeting our peers and trainers in the school canteen, the new recruits were sent off to change into our brand-new uniforms before meeting in the chapel, with orders to leave our shirts unironed, to signify that we were of the lowest rank. We were then issued with our shoulder numbers. From now on I would be known by a number, to my colleagues and the public alike. Stage 1 of a two-year-long probationer training programme had begun. To become a fully fledged police officer, I would have to complete six stages, which included initial training at Manchester, then National Police Training, then tutelage on patrol, and then independent patrol combined with various two-week courses.

The first week of my induction included learning the rank structure and phonetic alphabet, two things I had memorised with great enthusiasm as a child and which therefore didn't present a challenge to me. I was also issued with my Official Pocket Book. This notebook is a police officer's gospel and his Bible. A7-sized, with a black cover, it is used by an officer to record the details of the incidents they attend; its contents are admissible as evidence in court. The details I wrote down in it would become absolute truth in a court of law; they were unquestionable, because my status gave my word more weight than that of 'mere' citizens. A serious piece of the kit, as long as you didn't look too closely at all the penises officers drew in one another's books.

Printed at the front of the notebook was the caution we would iterate during every arrest: 'You do not have to say anything. But it may harm your defence if you do not mention when questioned something that you later rely on in court. Anything you do say may be given in evidence.'

With this notebook came the power to take a person's liberty and detain him or her against his or her will.

Immediately following the caution was the legal definition of a racist incident: 'Any incident which is perceived to be racist by the victim or any other person.' *Victim.* There was such humanity in this belief in the word of the victim. If anyone perceived an incident to be racist, it was. Simple as that.

In the second week of my initial police training, a memo was posted around the classes, asking for all the 'ethnics' to report at the school chapel the next morning before class. I smiled, cringing from second-hand embarrassment at the bad joke.

The training school normally took in new recruits every five weeks. My intake was one of the biggest in GMP's history, as a direct result of the Labour government's drive to recruit more officers of colour, which meant that a larger number of ethnic minorities than usual had been recruited.

There were a handful of us out of sixty-plus recruits, and I made friends with each of the new officers of colour: one South Asian, one East Asian and the three other black and white mixed-race recruits.

The memo about gathering the 'ethnics' proved to be serious. The leadership wanted a photoshoot for a media campaign, to show the public they were committed to equal opportunities. I could see why this might be an instant public relations hit, but I didn't want to be part of it. I hadn't joined the police to have my face plastered around train stations and shopping centres. The publicity could have put me in danger and jeopardised any future operations I was involved in. I told the press and publicity department that I wasn't doing it and I left, returning to my class.

The photoshoot marked an immediate racial divide between the cops. The police chiefs calling the minority officers for duty half an hour earlier than everyone else led to white officers feeling excluded, especially those who had already perceived the photo op as special treatment. Some were furious. Back in my class, the tension was tangible. Though I had declined to take part in the shoot, I was not excluded from suspicion. I couldn't ignore the quiet exchanges taking place between my white peers in Class A, where I was the only black or mixed-race officer out of approximately fourteen students, and the heaviness that hung in the air. It didn't matter that I didn't want to be singled out. I had been asked to be part of something and they hadn't.

The first two weeks of my training focused on procedural inputs and the Police National Computer (PNC) warning signals, used to identify those potentially carrying firearms (FI), 'mental' people (MN), those 'impersonating' a male or a female (IM or IF) and those carrying contagious diseases (CO), HIV amongst them. The warning signals were used to help officers know who they were dealing with after a stop, and if that person posed a threat.

We also had to learn the Identification Codes. These codes are used by officers to describe the apparent ethnicity of a suspect, including IC1: White European and IC2: Dark European. IC3: Afro-Caribbean was the one most frequently used.

We also received equal opportunities training, learnt the procedure for a grievance – for example, the procedure to follow if you experienced racial discrimination in the Force and how you would go about resolving it – had a presentation on appropriate language, and were given a talk by the internal affairs department suggesting subtle ways to keep ourselves out of trouble.

To become police constables we had to attend the attestation ceremony, presided over by a magistrate on behalf of the Queen. Ours took place in the training school's chapel, as was customary. My colleagues and I stood in smart rows facing the judicial officer and the Union Jack, taking it in turns to swear our allegiance to Her Majesty and all her heirs apparent. We had our police application forms in our hands, which confirmed our status as constables, and showed them to the magistrate whilst being attested. We couldn't speak to one another or sit down during the ceremony. There was nothing to do but stand and wait. Idly, I read over my completed form. On the back were details about my family, including my siblings. By the name of one of my brothers were some notes in pencil. I hadn't written them; they could only have been added by HR or some other department at police headquarters. I squinted at the grey words to make out the note, and my stomach dropped.

My brother had not long ago been arrested for disorderly conduct and police assault.

My cheeks started to burn and I lowered my head, not wanting to betray any emotion. I was about to be sworn in as an officer of the law, yet here was written testimony that my brother had assaulted someone in the same uniform I was proudly standing in. I tried to make sense of what I had just read. My brother was a quiet, passive, unaggressive, small man, not the sort to attack anyone, with or without provocation.

Could it be possible that the police had made a mistake, or mixed him up with someone else? My turn to be sworn in came, and I solemnly approached the magistrate. My colleagues were beaming, but I couldn't share their excitement. I just wanted to leave the chapel and go home.

When I returned to Liverpool that evening, I sat with my mum in the dimly lit family room at the back of our house, for one of our regular chats. I told her what I'd discovered on the back of the form. She just nodded. She knew what had happened.

A month before I had sent off my application to join the police, my brother had been out walking when he was arrested by police in what the paper described as a 'case of mistaken identity'. An officer shouted, 'Steven!' Ignoring the shout, my brother continued walking. The officers, believing that he had been involved in an incident nearby, arrested him, breaking his thumb in the process. Then the officers realised they had made a grave error. Not only was this man not guilty of anything, including the nearby incident they had been investigating – after checking his identification, they learnt his name wasn't even Steven. No wonder he hadn't responded.

My brother wasn't a criminal, or someone threatening in any way. He was a BT engineer who had been with the company for seventeen years at the time of his arrest. He did, however, have brown skin. That was enough of a resemblance to 'Steven' for the officers.

One of the many unwritten rules I learnt soon after becoming a constable was that if an officer lays his or her hands on someone and acts unlawfully – because, say, he or she has the wrong person – the officer should arrest that person anyway, charging them with something like police assault or a public disorder offence. This is to mitigate against any future claims of liability on their or the chief police officer's part. In the eyes of the leadership, this is showing strength on the streets. My brother was duly arrested.

The police had hurt my brother so badly that it took several months for him to recover. Both BT and my brother received damages from Merseyside Police. My brother was compensated for the distress caused to him, and the telecommunications giant was compensated for having one of its employees off work (his broken thumb meant that he didn't have full use of his hand). Had I not glanced down at my form whilst I was waiting to be attested, I might never have found out. The thought of my brother's suffering was upsetting, but it was far from a unique experience.

I later found out Manchester Police had stalled my application to join the service because my brother was in dispute with Merseyside police, seeking justice for what they had done to him. The police had been accused of false imprisonment, assault and malicious prosecution. Merseyside Police never did apologise to my brother, and it was only after reading about him in a local newspaper after I had joined the Force that I learnt that he was dismayed by his ordeal.[1] He never spoke to me about his experience or about my joining the police, and our relationship was never the same.

On the final day of my two-week induction at Greater Manchester, we were given a lesson in the abuse of the warrant card. The warrant card is the gold card for police officers. Without it, we had no power; with it, we could do things we couldn't ordinarily do as citizens, like jump queues, gain free admission to nightclubs, and receive free meals at restaurants like McDonald's.

The card wasn't actually designed to grant the police those powers, but the proof of identity and the authority held by officers when they presented it to a doorman or cashier was intimidating and formidable. Not every officer used it to demand free food. But some did, knowing they could get away with it.

When the first two weeks were over I needed to take my first police procedural exam, in order to progress to Stage 2 of the two-year compulsory training. Those two years would see me in uniform. In those days all officers had to walk or ride the street beats in uniform for the first twenty-four months before they were allowed to move up the ranks or specialise (this is still the case for the majority of today's recruits). Because I scored 80% in my first police exam, I was allowed to move on to the next phase of my training.

I was sent to complete Stage 2 of the police training programme: the fifteen-week compulsory residential course at Bruche, the National Police Training Centre in Warrington that trained all recruits in the North West England police (Cheshire, Cumbria, Greater Manchester, Lancashire and Merseyside, and West Yorkshire) and others like the Isle of Man Constabulary. There were always three intakes at the Cheshire training school, with about a hundred and fifty officers in each one. Officers moved up an intake every five weeks until they completed the fifteen-week cycle.

The site was a former American army facility hidden amongst suburban housing. I was on intake 10/01, along with another 140 students, divided into eight classes. It had opened its doors in 1946, and was the largest (in terms of student population) of the six Foundation Training Centres in England and Wales. The Probationer Foundation Course was introduced nationally in 1998, and its purpose was to develop the skills, abilities, knowledge and qualities of judgment necessary for the effective performance of the police in our society. The working facilities included an assembly hall, classrooms, a mock courtroom, a mock station, a training support unit, a gymnasium, a recreation hall and a swimming pool. There was also a training village called Sandford – a mock village designed specifically for trainee police officers to role-play routine police activities. Upon arrival at the government training site, each recruit was allocated a private room in the residential blocks, with male and female officers separated. The label on my door read: 'This room is allocated to – Name: K Maxwell, Class: A6, Force: GMP.' However, someone had flipped it over and written: 'Name: Bradley, Class: A6, Force: S Club 7 (after Bradley McIntosh, the sole black member of the British pop group). There was no toilet in the room, but there was a sink, which most recruits used as a urinal as well as the place where they brushed their teeth.

The other seventeen trainees in my class were white, thirteen men and four women. I had two class trainers, both female, and one of them a woman of colour – the only one.

We had to call our trainers 'Staff' – '*Yes, Staff, No Staff*' – and stand when they entered the room. In the canteen, as we prepared to start our careers, two of my peers complained that they didn't like women teaching them: as far as they were concerned, training officers was a man's role.

We were welcomed to Bruche by our trainers, then given a rundown of the rules of the centre, like wearing our hats outside the class at all times and walking around smartly dressed. My fifteen weeks at Bruche were crammed with new lessons. We watched *Police* – Roger Graef's 1982 fly-on-the-wall television documentary, in which the BBC followed Thames Valley Police, showing how badly officers treated a victim of rape, to learn about sexual assault investigations and how not to treat victims of sexual violence.

We were given a lesson in conflict resolution; for example, when attending domestics, the partner who called the police would often turn on officers when they tried to arrest their other half. We were told not to call women 'love', or any other patronising endearment, unless we wanted a thump. We attended thefts at the mock shop, road traffic accidents on the mock street and practised giving evidence at the mock court. The victims and witnesses were played by police and civilians.

There was more equal opportunities training too. We had to cover community race relations, racism awareness, and the controversial stop and search power introduced under the Police and Criminal Evidence Act (PACE) 1984. PACE instructed the police on how to treat people fairly, especially visible minorities, with respect and within the law. The police had resisted PACE coming into law because, as they saw it, it got in the way of them doing their job effectively, that is, arresting the 'bad people'. The leaders said stop and search was targeted and intelligence-led, but the reality was very different. It exerted social control. Section 1 of PACE was about the police suspecting you had drugs on you, or a weapon, or stolen property, or something used to commit a crime; the officer would have to have 'reasonable' cause to believe he or she would find something. But it targeted and marginalised black and minority ethnic people, like the sus law had done previously, through what the police called a 'fishing trip': that is, when you stop and search people in the hope of finding something. Police officers (mostly white) relied on a 'gut feeling', which often manifested around people of colour.

There is a fundamental difference between intelligence-led policing and racial profiling: one is specific and the other is not. But when officers are taught that dangerous knife-carriers are overwhelmingly black, and that potential terrorists are overwhelmingly brown, the two tend to blur.

For many minorities, their first interaction with the police is through stop and search, either from their own experience or that of a family member, and for many of my colleagues, policing was their first real interaction with people of colour. Many came from the shires. For some, their only experience of 'ethnics' was at the local takeaway on a weekend. They understood they had to arrest 'bad people', but a lot of them came with a preconceived idea of what a bad person looked like.

At Bruche, we learnt about the torture and murder of the young black girl, Victoria Climbié, who was failed by the police and other authorities, like the social services, in the lead-up to her horrific death. We learnt about the Human Rights Act, and how it affects policing. We had lesson after lesson about equality, diversity and social cohesion – which sounds good, but many officers were annoyed and irritated by the very fact that they were being told how to police non-white people, which then undermined the very training they'd just had. Race is a highly emotive subject, particularly in the police. So when officers see the word 'race', they become resistant to it.

The training had the accidental result of teaching white officers that black and Asian minorities *were* different and *would* cause trouble. Minorities, especially black people, were the reason there were all these equality laws and policies for the police to deal with and implement. Minority people were an 'issue' that needed controlling.

The personal protective equipment we carried, like the baton, was vital to our survival, but we were also taught unarmed hand-to-hand combat, and other self-defence techniques. The macho cops went in fists first, but I was more restrained. I thought that words were our best weapon. Some officers had to be pulled back by our self-defence trainers (also cops), as they got too 'hands on'.

When we were taught where on the body to hit someone, our instructors divided the body into zones using the traffic-light system: red, amber and green. 'Red' was any part of the body that could receive a fatal blow, i.e. the head and vital organs. Police officers are taught about deadly force and its use as part of standard self-defence training, and we were taught specific lines to include in statements after using force on a member of the public. For example, if we had intended to kill a person with a baton, then we had to say so. This sounds astonishing, but if an officer hits someone and they die and the officer later claims that they didn't mean to kill the victim, it is seen as undermining their actions, and leaves them open to criticism. Instead, we had to say that we had used deadly force because we were in fear of our life or the life of another.

There was psychological training too, to prepare officers for a career dealing with high-pressure situations. One of the exercises involved jumping into the school's swimming pool to save a brick which had sunk to the bottom, as if it were a person. Other physical training included running down streets, and standing for a long time hobbled together with our riot shields. There were regular beep test runs, which I enjoyed. I always placed first or second in these runs, my colleague from the Cheshire Constabulary being the only person who could keep up with or beat me.

We were taught how to arrest people, file reports and give evidence: the backbone of policing. We practised radio terminology, 'urgent assistance' (backup) being the most important phrase we'd learn. We continued to role-play traffic scenarios – both accidents and the issuing of tickets for motoring offences – in which our trainers acted as the complainants, injured persons or witnesses. We'd assess the situation, gather all the witness statements and work out what had happened.

We learnt how to write up our notes in the pocket notebook, which was regularly assessed. At any incident, the officer would have to write up the time of day, the location, what had taken place, and the personal details of any victims or witnesses, together with any action taken, such as an arrest. Since the information entered is admissible in court, officers could use the notes in the pocket notebook to 'refresh' their memory whilst giving evidence, and to support any statement they may have written down.

Finally, we learnt drill, with lots of boot-bulling (a military term for polishing) to make our boots shiny. I was familiar with drill from my two cadet forces, but in the police it was very militarised, as if we were being prepared for war. Having lots of ex-military and prison-service types in my class and intake, like my ex-army peer drill instructor (a student nominated by our class to lead the informal drill training, something which all classes did), must have helped.

Some of my colleagues in the accommodation blocks would stand in front of the mirror in the evening in their underwear and their body armour, with baton and cuffs attached to their belt, and say: 'Who's the daddy?' Some meant it tongue-in-cheek, but others were clearly experiencing a thrill of power from the uniform and equipment.

As I only lived twenty miles away from the school, I often travelled home after our daily law classes to see my mum in Liverpool, and returned late at night to sleep. On one occasion I opted not to go home, staying in my room to revise for my weekly law knowledge test. It was early evening, and my colleagues had entered the communal landing after a trip to the training school bar, whilst one white cop blasted out R & B music in the next room to mine. Someone shouted: 'Turn the coconut music off!' There was an outburst of laughter, some slammed doors, and a few voices started whispering.

Coconut. I'd heard the term before. Black people who joined the police were known as 'coconuts': black on the outside, but white on the inside. Though the officer who shouted it didn't know that I hadn't made my usual trip to Liverpool and that I was still in my room, some of the officers who hadn't gone to the bar knew. Someone knocked on my door, and when I opened it, the white officer who'd shouted the word was standing outside. He took a step towards me, and said: 'You heard what I just said, didn't you?'

'Yes,' I said, and closed the door.

I didn't know what else to do. Was I supposed to hit him?

Shout at him? I heard him walk into the room to the left of mine. I sat at my desk staring at the lamp, and listened to him and some others burst into another fit of hysterics. Uncomfortable and unsettled, I left the floor.

I went to sit in the classroom to think. En route, I saw my white class trainer. I sat down with her, to tell her what had happened. Taking solace in the privacy of the room, I confessed that I didn't know whether to quit the police then and there and return home to Liverpool, because I didn't feel comfortable in such an unaccepting environment. I had gone from being an ethnic to a coconut.

One of the officers laughing in the next room, an ex-army man, had once told a group of us that a former army colleague of his had accepted the nickname 'black bastard'. It was just banter, he said, everyone had a nickname in the services. I knew I couldn't be protected from this behaviour that was seen as normal, but felt I shouldn't have to subject myself to it for the rest of my career.

My trainer suggested that I spend some time with a female officer I had joined with, whilst she sought some advice herself. This officer and I had bonded not long after joining – she was glam and I was gay. I followed my trainer's suggestion and went to find my friend, feeling a little better about having got things off my chest.

Several hours later, it was suddenly becoming campus news that the two male officers – the one who had shouted 'coconut music' and one of the ringleaders from the group laughing in the bedroom – had been 'marched off' the police training site and sent back to their respective Forces, at Manchester and Cheshire, a process known as being 'back-classed'.

Those living in my accommodation block were questioned. The spotlight was on me, the black cop that other officers were starting to suspect was gay. People wanted to know what had gone down and why all the others who had laughed at the 'joke' weren't sent packing. I didn't know. It was as much as a surprise to me as it was to them.

One day not long after, early in the morning, an internal affairs inspector and a sergeant from GMP arrived at Bruche to interview me in the company of my class trainer. Internal affairs are meant to investigate wrongdoing by officers. After pulling me out of class in front of my peers, the internal affairs officers told me that if I proceeded with a complaint against my colleagues it would be my word against theirs, and I would have to deal with the consequences. I hadn't filed or even suggested making a complaint. My trainer called a halt to the meeting and sent me back to class.

Later that day, I learnt that my trainer, wanting to do the right thing, had reported the internal affairs officers' conduct to GMP's headquarters, without my knowledge. The assistant chief constable for personnel and training, Vincent Sweeney, personally took charge of the matter and instructed a female police superintendent and Paul Bailey, a member of the Force's Black and Asian Police Association (BAPA; a GMP-specific association operating separately from the national Black Police Association based in London), to visit me. It was unheard of for a superintendent to visit a new recruit. Although the police superintendent displayed some empathy, she made it clear that the onus of sorting this situation out was on me. She said I had to make a decision about what to do, as she and the others weren't going to 'lose any sleep over it'.

I knew that a complaint from me wouldn't make a difference for the better, but it would mark my police career. I didn't want to be isolated any further. My white classmates were agitated about the predicament of the two officers who had been sent back to their Forces, and I knew that if I wanted to survive as an officer of colour in the police and complete the residential training, I had to keep my mouth shut and head down.

I could have accepted BAPA's support and made a stand, but I would have been ostracised by my class. The black staff association was seen as militant by my white colleagues. Signing up for 'black help' would have been a nail in my coffin.

I was asked to sign a 'negative statement', confirming I was making no complaint against any person or the Force, and that I just wanted to get on with my training and work hard towards becoming a successful police officer. After my statement was signed, the two officers were reintegrated into the next intake, though the back-classing was undoubtedly a blow to their egos.

After the 'coconut' incident, my class held an open forum. These existed for people to express their opinions in a 'safe' space, and no opinion or observation was invalid.

The class challenged our trainers on why staff associations for women, black people and gay people in the police even existed. Why, they argued, wasn't there a straight white man's police association? I rolled my eyes, but the white class trainer was quick in her rebuttal. She pointed out that my colleagues were already in one, and it was called 'the police'. This was the mindset of white, straight male police officers in an overwhelmingly white, straight male organisation.

During another forum, our class trainer asked us whether we'd be able to arrest our mothers, if we knew that they had committed murder. As she went around the room, asking each recruit the same question, each answered yes. When it came to my turn and she repeated the question, I said no. My peers stared at me. My tutor asked me why. 'If my mother committed murder, as her son, I personally couldn't arrest her. Of course she would have to be arrested, but I would be lying if I said I could do that, because of our relationship,' I explained. The room was silent as they chewed this over.

Many of my colleagues went about their duties as though they would say anything to be accepted and to defend the system. But this was expected by the leadership. We were to identify with the uniform, power and authority, like good soldiers; in fact, internally, a 'group' of police officers was known as 'troops'. The leadership wanted unthinking loyalty and, above all, obedience. Many of these officers had fathers, mothers, brothers and sisters who were cops. (The glam cop I joined with for example, was the daughter of a seasoned detective.) Before joining, they had already been told how things rolled in the Force. They'd been taught that those shared values, ideas and attitudes were what policing is meant to be about.

In just short of four months, I completed my fifteen-week residential training. I had my end of stage review, and was finally passing out on 19 April 2002. I put on a smile for the last photo, as I had for my first class photograph at the beginning of my training. As I marched around the parade square with the Merseyside Police band playing and horses trotting, I saluted the Union flag and stood to attention. Out of the corner of my eye, I saw a proud Mum, sister, niece and boyfriend. I hadn't told any of my colleagues that he was my boyfriend, but I am sure they guessed it.

Although my start in the police had not been quite what I had wanted, I tried to remain focused; after all, this was my dream job. My pass rate on all the evidence files I had submitted in preparation for my career – which included the national MG (Manual of Guidance) forms like the MG5 (case summary) and MG12 (exhibits list) used in prosecutions – was 100%. I was a natural investigator. I was made for the Force.

3

Ways and Means

I arrived for my first patrol shift at Wigan Police Station – a tall, grey and depressing 1960s-style building in the town centre – as the only black uniformed officer. Wigan, a predominantly white and working-class town, was historically part of Lancashire, but the town and borough now came under the Greater Manchester county and its police. The superintendent who had interviewed me at Bruche after the 'coconut' incident was part of this division.

My working days were long and tiring. I was back living in Liverpool for the time being, and Mum would get me up at 5 a.m. each morning so that I could shower and catch the train to arrive at work and change into my uniform for a 7 a.m. start. When I first arrived at the police station, I was under no illusion that the Bruche incident would not be known here, remembering that the shouting officer had a cousin who was a detective at the station. The police is a small, close-knit community.

My first tutor constable was a good man. Tutor constables are responsible for the supervision of individual probationers. This tutor would supervise me for the first five weeks of my ten weeks of street duties, under Stage 4 of the probationer training programme. I'd then move on to another tutor for the final five weeks. If either was off-duty when I was on, somebody else would look after me. I'd graduated from the fake streets of Sandford to the real streets of Wigan.

One thing probationers are told during their tutoring stage is to forget 'everything' they'd learnt at the police training school, especially all the 'political correctness crap', the race training we'd received. Many people assume that new intakes of police officers will change the Force for the better and for the greater good, but they forget something important – old-school cops teach new-school cops, and new-school cops teach newer-school cops the same old tricks.

My class trainers at Bruche had been outstanding, but to most cops the training they gave us was only so much playing in a sandbox.

During these street weeks, trainees are taught something called 'Ways and Means', by tutors often not much more experienced than they are. The 'Ways and Means Act' isn't an actual piece of UK legislation, but another one of those unofficial internal policies inflicted on members of the public. Unlike most laws, the WAMA wasn't complicated, and only had one section: 69. If you can't screw 'em one way, flip 'em over and screw 'em another. You pulled somebody in a car over, and they had all their motoring documents in order but were being a bit too lippy? Then you went about checking the car itself, for example to see whether the tyre treads were the legal depth.

I was issued with a man-sized grey locker for my uniform and equipment. Officers often stole one another's things, but jokingly referred to this as 'redistributing police property'. I received a radio and CS spray, and was shown where my correspondence tray was. A correspondence tray was the main place where officers miraculously lost paperwork, like court files they were working on, or road traffic accident reports they had been given to deal with. CS spray, an incapacitant 'pepper' spray, is classed as a Section 5 firearm under the Firearms Act of 1968. Giving CS spray to a cop who actually wanted it was like giving a match to an arsonist. Some officers would spray each other in the station as a joke.

It wasn't long before I made my first arrest, for a breach of the peace. The detainee didn't make a reply to the caution, which I had executed perfectly. He was a man who had got into an argument with his wife, a 'domestic incident'. Not long before I joined, the police policy on domestic violence incidents had been not to get involved. The position was that the woman usually forgave her partner, even when she sustained an injury, and refused to press charges; so the Force left them to it. In this case, my detainee, incredibly drunk, had refused to leave the family home. To ensure his wife's safety, I removed him to the police station until he was sober and calm.

Traditionally, officers with longer service years 'handed over' prisoners to their probationary colleagues. This meant junior officers had to go to court and tell a judge or magistrate that they had arrested this person on the date and time in question, even if they hadn't been there and it never actually happened. Many of the people detained were so drunk that they didn't have a clue who arrested them anyway.

Like most cops, the first dead body I saw was a 'sudden death'. Recruits are watched over by their tutor as they check dead bodies for signs of foul play or violence, like a knife in the back or wound under the armpits, for example. I was a few weeks in, when we were called to a flat. The occupant, a large man, was lying on his back on his bed with blood and excrement all around him and his bedroom walls. It looked so much like a murder scene that, to begin with, it was treated as one. Senior detectives attended the scene, putting on protective overalls so as not to contaminate any potential evidence. For continuity, I travelled with the body in the back of the ambulance and was present at the post-mortem, where I watched the man's skin being pulled back over his skull. The stench from the exposed internal organs was overpowering. In the end there was fortunately nothing suspicious about his death. The man had 'exploded'. His stomach had combusted from the overconsumption of cider – I'd noticed numerous litre bottles around the flat. This type of incident, I learnt quickly, was policing at the sharp end. I saw my fair share of dead bodies, and not much of the glamour shown on television. It was the daily reality for most cops.

My second five weeks of being tutored were more interesting. On one shift, I was taken out on patrol by a stereotypical cop – testosterone and masculinity at the forefront of everything he did. Patrol involves being out in a marked police vehicle, a car or a van, waiting for control to allocate you a job, like a 999 call or something else – unless you happened to come across a job yourself, of course.

Policing consists of three parts: (1) proactive – prevention through patrol, (2) reactive – responding to incidents, and (3) investigation. Most of the action on patrol happens on a Friday or Saturday night. Macho Cop was all swinging arms, throwing his weight about. He told me that he and his colleagues looked forward to the weekend shifts and the scraps they would have with the locals, mainly outside the Liquid nightclub on King Street. The cops, wearing white short-sleeved shirts and black leather gloves, had to show the local rugby supporters who was in charge in the town. On duty in the town centre, Macho Cop chatted to a woman and managed to get her number and address. In the early hours, we drove over to her house and he had a little fun with her inside whilst I sat in the police car waiting for him. On another night shift with a tutor, we parked up in the local retail car park. He turned the car lights off, pushed his seat back and went to sleep. I just sat looking out of the window.

On another night, I was taken by a tutor to attend a reported burglary. I was instructed to listen and learn. The woman who had called the police told us that she'd been burgled, but whilst my tutor questioned her, her eyes never left mine. We learnt that nothing had been taken from the property, but someone had definitely been inside it. Things had been moved in the kitchen, but without a theft, we couldn't call it a burglary. We were taught mnemonics at the training school, to make it easier for us to remember the law. Burglary fell under DIRT: damage, inflict harm, rape or take (steal). One or more had to occur, for an offence to have been committed. Nevertheless, my tutor asked me to take down the report. To be confirmed in the rank of constable, officers had to have 'proficiencies': experience of various tasks and incidents, such as sudden deaths and burglaries. It would reflect well on my tutor if I got a burglary in (regardless of whether or not it had happened).

I was dissatisfied with the situation. I asked my tutor if I could ask the woman some further questions, and was given the go-ahead.

'Does anybody else have a key to the property?' I asked.

'Yes,' she replied.

It didn't take me long to unravel the fact that no burglary had taken place, but that her estranged husband had been on the property. As we left, my tutor congratulated me for solving the non-existent crime.

The new chief constable of GMP, Michael Todd – who took charge of GMP after the retirement of David Wilmot – had transferred from London's Metropolitan Police, where he had been an assistant commissioner for territorial policing (in charge of front-line policing in all thirty-two London boroughs), leading operations during the May Day demonstrations and Notting Hill Carnival. He later said that members of the public who watched television cop shows like *Inspector Morse* were better equipped for questioning suspects than some of his own officers. *The Independent* reported his comments, followed by other newspapers,[1] which led to him having to respond internally to the Force the same day, about his 'damning verdict on some officers'. The chief constable, known as the 'copper's copper', said that when he studied taped interviews with some suspects he was 'shocked' to find that even the most basic questions were not being asked.[2]

After my ten weeks of supervised street duties, I had two weeks of Stage 5 probationer training. The Stage 5 training consolidates what you have learnt from being tutored, prior to going out on your own on independent patrol. During Stage 5, we undertook riot training in the mocked-up purpose-built streets, shops and alleyways at the public order training centre in Manchester. I had to wear a NATO-style riot helmet (a motorcycle helmet with a visor) and a fire-resistant overall with elbow and knee pads, and walk through petrol bombs and thrown wooden bricks, which could break bones.

Now it was time to begin my independent patrol, Stage 6. This meant I was now going out on foot, on my own, into the big, bad world. When probationers were out on independent patrol during their training, the leaders preferred them to be on foot rather than in vehicles, especially during day shifts. Probationers were often allocated all the jobs the longer-serving officers didn't want to cover, like thefts and sudden deaths.

As I stepped out of the police station in my smartly pressed uniform, complete with body armour, pepper spray, handcuffs, baton and radio, with the bright sun beaming down on me, I placed my chequered cap firmly and low onto my head and walked up the town's main King Street alone.

I soon began to feel confident in my role. Whilst on patrol in a car with a female colleague, I had spotted a man following two young girls on a road with a kitchen knife strapped to him, like Rambo. I jumped out of the car and was on him before the wheels had even stopped rolling. We struggled violently, but I was able to restrain him. I hadn't felt afraid or thought about my own safety. My training kicked in and I just did what I had to do: protect life and property. I'd only been on patrol for a few months, and the chief superintendent noted my actions.

In 2002, I received my first commendation from the divisional commander in recognition of my 'bravery and dedication to duty'.[3]

Those first few months weren't all rough and tumble, though. I was once called to a house in Scholes, to a case of two 'brothers' who lived together, both of whom I suspected were gay. They'd suffered an assault which had left them battered, and endured repeated harassment from a neighbour. I did my best to get them justice in the courts, but the offender was found not guilty. It was disappointing, for them, and me. However, they still had the good grace to send me a letter: 'Dear PC Maxwell, we would like to thank you most sincerely for your help and prompt attention. We are sorry the case didn't go our way. We appreciate all you have done and the time you put into the case. Thank you very much indeed.'[4] I felt I had done them proud.

My time on patrol was also the first and only time I received a complaint – for incivility. (A little incivility was encouraged, just to remind the public who the police were: for example, if a member of the public asked an officer for directions, you'd get cops who would point to their hat and say, 'It says E to R, not A to Z,' referring to the 'EIIR' on the cap's badge – for Elizabeth II Regina, the queen to whom we'd sworn loyalty. The member of the public would just walk off, unamused.) The complaint went nowhere, but the way it arose is an interesting example of the culture in the police: I had been on the computer in the station writing room, when the inspector called for me to attend the front desk. The front desk is normally all the public see in police stations (unless they are under arrest). The duty officer told me that a young boy, waiting for his mother and sister, had drawn on the station wall with a pen. I was ordered to arrest the boy for criminal damage. Although there was visible damage, spit or water would have removed the marks; but this was seen as an opportunity for me to get another proficiency to complete my probation. I gritted my teeth and arrested the poor boy. His mother was rightly furious. Unfortunately, no junior officer was going to go against the leadership who directly controlled their future, and especially not during their probation. I was later congratulated by my peers for a job well done. Any officers who weren't racking up complaints weren't good cops – they couldn't be trusted.

If you think this is ridiculous, bear in mind that arresting people on tenuous grounds can also line the pockets of the officers making the arrest. For example, they may be additionally charged with assaulting, or disorderly behaviour towards, a police officer during the arrest. For the former, the trick is to simply get the detained person to touch or push you, even if only slightly. If found guilty by a court, they'd receive a criminal record for assault, and the officer would get something like £50 in compensation, and £100 if they had some visible marks, like a slight reddening. For the latter, the officer just needed to wind the detainee up enough for him or her to swear, which constitutes a public disorder, an offence for which they would be arrested. One of my colleagues often went 'cha-ching' after accusing those he arrested of causing him harassment, alarm or distress under Section 5 of the Public Order Act 1986. The officer would then continue to wind the person they'd just arrested up, saying that they were going to tell the magistrate that they had been a 'naughty boy' (or girl). Probably unsurprisingly, many people responded 'fuck the magistrate'. The officer would then ask the detainee if they were willing to sign the police pocket notebook to confirm they'd said this. Anger, brashness, and often alcohol, led a fair few people to sign. Some time later, sitting in front of a magistrate would be a smartly dressed police officer and an often smelly and scruffy prisoner (especially if they'd been in the cells overnight), who had signed a statement in the pocket notebook that they'd told the judicial officer to go fuck themselves. And, as I've said, that notebook was the Bible for cops. It contained the truth, and nothing but the truth. It was an easy catch for the police.

During my service, I heard officers getting people to confess to crimes they knew nothing about, sometimes in return for favours, as it made the Force's detection rate look good. In interviews, some officers would try to persuade detainees not to have a lawyer present, telling the prisoner that it was in their best interests. Lawyers only got in the way, they would say. They never trusted 'duty' solicitors, the state-funded lawyers who advise those detainees who cannot afford a private lawyer. All interviews were recorded on a double-cassette tape recorder. At the end of the interview, one of the numbered tapes would be sealed with a serialised label (only to be opened on the order of a judge) and the other used as a working copy. This system was supposed to make the interview process fail-safe and incorruptible, but even with recorded interviews it's possible to 'stitch up' a detainee, by framing what they said in a particular way, or by pressuring them to admit to crimes they hadn't committed. In 2002, the *Manchester Evening News* reported on the 'villains' who had escaped justice, after lying cops claimed that crimes had been 'solved' in my Force at the Stockport division. Under the headline of 'Scandal of the bogus crime figures', the paper highlighted how 'crooks' responsible for more than a thousand crimes were to get away scot-free, after GMP falsely claimed they had cracked the cases.[5] One man on remand in prison allegedly admitted to more than two hundred crimes that he did not commit. As a reward he was taken out of prison by police officers for visits to McDonald's and allowed to see his girlfriend. Two detectives were found guilty of lying, after the Force had been publicly embarrassed by the newspaper. One officer was found guilty of thirty-four offences of dishonesty, and another of seven charges of dishonesty. The first was fined ten days' pay, and the second five days'. Both were allowed to keep their jobs. None of the 'solved' crimes were reinvestigated.

Just as biased paper trails can be used against suspects, so too can unofficial meetings, where no records are kept at all. Plenty of case-sensitive talks take place in the police canteen, where the unofficial, off-duty vibe can hide serious conversation. On one occasion, my colleagues got together to discuss what they were going to say about a suspect who had been arrested and sent to court for public disorder, and who'd had the cheek to plead not guilty. Statements would often not be written up straight away, so that conferring could take place and officers could get their stories watertight. In this case, the officers' statements in court were so similar to each other that people laughed after each one gave their evidence. The police case was such a farce that it was thrown out.

I hadn't been very long at Wigan, when I started to become uncomfortable with the homophobic slurs that were frequently used at the station, mainly by my supervisors, the sergeants. I didn't want to be bothered by it, but it was getting me down. At Bruche, I wasn't officially out, and on days when I stayed with my boyfriend in Manchester overnight (whilst we were looking for a flat together there) my boyfriend used to hide in the car park across from the police station when he met me after work.

Amongst the talk about 'puffs' and 'queers' – words that were casually tossed about – every other day one of my colleagues would say to me 'Is it because I'm gay?' in a strong Lancashire accent, a line he used on anyone who complained about any unfairness from him or our peers.

My colleague was only joking, and I sensed no malice from him towards me, but it got on my nerves after a while. I mentioned the homophobia in a private conversation with a female colleague who was on my shift, unaware that she was allegedly having an affair with a police superintendent, and the information was likely to be relayed to him.

One of my sergeants began giving me workloads that were unsustainable, in comparison to my peers in the same service, and regularly took me into an empty room to discuss my progress, or lack thereof. But I was progressing fine. There were no reports or comments that proved otherwise, and I had just been commended for the attempted knife attack I'd foiled. I had also just been signed off as competent for independent patrol by my two tutor constables. The sergeant would not explain that I was doing badly, or that I wasn't doing my job – only say 'I'm watching you'. Bear in mind that being seen to be attracting negative attention from a sergeant could affect how the rest of the team saw me. The sergeants, that first line of management in the police, set the standards, culture and tone of the Force, as well as the expectations of the mass of officers under them, and many of them (including him) were old-school.

One day, having had enough of this sergeant, and hearing yet another comment about 'those queers' in the writing room, I found my patrol inspector in the station corridor and came out to him, then and there. 'I'm gay,' I said.

Without missing a beat, he replied, 'As a Christian, I cannot condone what you do. But as long as you're a good police officer, that is all that matters.'

After coming out, I knew my time at Wigan would be coming to an end. After my female colleague mentioned the problems I'd had because of my sexuality to the superintendent, I was ordered to go and see him. The superintendent asked me to write down my experiences in a report for him, and hand it in before I left the station that day.[6] Mentally and emotionally exhausted, I wrote the brief report in the station writing room, sitting there in my uniform but with my tie off after attending an incident. I wrote down when I joined the police, why I joined and my experiences so far. I didn't name any officers, I just described my reality. I was sent to see the chief superintendent, who was our divisional commander. Like someone suffering from Stockholm syndrome, I gave him a genuine apology for making waves and causing so many problems. Although the divisional chief empathised with my plight and did his best to make me feel valued, his suggestion that I stay at the division but be supervised by a (white) lesbian custody sergeant (the person who books in a prisoner and authorises their detention) at the neighbouring Leigh Police Station was short-sighted. I didn't want to be supervised by another person simply because they were gay. I wasn't in the gay police, but the police. And, crucially, what did my lesbian colleague know about being black? Nevertheless, the Force HQ had already been contacted, and the assistant chief constable, Vincent Sweeney, authorised my move to a central Manchester police station where they felt the environment would be less 'small town'. I was to take immediate annual leave and move.

In his letter to the Force chiefs, the divisional chief superintendent wrote: 'I am satisfied from what the officer told me and from other issues which have also recently come to light that the standard of guidance, direction and support given by supervisors on the relief, particularly to younger officers, has fallen short of my expectations.' Summing up his report about me to his bosses, the chief superintendent finished with: 'He is a promising officer who understands he will need to show a degree of personal resilience.'[7]

I wondered how many of the white straight officers had been told that they needed to show more of this.

At Wigan, I was often racially abused by the public when arresting people, but took this as part of the job. One memory sticks with me: a young white woman, who had assaulted an asylum seeker during a large-scale disturbance that saw twenty to thirty people attacking him, punched me twice in the face as I was arresting her, and screamed in front of the large crowd that I was a 'blacky bastard'.[8] After a brief search, I found a knife on her.

I sent the compensation I received for the assault, which wasn't much but all she could afford, to the Lesbian and Gay

Foundation (LGF), as I did not wish to keep it. I didn't know of any black equality organisations.

I didn't join the police to be assaulted, or turn those inevitable assaults into profit. I didn't know what drove a white woman to attack an asylum seeker, and then a black man wearing a uniform. I wasn't devastated by it, but wanted to understand the social problems behind it – I witnessed great poverty and awful housing conditions as I went about my duties.

But the racism and homophobia from my colleagues was throwing me off.

I was now painfully aware of a reputation that would follow me from Wigan to Manchester, just as it had from Bruche to Wigan.

What had I done wrong? How much more 'personal resilience' would I need to show?

4

Pride and Prejudice

After a week's annual leave, with no goodbyes, I transferred to Bootle Street Police Station, a grand old stone building in Manchester's city centre, the headquarters for the old City Police. Moving during your probation was unheard of, except in extenuating circumstances, granted by an assistant chief constable or above. During the week off, my mum and partner supported me, but a strain started to develop in my relationship with my partner, who was now a junior doctor.

I soon learnt the inner-city police was in competition with other local stations like Longsight, which covered Moss Side in south Manchester, a predominantly black area that had had its own Toxteth-like riots. My new station was called 'Brutal Street' by my colleagues, a reputation it lived up to. I arrived at the station's front desk with my uniform and equipment, and was sent straight to see the sub-divisional commander, who held the rank of superintendent, in his office on the first floor. The first thing he asked me – in front of his deputy, the sub-divisional chief inspector – was, 'Have you come to my station on a crusade, waving a gay and black flag?'

Alarmed, I said that I hadn't. It was the Union Jack that stood proudly on my bedroom shelf back in Liverpool, along with the flags of the Commonwealth that I collected. I was not a member

56

of any political association, staff or otherwise. I just wanted to do my job.

I was placed on a patrol shift, known as a 'relief'. The shifts were either from 7 a.m. to 5 p.m. (day), from 1 p.m. to 11 p.m. (afternoon), or from 9 p.m. to 7 a.m. (night). There was also a 5 p.m. to 3 a.m. afternoon shift on the weekend. There were five patrol reliefs at my station, A to E, as well as other units, like plain-clothes and the criminal investigation department (CID). My relief shift had more than twenty other constables, three sergeants, an inspector and a dog handler; my station had the biggest reliefs in the Force. I was, once again, the only black officer.

There was another gay officer at the station, who had experienced homophobia and as a result was now office-based. We paraded on (i.e. they took roll call, checking who was on duty or on annual leave, etc.), and were given our duties and our intelligence briefings in the parade room, for which we could now sit instead of stand, as used to be the way. The parade room was a place of banter, complaints about 'the job' ('like no other') and easy chat.

I settled into life at Bootle Street, working uniform response '999' policing (i.e. attending emergency calls), but quickly realised that it wasn't very different to Wigan. Members of the public would often turn on minority officers, especially when they were being arrested. They were very vocal when it came to race, and more so when it came to religion, which I believe worsened as a direct result of the 9/11 attacks.

I was once called to a disturbance at an entertainment complex called The Printworks in the city centre. I ended up arresting a drunk man who was causing trouble. As I was placing him in the back of the police van, he loudly snarled at me, in front of my peers and the watching public, 'Get your stinking Muslim hands off me.' Although I was a Catholic, my dark skin was reason enough for him to assume that I was Muslim.

In fact, the inner-city police could have taught the small-town police a thing or two. Manchester was policed by people from the small, predominantly white Lancashire towns that surrounded it. When we policed a white working-class area, those we came into contact with were known as 'chavs' or 'scum', those we called 'shit-bags' in Wigan. When we policed a black or Asian area, they were 'niggers' and 'Pakis' respectively, and in the gay area they were 'queers'. In Chinatown, they were 'Chinks'. Many people didn't even know the difference between a Sikh, a Hindu and a Muslim. It all came with the territory.

Sometimes this sort of behaviour could backfire. I was on the 5 p.m. to 3 a.m. weekend shift in the nightclub riot van, when our vehicle pulled up alongside a black motorist on Deansgate, outside the bars on the strip. One of my colleagues opened the van's side door and started to berate the driver of the vehicle, though neither I nor my colleagues could see a reason why. Whatever it was, the sergeant sitting in the passenger seat encouraged my colleague, whilst everyone laughed. That is, until the driver got out of his vehicle and identified himself as a lawyer who worked with the Force. He asked for my colleague's number and that of my sergeant's. After my colleague apologised, the sergeant was left red-faced. We drove off in silence.

One day, a white female colleague and I were leaving the station yard in a marked police vehicle when an Asian taxi driver drove by blocking our path. At the top of her voice, my colleague shouted out to the taxi driver, 'You stupid Paki!' Embarrassed and disappointed, I gave an imperceptible shake of the head, but couldn't find it in myself to do more. What could I have done? I thought, as I sat next to her. She was well connected and popular, especially amongst the male officers. Had I said something to her, or to someone else later, I would have been ostracised for having challenged or reported her – being a grass, untrustworthy, not a team player. And the careers of cops who weren't trusted by other cops would stall.

This close-knit camaraderie bred some more intimate

relationships. Many cops at my new station were having extramarital affairs with other officers and police staff. It wasn't my business to question the morality of these relationships, but they strengthened bonds in the police, including between junior and senior members of staff. Some tutor constables were sleeping with their tutees. Some officers even got together with people they had dealt with as victims of crime, including domestic violence. There were officers who didn't care that others knew, as long as their partners didn't find out – and of course they rarely did, because of that blue wall of silence, because no one trusts a snitch. Cops 'did' cops because they understood 'the job', they said. I was privy to several extramarital affairs between those in the highest ranks down to the lowest, on duty and off duty, in police offices, toilets and cars. The safest option seemed to be to turn a blind eye, especially as some of the people engaged in affairs were dictating my career.

These affairs didn't stretch to gay relationships; I knew several straight officers who had gay tendencies – some 'played' (i.e. experimented) with gay officers – but homophobic attitudes still continued. For example, one Christmas, when I was working on a crime report in the station writing room, a female colleague began to complain about not wanting to go to Via Fossa, a bar in Manchester's gay village, and deal with a theft. Apparently she didn't want to be dealing with 'queers' and their 'drama' anymore. Within the safe confines of my mind, I challenged her, calling her out for her homophobic language – but fear kept me from actually saying anything. I did not want to make any enemies.

On another night, after work a group of us went to the local nightclub, 42nd Street, which was on the same road as the police station. I went to join a circle of my colleagues, just in time to hear one of the male officers announce, 'If a gay guy ever tried to hit on me, I would break his nose.' His words were meant for me; it was an observation he felt it was important to air as I joined the group. This officer had tested me previously, by asking me in front of others if I liked women. My brain shouted, 'So, just because I'm gay I'm attracted to you?' But again, I kept it to myself. He carried on, saying he didn't think what gay people did was 'natural'. I held my tongue, smiled and drank my drink. Maybe he was scared that gay men would treat him like he treated women.

On another night, later, Officer Don't Hit On Me and I bumped into each other in the gay village at Sackville Street car park, when we were both on duty but working separately. He told me and my van partner that he was annoyed by 'queers' and their 'problems', having just gone to an incident in the area. His eyes were on me as he said it, and I could sense his satisfaction. He knew I wouldn't say anything, just as I hadn't the last time. Anytime I tried to make friends with my new colleagues and had to sit through more of this, I came away feeling isolated. It impacted on my relationship with my boyfriend, who had already felt the pressure of my experiences at Bruche, Wigan, and now Bootle Street.

Sometimes my feelings of isolation were compounded by the fact that, seen from the outside, I was part of that blue wall. During the spring 2003 protests against Tony Blair, George Bush and the Iraq war in Manchester – the biggest political demonstration in the city since the Peterloo Massacre in 1819 – three separate marches converged at the city's town hall. I was on one side of the police line, and my friends from university, including my best friend and confidant Dan, were on the other. We smiled as we pretended we didn't know each other, to save any embarrassment.

A Chinese officer at my station was in a situation similar to my own. He was struggling to fit in, and I sat and listened as my colleagues talked about how they would let him struggle and fail, in the hope that he would leave the police and return to the chip shop in Manchester where he came from. He was tutored for much longer than was normal, and as a result they described him as useless, lazy and incompetent. He did fail, did resign, and did return to the chip shop, to their utter delight. Whilst they roared with laughter over his resignation, I just stayed silent.

I was starting to resent myself for the way I kept quiet. I wanted to scream. But what could I have done and who could I have spoken with? The sub-divisional chief already warned me about 'flying the flags'. As the most senior officer on the sub-division, he set the tone, and the other officers, especially the most junior ones, followed. I found myself eating in the writing room during my breaks, whilst my colleagues ate in the rest room next to the gym. The rest room was an uncomfortable place, pumping with testosterone. There was a television and when particular programmes came on – any programmes to do with gay people or rap music – my colleagues would circumspectly air their views, cautious of using fully racist or homophobic words.

Once I was with a male colleague who had pulled over a female motorist on Newton Street outside the police museum, for committing a minor traffic offence. She asked why he had stopped her. He replied, 'Because I can.' She fired back that he couldn't stop her for no reason, so she received a ticket for failing her attitude test. When we got back in the car, out of earshot, I told him that he was completely out of order.

'What are you going to do? Snitch? If you do snitch, you'll be on your own.'

I knew what he meant. It meant no one trusting me or wanting to associate with me, no one coming to my assistance, if ever I needed it, on the radio – or driving over so slowly that it would ensure I got a little banged up first. Being liked on relief wasn't just important, it was essential to your survival. This was the reason good cops would say nothing about bad cops. One of the unwritten rules for cops was valuing our brotherhood before anything else. The police badge wasn't just a shield, but a family crest. The only thing I could do was to avoid working with that officer again.

I remembered the case of Detective Sergeant Gurpal Virdi of the Metropolitan Police. In 1998, Virdi had been wrongfully arrested and sacked by Scotland Yard after an internal police disciplinary board found him – an Asian sergeant who had suffered racial abuse – guilty of sending racist hate mail to his ethnic minority colleagues and even to himself. Delivered via the Met's internal mail system, 'each envelope carried a picture of a black man's face and the initials of the National Front'. One of the letters read: 'Not wanted. Keep the police force white, so leave now or else!'[1]

In a statement to *The Guardian* after the internal police disciplinary board ruling that justice had been done, my chief constable, Michael Todd – the Met's deputy assistant commissioner who coordinated the investigation at the time – said: 'The ruling is very fair when you look at the effect of what Sergeant Virdi did.'[2]

Virdi succeeded in his discrimination claim against the Met. An employment tribunal ruled that he had been falsely dismissed by a racist employer, for an offence that he couldn't have committed – he never sent any racist hate mail at all. The Virdi Inquiry, commissioned by the Metropolitan Police Authority (MPA) to look into the matter, delivered a 200-page report which showed that Virdi had been 'convicted' by a kangaroo court.[3] He received an apology and compensation. Surprisingly, following the success of his claim, he returned to the police after being reinstated: the *Evening Standard* reported that Virdi 'accused the force of setting out to "destroy" him'[4] for standing up to racism, but he still decided to go back.[5] Some of the officers in Virdi's case who had played a part in the campaign against him were promoted.

In 2003, in an interview to mark the tenth anniversary of Stephen Lawrence's death, Commander Cressida Dick, head of the Met's diversity directorate, said that Scotland Yard remained 'institutionally racist', ten years after the murder. 'It's very difficult to imagine the situation where we will say we are no longer institutionally racist,' she told *The Independent*. 'The point about racism is it's about the structure of society and power differential and how institutions operate.' Dick said she did not believe there was a single institution able to say 'we are not racist'. Responding to the figures about the disproportionate number of black and Asian people being stopped and searched, the Lawrence family's solicitor Imran Khan said, 'We may have individual officers who have taken on board the recommendations from the Lawrence inquiry – but it has not produced a structural change.' Baroness Howells, the racial equality campaigner, said that the police were undergoing a 'process of unlearning', 'because Britain never had an apartheid system we never realised how deep the prejudices were.'[6]

It is no coincidence that there was a massive recruitment drive in Greater Manchester after Chief Constable David Wilmot's comments at the Stephen Lawrence inquiry. The GMP was a Force that struggled to attract minority recruits: I was one of approximately 40 ethnic minority male officers out of 8,000. After I'd joined Bootle Street, another black officer was placed on my shift. I thought it strange, placing two of the few black or Asian officers at the station – and amongst the more than nine hundred staff at the division – on the same shift, but of course it wasn't done at random. Management even sent us out together on patrol, making it look as if there were plenty of black cops in the division.

Out on patrol together, this officer told me that he had moved divisions after encountering difficulties with his colleagues and supervisors, just as I had. It was as if all black and Asian officers ran into trouble – but surely, I thought, not every black and Asian officer was a 'problem'? The few people I had seen challenge the culture and behaviour, like Virdi, were vilified. I heard my white colleagues describe black officers as radical for challenging racism. I heard my straight colleagues describe gay officers as activists, for challenging homophobia. I was a young man with my future ahead of me and I didn't want to go down the same route as Virdi, so I forced myself to remain *one of them* instead.

Those in the same leaky boat as me kept their heads down, and I empathised with them. Some would go further, and deny the very existence of racism or homophobia in the police, emphatically repeating that it was not a problem in the Force. However, this attitude could undermine the experiences of other minority cops, and those members of the public who complained about racism and/or homophobia at the hands of officers.

Michael Fuller, a deputy assistant commissioner with the Met Police, was appointed the UK's first black chief constable in 2004, leading the Kent Force.[7] I was happy for him, but I knew he'd got ahead by toeing the 'white' line. I agreed with Darcus Howe, the broadcaster, writer and civil rights campaigner, on the appointment: 'I am pleased that Fuller has broken the glass ceiling. But I have no great expectations that he will be part of the revolution in policing that this society so desperately needs.'[8] Upon taking up his new job, Fuller said, 'I am a very professional police officer'.[9] Why, I wondered, did the black chief have to remind the public that he was 'professional', and 'very' much so? In his 2019 memoir *Kill the Black One First* – written after he retired, and was no longer in a position of influence – Fuller says, 'I had come this far in the Met by not talking about my colour. By not discussing racism . . . Police racism was an ugly beast in the corner which I didn't want to poke.'[10]

I was amazed by the account of one black cop, who insisted he had never encountered racism of *any* kind in the GMP. Detective Inspector Tony Alogba from Ashton under Lyne said he had never been the victim of racial jibes or taunts, and had always believed that the Force had done everything possible 'to eradicate alleged racism'.[11] But although the officer had a

Nigerian surname, when I saw a picture of him on the Force's external 'local policing' website, my first impression was that he was white. He was almost certainly mixed-race, with much lighter skin than mine. He had the privilege of 'passing' – being perceived as white – and his experience in the police was different to that of darker-skinned people.

The account of former Inspector John Phazey of West Midlands Police confirmed for me how widespread racism was, when, after completing his thirty years (of basic service required to receive a full pension), he said that he routinely heard officers using derogatory terms for Asian and black people. But he went on to say that the derogatory terms weren't racist: 'It didn't mean any more than someone saying Paddy for an Irishman or Jerry for a German.'[12]

I began to realise that officers of colour could often be deeply conflicted, particularly seniors, who were insensitive to those below them. They did not necessarily feel solidarity with other black and Asian officers, especially as they had been trained to serve as enforcers of an institution that has historically been anti-black and pro-white. Some were ignorant of the structural racism around them; some were aware of it, but thought the best way to get ahead was to emulate the attitudes of white colleagues.

Two of the other mixed-race officers who had joined with me struggled with identity crises. One hated everything about 'blackness' and the BPA; the other refused to be called black, accepting only that they were mixed-race. Though I respect their choice of self-identification, it was alien to me. I was mixed-race, but had always identified as black too. I had never wanted to be white, and had never been ashamed of being dark-skinned.

Gay officers also faced challenges in the Force. Many of my colleagues speculated that being gay was a lifestyle choice. They saw gay men as effeminate and as the job was for 'masculine' men, thought that gay men were bad officers. According to the officer who had shouted 'Paki', whenever court cases didn't go the police's way, it was because the judge was a nonce and 'down the gay canal, getting noshed off' by a male sex worker. 'Feminine' traits, like active listening and rapport-building, were considered weaknesses. Lesbian officers, and women officers in general, faced similar prejudice. They were either bikes or dykes – you rode them, or they rode one another.

It was lonely, living inside this mad world, and I never found any gay allies. The majority of gay officers I knew of were working in offices, away from operational colleagues and their extreme views. Prior to 2003, the police were at war with the gay community. Over thirty gay men were murdered between 1986 and 1990, but the police did nothing or little about it, despite concerns from the community. The Sexual Offences Act 1967 saw the partial decriminalisation of male homosexuality for consensual sex between men over twenty-one in private, but afterwards gay men were targeted more than before, under the homophobic laws concerning 'gross indecency' and 'buggery' – until May 2004, when the Sexual Offences Act 2003 repealed them. After this, homophobia in the police went underground. Homophobes simply found other ways to vent their hate, like targeting gay men under the still used law against 'outraging public decency'. Instead of protecting gay people and addressing hate crime, the police directed resources towards raids on public toilets, saunas and bars. The former chief constable of Greater Manchester, James Anderton, said that gay people were 'swirling in a human cesspit of their own making'. Despite facing criticism for his remarks, he continued: 'The law of the land allows consenting adult homosexuals to engage in sexual practices which I think should be criminal offences. Sodomy between males is an abhorrent offence, condemned by the word of God, and ought to be against the criminal law.'[13]

Some of my colleagues told me they had blackmailed bars on Manchester's Canal Street (in the gay village), getting crates of liquor out of them in exchange for not being raided. Many gay men were arrested for victimless behaviour.

When I joined Bootle Street, my colleagues and I often targeted gay men under the now-outdated anti-gay laws, like the one against 'gross indecency', which was used to criminalise sodomy. We knew we could find men on the canal towpath and punish them for sex acts. The police leadership directed us to do it, stating that these homosexuals were causing a public nuisance, thereby dividing the LGBT community into the 'workable' gays and 'the degenerates'.

In 2003, the gay community started to become complacent, even though there was still much distain and prejudice towards lesbian, gay, bisexual and trans people. Many of my queer brothers and sisters believed that they were now equal in the eyes of the law, forgetting the dismissiveness, lack of interest and victim-blaming many LGBT people had gone through at the hands of the police. Some gay people even praised the police's 'cleaning up' of the canal. As a gay man on the scene and an officer frequently policing Manchester's gay area, I was aware that many LGBT people didn't report incidents or hate crimes to the police because of their experiences, like being brushed off by the Force, including by gay officers.

During football matches we worked in 'serials', consisting of three riot vans – which were hotspots for homophobia – and each serial included an inspector, three sergeants and eighteen constables that policed the city before, during and after the match, as well as the stadium itself. Internally, the full-time riot officers, the Tactical Aid Unit (TAU), were known as 'knuckle-draggers'. Officers swapped shoulder numbers to confuse the public, whilst other officers might not wear them at all.

Three years after I joined the Force the overt homophobia started to change, as a direct result of the Labour government's repeal of outdated laws like the one against 'gross indecency'. In the year I joined secondary school, in 1989, the number of convictions for the consenting gay offence of 'gross indecency' was greater than in 1966 – a time when male homosexuality was still illegal in Britain. Ensuring that people forgot this chequered history was a strategic public relations exercise on the part of the police, and many white gay men jumped on the bandwagon to further their own police careers. The police created public relations departments devoted to LGBT issues, which they wouldn't have dreamt of doing for the black community, knowing that a good, public-facing relationship with the LGBT community mattered if they wanted to clean up their image. As part of this new deal, police officers were allowed to parade in uniform at Pride for the first time in 2003, and officers would blow their whistles whilst handing out sweets to the clapping public. Constable Andy Hewlett headed the Gay Police Association's uniformed contingent as part of the National Pride Parade in London in June 2003. He was one of thirty-five officers who paraded in uniform at the event for the first time in the history of the police. Another forty-five non-uniformed officers took part. Together, they walked from Embankment to Hyde Park.

Later, Pride became militarised and corporatised, moving far from its riotous foundation. (By contrast, black carnivals like Notting Hill were prepared for and seen as a 'battle' by the police.) However, gay friends of mine outside the Force, especially older gay men, thought it important never to forget the mistreatment of LGBT people by the police, in order to ensure that it never happened again.

At the beginning of 2003, I'd heard that the Force's Lesbian and Gay Staff Affiliation, LAGSA, was having its annual general meeting at Bootle Street, and decided to attend. The lesbian sergeant they had wanted me to work with at Leigh was one of the leaders. LAGSA, which was founded the year I joined the police to address issues of sexuality across the Force, was run by white lesbian officers. Though I didn't realise it at the time, there was friction between LAGSA and the white gay men who ran the national Gay Police Association from London, which the Manchester affiliation hadn't signed up to, and the local LAGSA and the national GPA were run separately. My only hope in attending the annual general meeting was to find like-minded people who would understand my difficulties as a gay man. Whilst I did find some sympathetic ears, there was one big problem. I was a different colour to everyone else in the room. They were all white.

LAGSA were annoyed that the BAPA had been provided with a ball at Manchester's Town Hall by the Force. As I sat in the back, listening to the general discussion, a lesbian member of the executive committee remarked, 'If the blacks are getting it, so are we.' Mine was the only face in the room that fell at her words.

Throughout my time in the police, I'd heard the term 'The Gay Mafia'. It struck me as a tasteless joke, but it was actually a reference to the power some white gay police officers, in and out of the closet, held in the police and other public institutions, like the government. Many affluent, white gay people were ruthlessly ambitious. Strikingly, many would distance themselves from the LGBT movement (and 'activists') and the struggle for equality, focusing on their careers and only coming out after achieving rank, power and prestige. This lack of solidarity could be damaging for the visible minorities – whether it was LGBT officers who wouldn't toe the line, or the officers of colour who had no way of *not* being 'out' as non-white.

There was a hierarchy in the police. First came the white straight male, then the white straight female, then white (male) gay officers, then white lesbian officers, then 'straight' officers of colour. Black gay officers didn't make the list. Disabled officers weren't even considered. It was becoming such a lonely existence in Manchester's Police, that I started to look into London's police force. I thought the capital – diverse and multicultural – might suit me better.

In the years after the 9/11 attacks, a new fear of global terrorism also saw a creeping tendency towards militarisation in the British police forces. Many gay officers started wearing the black-and-white Union Jack on their uniforms at Gay Pride Parades, which originally symbolised the 'thin blue line' officers killed in the line of duty, but had been repurposed as a patriotic symbol. There was a fetishism, almost an obsession, with uniform amongst some LGBT people. It was as if the uniform made them think they knew who they were and what they belonged to, and the royal family played a part in the ideology of many white gay and lesbian police officers. Many spoke about the 'good old days' of the British empire – most black and brown people would never speak about colonialism, slavery and apartheid with such fondness.

I wanted to be accepted into this brotherhood, but I was aware of what it was costing me. I felt so ashamed. Like the majority of officers, I was rapidly becoming institutionalised. Once, I was driving alone along Princess Street in the city centre when I stopped a driver for a genuine routine vehicle check. I pulled over the car. The driver was black. Despite our shared skin colour, he accused me of stopping him simply because of his blackness. I hadn't victimised him in any way or done anything else untoward to him – but in my uniform, I wasn't black. I was blue. To him, it didn't matter what colour my skin was, he was just tired of constantly being stopped by the police. Despite my own experiences with racism, I failed to empathise with him. It took some time for me to realise this, and with a deep sadness I understood just how different the experience would have been if he had been white.

Our work was dominated by performance indicators. The Labour government had started to focus on 'narrowing the justice gap', creating its own league tables for police forces; and performance indicators ruled these figures. They were how we demonstrated our worth to the management, as well as to our colleagues. Being the best cop in the station no longer meant being the one who could talk someone down from a rooftop or comfort a family after the death of a young child. Now, the best cop was the one who made the most arrests, gave out the most traffic tickets, and produced the most paperwork. To the leadership, not producing paper meant not doing the job. Arresting beggars was seen as a waste of time, because nobody cared about them, and it didn't earn you a reward, so the homeless were continually picked on and moved on – hopefully to someone else's patch. To meet the quota, we had to go out on the streets and find ways to issue tickets, by any means necessary. The paperwork could be for anything, from vehicle offences to the newly introduced public order penalty notices. Some colleagues would search back alleys in the early mornings, just looking for drunk people they could fine for urinating after a night out. Urinating in the street was an easy find, but if you wanted you could up it to indecent exposure (because they had their penis out), and so potentially put someone on the sex register for having a pee in the street. The targets were meaningless and achieved nothing.

The big performance indicator and gold standard was 'stop and search' and later the so-called stop and talk, which the police leaders said was an 'essential tool' in combating crime. Unsurprisingly, it was predominantly young black men who were stopped. For so many of them, just speaking to an officer in a wrong tone landed them a disorder ticket and a record. It's how many young black men end up in the criminal justice system, in which the police is central. To give you an example: a young black person is walking or cycling along a high street when he is stopped by the police. The reasons for the stop don't matter. The officer asks if he is known to the police. The young person says no. Because this is how he is programmed, the officer doesn't believe this. After the officer has made his checks, the young person is confirmed as 'not known' and sent on his way. The officer, not wanting a complaint, places the young person on the criminal intelligence database by recording the stop. Now we have a young person who is not a criminal, and has never been in trouble with the police, appearing on a criminal database. Two weeks pass, and the young person is walking along the same or another street. Again, he is stopped, by different officers. He is again asked to account for his presence and if he is known to the police. He says no. Technically, he is right. He has never been arrested and is not a criminal. But to the officers, he has lied. The database lists him as known. The young person is confused. The new officers say he is known because he was stopped two weeks earlier. The officers ask the young person why he was stopped. 'For nothing,' he replies. The officers say it 'couldn't' have been for nothing. Everyone is getting agitated, the young person is getting upset. He feels oppressed and he doesn't understand why this keeps happening. He swears. The officers tell him to calm down and stop swearing or he will be arrested for public disorder. The young person gets more upset and angry. He swears again. He is then arrested for public disorder. During his arrest, he struggles with the officers, because he is upset and angry. He is additionally arrested for resisting arrest and/or police assault. The case goes to court and, naturally, the officers' word is taken over the young black man's. He now has a criminal record for walking down the street, jeopardising his future job prospects. All of this was lawful. In 2015, more than 40,000 of the UK's 16 to 24-year-old BAME were long-term unemployed, a 50% increase under the coalition government.[14]

At Bootle Street, each relief had charts on the writing room wall showing how many tickets, arrests and so forth each officer had accumulated for a particular period. The chart was coloured according to the traffic-light system: green meant we were good, amber meant we could do better, and red meant that we were going to have a chat with the inspector soon. We were encouraged to compete with each other, like salesmen or prize fighters. If the indicators for a team were low, it meant the shift inspector wasn't performing, and he too would be having his own chat with his seniors. So his sergeants got it in the neck, and in turn, their constables bore the brunt. It was very much like a business, and the criminals were our merchandise. When they threw in monetary bonuses, the competition became intense. Situations were manipulated, so that offences suddenly appeared, and most often the victims of this manipulation were minorities. For me, the hardest pill to swallow was the realisation that I was part of the problem. That black man I'd stopped for a vehicle document check had poignantly confessed how much he hated being a black man in Britain. I had smiled at him, thinking that my reality was different from his. I had become the coconut. I had suppressed my misgivings and began to feel it was 'us' against 'them', imagining that I was part of 'us'. I am still deeply ashamed of what I said to that young black motorist: 'If you don't like living in the UK, why don't you go and live somewhere else?'

I had become all that I hated. And I had started to dislike black and Asian people for making my existence in the police difficult, especially after 9/11. Police chiefs used the words 'war on crime' (like the 'war on terror') to describe their purpose. They commented on television that they, the police, had the 'biggest gang' in the fight against the baddies. Cops saw themselves as soldiers in a street war – all the more so because many of them had actually been soldiers. Some compared their experiences on the streets of wet, cold and windy Manchester to their tours in desert countries. Many officers would adjust their uniforms or personalise them to look more militarised, with Union Jack badges and the St George's Cross cropping up a lot. All this talk of war, gangs and fights fuelled them with adrenaline. This adrenaline could cause rage and excitement to spike – the 'red mist' that sometimes descended during arrests, and at other incidents. Sometimes five, six, seven and even eight officers piled on top of a person being detained. Blinded by that red mist, officers would lose their sense of judgment. This is one of the reasons why the number of deaths by asphyxiation in police custody is so high. When people struggle violently over a long period, the metabolic process becomes anaerobic and they don't take enough oxygen into the lungs. During the struggle, high levels of lactic acid build up, and if officers constrain a detainee's breathing, preventing them from taking in oxygen, the person loses consciousness and cannot be revived, which leads to positional asphyxia.

When someone was detained and handcuffed, if they were being 'mouthy', the handcuffs were tightened. If the prisoner shouted out that the cuffs were hurting, the reply was: 'Then stop struggling.' If a prisoner was still mouthing off as they were placed in the back of the police van, his or her head would deliberately be banged against the roof of the vehicle. If they were injured, officers would explain that they had attempted to resist entering the vehicle and had injured themselves in the process. Any more attitude? Easily fixed by slamming on the brakes to make the prisoner, not wearing a seatbelt (there were none) and hands cuffed behind the back, crash against the cage doors. The excuse? The traffic lights changed suddenly, or something ran out into the road.

There were prisoners who entered the police custody area with a full set of teeth and left with some missing. Others were strip-searched and asked to bend over, just for humiliation. CCTV was introduced in Britain in the 1970s to combat crime and antisocial behaviour, but if there was CCTV at the station that might record something which would contradict an officer's testimony, it was found to have been switched off, lost or malfunctioning at the time of the incident.

Later in court, detainees might complain about their treatment to a magistrate or judge, but to no avail. An officer's word always had more merit. What judicial person is going to believe the word of an alleged offender, a scroat (police slang for the scrotum), over an officer? The truth is, an officer's word shouldn't have any more bearing than an ordinary citizen's. It's not as if cops are born with a truth pill on their tongues. But the truth and reality are often two different things, especially for those up against the Force.

In 1998, the former British army paratrooper Christopher Alder, who was a trainee computer programmer, died whilst in custody at Hull Police Station. CCTV had recorded chimpanzee and monkey noises being made in the background whilst the Falklands veteran was handcuffed and face down on the floor, surrounded by officers. The footage showed him gasping for breath, his trousers and pants pulled down to his ankles, as the officers chatted and joked around him. They later said they believed Alder was 'play-acting'. After being put on trial for manslaughter and misconduct in public office, all of the officers were acquitted on the orders of the judge.

During one of our night shifts in June 2003, shortly after 3 a.m., we received a call over the radio about a man who had smashed a bus shelter on Piccadilly, in the city centre, near the main train station. A team from my shift arrived and the man was subdued on London Road. His name, we found out, was Delbo King. King, a black man, was pepper-sprayed and dragged to the ground by four of my colleagues, as another stood by and watched. Once he was pinned to the floor, one of my patrol sergeants began to kick a handcuffed, restrained King. The junior officer involved was accidentally pepper-sprayed in the confusion. The entire incident was caught on Manchester City Council's CCTV.[15] The video footage also showed King's head being banged against the door frame of the back of the police van as he was being put into it (the 'subduing' tactic). After the altercation, back at Bootle Street in the early hours, the video footage capturing the incident was played in the patrol briefing room for my shift, for us to have a laugh at the sergeant and some of my team kicking King's arse on the street. The twenty-minute camera footage later shown in court clearly showed

King being booted by my sergeant.[16] After his arrest, he received bruising to his genitals and one of his teeth was broken. King admitted to damaging the bus shelter, but the police said King had abused officers and resisted arrest. This was easy to 'prove': during training, we were taught to shout demands like 'stop struggling' or 'get back', even when the person had been forcibly restrained or was nowhere near us.

Anthony O'Donnell, King's solicitor, said he had been the victim of 'gratuitous violence' by the police. GMP received a lot of negative press for the incident, triggering nationwide outrage.[17] Mark Littlewood, a spokesman for the human rights organisation Liberty said, 'On the face of it, the police have some serious questions to answer. Clearly these officers have to be given a fair opportunity to explain their actions, but it is hard to see what could justify this kind of violence.' Graham Stringer, the MP for Blackley, called for an independent inquiry, stating: 'If people see things like this taking place, they could lose trust in the police, so there has to be an independent investigation into what happened and why management within the Force didn't take action sooner.'[18]

King said he just wanted my colleagues to be brought to justice: 'I am sickened about the whole affair and I intend to seek justice.' A former British Paratrooper who had served in Northern Ireland, he went further: 'I am not some scumbag drug dealer. I have served Queen and country. I admit I was drunk but I wasn't violent towards the police and after they cuffed me that should have been the end of the matter.' He finished by adding, 'They seemed to enjoy what they were doing.'[19] I often saw this behaviour. It was toxic masculinity at its worst.

The deputy chairman of the Police Complaints Authority (which took over from the Police Complaints Board in 1985), Wendy Towers, promised 'a full and impartial investigation'.[20] A criminal investigation found that my sergeant had no case to answer.[21] He was moved from patrol to an administration role, and then to the divisional tutor unit, as a supervisor of new recruits to the police. He was later named a 'diversity champion'.

It reminded me of the case of Rodney King (no relation) in 1991. Rodney King, a black taxi driver, had taken a beating from officers of the Los Angeles police department after he refused to stop when they tried to pull him over on the freeway. They were later acquitted of the assault, sparking the 1992 Los Angeles riots, which resulted in the death of over 50 people and more than 2,300 injured.

LA 92, a documentary about the riots, shows archive footage of Sergeant Stacey Koon, the officer in charge of the scene and one of the defendants in the assault case, responding to questions about King's treatment with the words: 'It's violent and it's brutal ... Sometimes police work is brutal.'[22]

It wasn't only black people who were on the harsh receiving end of police brutality, but poor white people too, as I'd seen growing up. In 2010, an officer from my old uniform patrol shift was jailed along with a custody sergeant for eighteen months each over the arrest of 18-year-old Amy Keigher. Keigher had been arrested on suspicion of carrying out a racially aggravated assault in Manchester city centre. One of my police constable colleagues had held Keigher in a painful 'restraint position' at the station that put her at risk of suffocating, forcibly holding her head down on the custody desk whilst she was handcuffed, snarling at her, 'I'll rip your fucking skull off.' When Keigher began crying and telling the officers they were hurting her, the custody sergeant said: 'If you misbehave you will be hurt. It is the technique we are trained to do – hurt'. This entire incident was caught on CCTV, and couldn't be explained away, though my former colleague claimed that he had acted in the interests of safety – his own and his colleagues'. The case came a decade after my skull-ripping colleague had previously escaped dismissal, having been convicted and fined £100 for punching another prisoner in the face. Keigher pled guilty to a charge of common assault – the reason she was arrested – but the judge in the Keigher case, Anthony Gee QC, told the two officers that what they did 'was little short of torture'.[23] He went on to say that 'anyone seeing that CCTV footage could not be anything other than appalled' at how Keigher was treated, and that the sergeant, 'as the senior officer, could have put an end to it immediately – he didn't'. The judge said that Keigher 'represented no real threat to anyone'.[24]

Naseem Malik, a commissioner of the newly renamed Independent Police Complaints Commission (the IPCC, which took over investigating police misconduct from the Police Complaints Authority on April Fool's Day 2004), said after the case: '[These] actions were what you might expect from a street gang, not professional police officers.'[25]

My former colleagues had denied misconduct in public office, but were found guilty in a three-week trial. Three of my other colleagues – one male police officer, one female police officer and a civilian detention officer – were all cleared of the same charge. A spokesman for the Police Federation, the police officers' union, said it was 'extremely disappointed with the severity of the sentences'. Both the judge and local newspapers called my former colleagues 'thugs'.

As a police officer, I didn't for a moment believe that Keigher got what she deserved, regardless of her admitting that she had assaulted somebody. Even more so because the police are meant to protect people from harm. But equally, I didn't believe that my two former colleagues were necessarily bad people either. The constable in question was a product of the system that had taught him to protect himself and his fellow officers, and I guess he genuinely believed that's what he was doing. Yes, police officers learn life-saving skills, but most of what they are taught relates to dealing with those in society who pose a threat. Disrespecting the police undermined their authority, and was a threat to them, and threats needed to be neutralised.

★

In addition to ordinary duties, officers can choose to apply for various courses, to build their own careers. During my Stage 6A probationer training, I applied for and completed a rape investigation course. In a rape investigation, trained uniform 'Nightingale' officers take the victim through the investigative process, explaining the early evidence kit, which collects and stores any initial forensic evidence (such as toilet paper, if the victim used the toilet), storing clothing as evidence, and taking down an initial account identifying the offender and location. A medical then took place, in an examination unit at St Mary's Sexual Assault Referral Centre. Once the Nightingales had collected their samples and a statement, the victim would be handed over to detectives.

I had also applied for a short attachment at the police headquarters' press and publicity department, to work on the national firearms amnesty. GMP was the lead Force for this Home Office initiative to get guns off the streets. The Force often advertised roles like this to aid officers' professional development, and cops were able to apply for them on their own initiative. Having studied media at college and university, I thought this would be a good fit for my skills and a useful addition to my CV. My application was accepted and I was to join the attachment for several months, alongside my normal operational duties. I was going to be doing more for the same pay, true, but I was interested in the work. Shortly after my interview with public relations, my patrol sergeants (including the one from the Delbo King case) said that I couldn't join the attachment because of 'low staffing levels' at the station, even though I had sought permission and received it before applying. Thankfully, my new inspector said he would allow me to join the attachment. I knew exactly why the problem had arisen with the sergeants in the first place. As I left their office, I had, after all, overheard one of them saying they were keeping me 'in my place' by not letting me go.

Following my attachment, I received a two-page letter[26] from my divisional commander, which had been sent to him by the superintendent in charge of the community affairs: I was to be commended for the work I did on the National Firearms Amnesty.

I couldn't keep bottling everything up. I confided in a station sergeant I trusted, an older, realistic man who knew how harsh the police could be. Not long after, early one morning, the new patrol inspector asked to see me. I went to his office and he explained that he had heard I was unhappy. I replied that I just wanted to do what I was paid to do and get on with my job. The inspector was the son of a former superintendent, and it was no secret that he wanted to achieve the same rank as his father. I thought he was hoping that addressing my difficulties whilst he was acting in the rank (as his substantive – i.e. permanent – rank was only that of sergeant, three ranks below a superintendent) would help him achieve this. Thanks to Labour's initiatives, box-ticking and paying lip service to 'race and diversity' issues on police forms meant brownie points, and that meant fast-tracked careers (for white officers). But cynicism aside, I also believed my inspector didn't like the culture of racism and homophobia.

He wrote a report about me to the chief inspector and asked me to sign it.[27] The report described my unhappiness in the Force and the way that inappropriate comments had left me feeling that the police was not the professional organisation I had thought it was. The inspector wrote that I had experienced issues that had left me feeling offended, but that I wasn't prepared to name specific colleagues, so as not to draw attention to myself. I left the inspector's office to join my team on patrol, with a copy of the report. I reread his words, folded it up, placed it inside my body armour, and got back to my reality of policing. The report travelled up the ranks. The sub-divisional chief inspector read my inspector's report and wrote his own memo to his seniors about me.[28] The chief superintendent then wrote his own note about the situation to the Force's personnel director, saying: 'This has the potential to turn unpleasant.'[29]

5

The Secret Policeman

Unbeknownst to all but the police leadership, the BBC was
going to broadcast an undercover documentary about the Force
on prime-time television, on BBC One in October 2003, called
The Secret Policeman.[1] The corporation had commissioned the
documentary after the 'institutional racism' comments made by
the former chief constable, David Wilmot. It revealed the extent
to which structural racism was a problem throughout the police.
There was much panic. It was going to be a disaster for the
service and a public relations nightmare.

The covert footage captured by the BBC Scotland journalist
Mark Daly was astonishing.[2] Daly had gone undercover as
a trainee police officer. He had filmed the footage during his
initial training at Bruche – my passing-out parade took place
shortly before his – and subsequently, whilst he was out on patrol.
The documentary covered the public inquiry that followed
the murder of Stephen Lawrence, and the internal reaction. The
footage was a brutal exposé. Daly had managed to capture the
police's bigoted views towards people of colour; even recording
one officer, Rob Pulling of North Wales Police, dressed as a
member of the Ku Klux Klan.

For the first time, the public could see the police on film
routinely denigrating ethnic minorities and expressing sympathy

for Hitler. The film also uncovered possible links with the far-right British National Party, at one point the fifth biggest political party in Britain. The Freemasons already had their funny handshakes in policing, like at Wigan, but no one knew how many far-right extremists were in the police. The BNP claimed several of its members were in the police ranks. Its spokesperson, Phil Edwards, said, 'I know we have several serving officers in our party and why not? I should imagine most police sympathise with the BNP's view that a multicultural society is not a stable society.'[3]

There were some remarkable ugly scenes. The KKK costume-wearing officer, Pulling, lunged towards the hidden camera, detailing his fantasies about attacking the only Asian recruit in his class. He described him as 'fat', 'smelly' and 'irritating', adding, 'I haven't even fucking started with him yet. He'll regret the day he was ever fucking born a Paki.'[4] His tirade continued. He went on to say that the gang who murdered Stephen Lawrence did their country a service: 'They fucking need fucking diplomatic immunity – they've done for this country what others fucking should do . . . Isn't it good how good memories don't fade. He fucking deserved it and his mum and dad are a fucking pair of spongers'. His reaction to the Macpherson report: 'A fucking kick in the bollocks for any white man, that was.' During the recording, Pulling received a text message: 'Trading standards have just confirmed why golliwogs were banned on marmalade jars – niggers were peeling them off and using them as bus passes.' On Hitler and the Holocaust: 'He's [sic] had the right idea but he went about it all the wrong way, mate. If he went about that in the correct way we could have a better world now.' On second-generation immigrants: 'A dog that's born in a barn is still a dog. A Paki born in Britain is still a fucking Paki.' Pulling's ultimate fantasy was to bury a 'Paki bastard' under a train track.[5]

Pulling complained to his course trainer about the only Asian officer, claiming that he had been playing the 'race card'. I was more shocked that it was the 'Asian officer' rather than Pulling who was summoned to see the sergeant, with the news travelling fast around the police campus; it felt so similar to my 'coconut' incident. Daly recorded Pulling and his colleagues discussing the Asian officer: 'Should be out now of a fucking job'; 'I just fucking hate him'; 'I'd kill him. I'd pull my fucking hood on my head and fucking chase him down the road.' In the event, the Asian recruit was back-classed, which was announced by the trainer to the rest of the class: 'I have some news,' (excited laughter). 'Well, the point is he's not coming back,' (to shouts of 'hooray'). The class trainer went on: 'I've been told I'm not to try and look too happy.'

Although I'd received exceptional instruction from my trainers at Bruche – perhaps because they were women, and one of them a woman of colour – *The Secret Policeman* highlighted numerous concerns about how police trainers behaved. An instructor was recorded saying: 'There's four words which you cannot say: negro, nigger, coon and wog . . . [laughs] Paki, that's five, totally unacceptable.'

Trainee officer Andy Hall (who had spent fifteen months in London at the Met, but had to retrain as he didn't complete his two-year probation period) called for immigrants to be shot, and for armed squads to shoot them as they came into Britain. Steve Salkeld boasted that he'd nick the sole Asian cop on the course if he saw him driving a Jaguar, 'cos it's built into your fucking brain'. Hall went on: 'He's a Paki and I'm stopping him cos I'm fucking English . . . If you did not discriminate and you did not bring out your prejudices you would be a shit copper.' Speaking of his experiences policing in London, he added: 'We used to drive down the road and say "he looks a dodgy cunt, let's stop him". That is practical policing.' He had no qualms about this behaviour: 'Police are racist mate, police are racist. They are, they fucking are.'

Constable Carl Jones called discriminating against black

motorists 'BAT', Black Added Tax. He said: '[In] my previous life of work I used to fuckin' rip 'em off and I did.' Constable Tony Lewin bragged: 'I'll admit it. I'm a racist bastard ... At the end of the day we look after our own.' Daly asked Adrian Harrison, a former social worker, 'Did you know then before you joined up that the whole Force was totally racist?' to which he responded, 'Definitely.' Harrison then went on to say he was 'cool' with racism, because 'I've been working for an organisation who [sic] is totally politically correct.'

Prior to the showing of the documentary, the new chief constable of Manchester, Michael Todd, sent this internal memo to staff:

> *I am extremely concerned by the events of the last 48 hours and the discovery that a BBC reporter has been working undercover as a probationary constable in Stockport. The incident/case is being fully investigated and as the individual is currently on police bail until November there are some restrictions on what can be said. Officers are currently investigating what possible offences may have been committed. But I have made my views of the tactics used in this case very clear to the media, it is deplorable and appears to be an outrageous waste of public funds. I feel, as I am sure many of you do, betrayed by what has happened. I will be making my views known to the director general of the BBC. We cannot let this incident undermine our determination to fight crime and protect people in Greater Manchester.[6]*

Despite Todd's defensive statement (he was the one who spoke out against Gurpal Virdi), the Force had to act. Ten officers resigned and a further twelve faced disciplinary action. I could understand one bad apple, but this made twenty-two, all convinced that the institution they had joined would turn a blind eye to, and even condone, their views.

After *The Secret Policeman* hit the small screen, life for its maker Daly wasn't easy. The police swiftly set about arresting him for collecting his police salary by deceit (obtaining pecuniary interest by deception) and damaging police property (for inserting the secret camera into his police-issued bulletproof vest). The BBC, smartly, had placed Daly's police pay into a separate bank account, not to be used, but returned.

Days after the screening, I was called into the chief inspector's office. I was informed that I had been selected to go on a secondment as part of Her Majesty's Inspectorate of Constabulary restructure team, after a critical inspection of the Force. My 'media skills' were needed, I was told. This secondment wasn't something for which I had applied. I was told by the Force headquarters that I had been selected because my divisional command had highlighted me as an officer with high potential. I was sent a letter by the Force regarding fast-track promotion, known as the accelerated High Potential Development Scheme, three months *after* the secondment was due to start.[7]

I told them that I didn't want to do it. The chief inspector responded that I had no choice but to accept. I was to be moved with immediate effect. The immediacy startled my peers and supervisors as much as me. We had only just been on football riot duty the day before, policing Manchester United v Portsmouth. I was being moved out of the way, again, during my probation.

The senior officers of my Force and others had been trying to work out how best to minimise the fallout from *The Secret Policeman*. One thing they needed to do was move people like me from key operational roles. The chiefs hadn't realised how far right-wing extremism was embedded in the service until the documentary pulled all of the evidence together. Ethnic minority officers were moved from their normal shifts into offices and other duties, not because of fears that racist members of the public would turn on officers of colour, but because of fears that there would be internal combustion, i.e. that white officers would turn on colleagues of colour. The Force was in turmoil and minority officers were extremely vulnerable.

After the documentary was aired, GMP's deputy chief constable, Alan Green, admitted that he feared right-wing extremists might have infiltrated the police and accepted that he had no idea how many may have slipped through the net. He said, 'I was shocked, sickened, ashamed and saddened by what I saw.'[8] Tony Lloyd, the MP for Manchester Central, who later became the county's police and crime commissioner, said the documentary was 'genuinely frightening'.[9] Sir Bill Morris, the trade union leader, who later chaired the Morris Inquiry and wrote a report about racism in the Metropolitan Police,[10] commented: 'Anyone who watched will be appalled at the depth of racism among public servants serving a multi-ethnic community.'[11]

I read much about *The Secret Policeman* and the reaction to it, but one letter to the *Police Review* stood out for me.[12] It was written by Constable Tony Chanda of Merseyside Police, and published in the police magazine. He wrote:

> *I trained at the Bruche training centre and as the only Asian found it very difficult to adjust to the military type of training. I made the necessary adjustments to fit into the establishment and finished with my head held high. Seeing* The Secret Policeman *and the racist hatred by those named in the programme, I felt for the Asian police officer. That would have been me 20 years ago, so I feel nothing has really changed. My first posting was at Southport as a probationary officer. I was told that the reason I was there was to show the ethnic flag.*

I started on the restructure team at Bootle Street shortly after *The Secret Policeman* aired. Just days before, I had attended the personal leadership programme, a positive action scheme run by the National Police Leadership Centre at Centrex for ethnic minorities. Centrex, the Central Police Training and Development Authority had taken over National Police Training. The law allowed for positive action, such as encouraging applications from disadvantaged groups, as opposed to positive discrimination, which was unlawful and, in my opinion, not useful. Filling the ranks with black and brown faces for the sake of box-ticking didn't improve policing but undermined it. The service needed black and Asian officers who had a passion to serve, not to meet government quotas. There was a reason ethnic minorities did not want to join the Force. More black cops wasn't the answer. More brown faces wasn't going to stamp out the racism.

There were five of us seconded to the strategic team: a chief inspector, an inspector and three constables, including me. The superintendent who oversaw it answered to the new divisional chief superintendent, Justine Curran, who had transferred back to Manchester from Merseyside Police; she answered to the chiefs of police at Force headquarters. The project was to restructure my division, North Manchester, from three sub-divisions into a unitary one, with local policing areas known as 'neighbourhoods'. It was to be a model for other police commands, locally and nationally, and I was responsible for the marketing and communication strategies to the 900-plus staff in my division – a division so big that it could have been a police force in its own right. It was one of the biggest basic command units in the country and covered some of Britain's most deprived council wards.

A month into the secondment, I was confirmed in the rank of constable. I had been a little concerned whilst waiting for this to happen. Within the first two years of your probation, the chief of police can get rid of you without giving a reason. However, just before my confirmation I received a letter from the divisional training sergeant that read: 'You have worked very hard during your probation and made excellent progress.'[13] This was an unofficial acknowledgement that I would be confirmed. I would have had to do something really stupid not to receive it.

At the division's carol service at the Hidden Gem (officially St Mary's Catholic Church) on 17 December 2003, I was asked to give the second reading along with the chief superintendent. Like Mum, I had always had a strong belief in God, though I didn't shout it from the rooftops. In many ways, I was and am a cultural Catholic. Revelling in the season of goodwill, and in high spirits after my rank confirmation, I attended my patrol relief's Christmas party at the Bootle Street Police Station bar. Many police stations still had a bar serving alcohol (for promotion and leaving dos) and a canteen for breakfast, lunch and dinner, and the 'canteen culture' of informal mixing and gossip was at the heart of day-to-day policing. A colleague from my patrol shift was doing stand-up comedy for the evening. Part of his routine focused on me. He had a bit about my sexuality. I was sitting in the front row with some colleagues, staring at the officer as he made up a story about finding me in the middle of a sexual encounter at the station. According to the routine, I had been on my knees giving oral sex to a male prisoner in the cells whilst my sergeant was looking for me.

I was one of only three gay male officers at the station now. My face and ears burned as the crowd laughed. I looked past several people wiping tears of mirth from their eyes, and saw my patrol inspector walk out. Shortly afterwards, one of my sergeants called me on my mobile. I was asked to see the inspector in his office. I went to see him. Since it was the Christmas party, we were both in our civilian clothes. As we sat in his office, he asked me what I wanted to do. I simply said 'nothing'. We had recently had a similar conversation, and he'd got a signed report from me. The inspector said that he would deal with my colleague, but I didn't have much hope; he hadn't, after all, said anything during the stand-up act. When serving, we are police officers. When we are off duty, we are police officers. The chief of police is vicariously liable for any unlawful acts following a shift, especially those committed within a station or building controlled by him or her. The inspector, no doubt, would have known this.

After our impromptu meeting, I returned to the bar. Though I was the one humiliated, I found myself reassuring my colleagues that I had not made any complaint against the 'comedian'.

On my next shift following the Christmas party, I returned to my secondment on the restructure team. There were now eight of us on the team, including two officers, still in their probation period, and a new sergeant. As demand for its work grew, the restructure team grew. I was in a foul mood, angry and confused. As I sat at the computer terminal in the restructure office, I heard one of the female officers on my team talking down to two male officers who had been seconded as additional resources to work with us. As I caught my colleague's tone, my head snapped in her direction and I leapt to the officers' defence. An anger that had been dormant inside me reared its head. My colleague was out of order – rude and belittling – and it had rubbed me the wrong way. As I called her out, I realised to my shame that I could stand up for others, but not for myself. Still, my words did something. They stopped her bad attitude in its tracks, and she never spoke to the two officers like that again in my presence.

Not long afterwards, a new male inspector joined the team. One afternoon, I was having an informal chat in the main office about women in the police, and said to my two female colleagues that female superintendents who had the experience and service equivalent to males should be given an opportunity to be a chief superintendent, on merit, to 'break the glass ceiling'. Overhearing me, the new inspector stormed out of his office and told me to stop talking about this. Unfortunately for him, the female chief inspector with whom he had already clashed once before overheard him and came out of *her* office. She said anyone was allowed to talk about anything they wanted to. Though I cheered for her internally, I stayed quiet and wondered how I had managed to ruffle so many feathers. Still raw from the Christmas party, I had somehow walked into two battles I hadn't wanted or planned. But I learnt from these experiences that cops have long memories.

At the beginning of the new year, I drove from Manchester to Liverpool to visit my mother. When I got home, the front door to our family home wasn't locked. I knew something was up. I went in, and found Mum in her bed. When I asked her why the door wasn't locked properly, she told me that she was feeling unwell and must have forgotten. This wasn't like her at all. I tried to find out how and why she was feeling unwell, but she couldn't say. We packed a bag for her and drove back to Manchester, so that Mum could stay with me and my partner for a few days. He was a doctor, after all. She didn't get better, and in the end I persuaded her to see her doctor. She had a urinary tract infection, so was referred to a specialist at the Royal Liverpool Hospital. We went there together. Mum was weak, so the doctor called me in to a room with him, to break the news: my mum had ovarian cancer and only three months to live.

My world collapsed. It was hard to comprehend what he had said to me. My mum was going to die soon and, as much as it hurt, I had to be strong, even though I was still at the stage in my young life when I desperately needed her there. I have never loved a person as much as I did, and still do, love my mother. She was my world: my rock and my best friend. I was her boy. Her baby son, as she often told people.

I gathered my ten siblings together at Mum's house, and told them all at once. Half of them didn't believe what I said, the other half couldn't take it in.

I'd never known our mum to ask anything of us, so when she told us that she wanted to die at home, of course we agreed. I would have done anything for her. I would have given my life for hers. After a few nights' stay in hospital for some checks, we got her ready to go home and she was discharged. I made up a single bed by the window in the living room, which we'd turned into a bedroom for her, and planned to stay with her for her final days. I cared for her and helped to wash her daily. It gave me some peace, knowing I had the opportunity to help my mother die with dignity and pride.

On her last night, it was just the two of us in the room. I sang 'I Just Called to Say I Love You' by Stevie Wonder to her, which I'd sung as a child, as she closed her eyes. The next day, surrounded by her children holding her hands, Mum fell asleep for the final time, never to wake again.

My siblings and I were naturally upset by the loss of our sole parent, but we tried to remember that she had lived a good and rich life. We would never know a love like the one she had shown us, and we were better, stronger, happier people because of that love. Although she was only sixty-seven years old when she died, she left a great legacy, with many grandchildren and great-grandchildren who adored her. We were thankful to have been able to say goodbye properly, as we knew many others didn't have this chance.

After the funeral – with its hundreds of mourners, and the tributes that had poured in from neighbours and friends who had admired, respected and loved my mum all through her life – I returned to work. It was the only thing I could do, although I had lost my biggest 'police supporter'. Her passing also marked the final chapter in my relationship with my partner, the doctor.

A lesbian colleague at Bootle Street, who was from Liverpool, arranged for a collection whilst I was away, and I asked that it be sent to Macmillan Cancer Relief, who had supported Mum. My colleague had also asked the Police Federation to send some flowers, but they initially refused. A week after burying Mum, on what would have been her sixty-eighth birthday, I received a letter from my police commander congratulating me on my 100% attendance record for the previous twelve months.[14] It was a bittersweet moment. In the three years of my entire service, I had never taken a single sick day.

After using up all my annual leave, my divisional commander, Justine Curran, authorised some special leave, which was allowed when a member of your immediate family dies. But my new restructure team inspector was keen for me to return, as the marketing and communication strategies I had been responsible for had not been as effective as they'd hoped. Besides, I had to get back to some sort of normality. I had worked hard to become and remain a police officer. I didn't want to fail myself or my mum, especially with the encouragement she had given me to serve. I could sit around crying or get on with the life she had given me. I chose the latter.

My work on the restructure team came to an end once the new division was in place. As an original team member, I was asked to stay on for an extra two weeks to handle any queries and make sure that everything went smoothly. I was to be awarded a divisional commander's commendation for my duties on the team, being cited for 'outstanding work in connection with his exemplary performance whilst involved in the restructure of the North Manchester Division'.[15] I also received a monetary award from the 'Bonus Panel' (the chief superintendent and senior management team) for my 'dedication to duty', and 'in recognition of your excellent work in delivering the divisional restructure'.[16]

My appraisal consisted of three 'exceptional' ratings and four 'fully competent' ratings.[17] I had to apply for a post-restructure role, and choose an area I was particularly interested in. I successfully applied to join the plain-clothes unit, otherwise known as the Area Support Team. The plain-clothes unit – officers who police the streets in their own clothes, blending in with the public – deals with intelligence, planning and organising operations, searching premises and dealing with any 'exhibits' such as evidence of crime. I had the experience, strategically and operationally, to fit the criteria. I visited the plain-clothes office to get a feel for it, as it was going to be a two-year tenure.

Later that day, I saw the plain-clothes inspector in the restructure team office. He approached me and said that some officers in the unit had told him I was not keen to join it. I was baffled. My visit had been brief and I hadn't even spoken to anyone. I had only been there to make sure I made the right choice in my application. I told the inspector that it was always my intention to get some plain-clothes experience and that I would be joining him after my time on the restructure team came to an end.

So I started in plain-clothes shortly after the July 2004 restructure. The squad blended into the community by sitting in coffee shops, walking through shopping centres like the Arndale, waiting for something like a robbery – a street crime, a theft with use of force – to happen, so that we could step in. Now out of uniform, I no longer carried out the ad hoc initial Nightingale rape-investigation duties. Unlike uniform policing, which was reactive, plain-clothes was proactive. We worked to prevent crimes from taking place by stopping known robbers. We were usually found at crime hotspots like the main shopping areas.

Since the restructure, the plain-clothes unit had become quite big, with around thirty officers. Most of the staff on the team I was placed on already knew each other, having worked together at Collyhurst and Grey Mare Lane police stations. They were friends at work and outside of it.

After a couple of months, the remit of the new unit was changed. The way we were combating crime wasn't effective enough, and my sergeant had to select a new team. Everyone on the team was asked to state (verbally) whether they wanted to stay on his team, which I did. However, I wasn't taken on in the new selection. When I asked him why, he told me he wanted people he knew and could trust. I later found out that I'd only been asked to state my preference so that the process would look fair; a colleague of mine told me that the decision to move me had been made before I was even asked to state it.

I decided to apply for a five-week attachment in the Tactical Aid Unit that was being offered to constables, away from plain-clothes. It was the riot squad that dealt with public disorder in the county on a full-time basis, and as I'd not long passed my advanced level public order training, this was ideal for me. I thought that some time away from the plain-clothes unit would do me some good, and learning new skills would greatly assist me in my development as an officer. The TAU accepted me and gave me a start date. Not long after I was told that I could go on the attachment, the plain-clothes inspector cancelled it, and told me that it was due to 'low staffing levels'[18] (I'd heard this before whilst in uniform). A (white) officer from my team applied for an attachment to the Force's Vehicle Crime Unit after me, and had it approved by the inspector.

I then applied for a permanent post as a trainee detective in my division, supported by my new female sergeant (whose plain-clothes team I had now been moved to). My interview was at Bootle Street, with two old-school inspectors. I knew I would be unsuccessful even before I applied, but still pushed through. Unsurprisingly, I was not accepted, despite my having that 100% pass rate on all my evidential crime files. I came out of the detective interview like a dog retreating, tail tucked between his legs.

My glam colleague from Bruche had become a detective not long after her probation period, in the same office where her dad worked as a detective. I was very happy for her, but I couldn't think of any qualifications or experience that she had and I didn't. The plain-clothes inspector wanted me out, and I wanted out, but I had nowhere to go. As I weighed up my options, I decided to put myself forward for the National Investigative Interviewing Course. The NIIC is an advanced course that focuses on suspect and witness interview skills. I completed it outside my normal shifts. I also completed the National Optical Evidence and Intelligence Gathering course, which focused on how we gathered intelligence, and on 15 December 2004 did my second Christmas reading alongside the chief superintendent, Justine Curran. The plain-clothes inspector might not have wanted me in the unit, but it was harder for a manager to turn down an officer's request to attend a development course in their current role, than requests for attachments and trainee detective posts.

Whilst I was on one of those courses at the Force's training school, Sedgley Park, I was approached by a man in the police canteen as I ate my lunch. He took me to one side and identified himself as a detective inspector from covert operations. He said that he had been watching me, and asked if I had ever considered becoming an undercover officer – a police spy. I hadn't. I did, however, know that police officers infiltrated and spied on groups they believed to be 'disruptive' or anti-establishment, such as those supporting black rights and gay rights. Many of the political groups and social movements I knew of were under the observation of undercover police. Often, when I was out in Manchester's gay village, I would see undercover cops acting as 'test purchasers' for drugs. Officers would approach people and ask if they had any drugs to sell, then arrest them if they did. If we recognised one another, I always turned the other way, so that I wouldn't blow their cover.

After several meetings with the inspector and other senior covert detectives, I was asked to apply for the United Kingdom Undercover Officer Training, which was led nationally by the Metropolitan Police's specialist crime directorate SCD11(10). I completed my application form at GMP, and attended a pre-assessment briefing with around forty other applicants. We undertook a series of video-recorded role plays which assessed how well we acted around infiltrated groups, and how we would cope in dangerous situations without revealing our undercover

identities. We were then sent for external psychological testing and independent non-police panel interviews. This was an intense day, with three hours of questionnaires and tests to complete, including a decision-making test and four personality tests – the 16 Personality Factor Questionnaire, the NEO Personality Inventory, the Eysenck Personality Questionnaire and the California Psychological Inventory. I then received my result and detailed feedback sheets. I had been successful. Out of forty applicants, I was one of only two who had passed all the assessments, the psychological testing and the interview. The assessment by the Devon-based chartered occupational psychologist Dr Felicity Gibling highlighted that I was

> in favour of working with the support of a team rather than in isolation . . . He seems to have a very warm and receptive nature and this suggests he will want to spend much of his time with others. He is likely to rate relationships as one of his highest priorities, and he should be both cooperative and considerate towards his colleagues . . . Kevin seems to be quite an assertive person, so he will generally be prepared to stand firm and defend his views, particularly when they are important to him . . . He would probably be unwilling to countenance breaking rules even if there appears to be a good case for it. Kevin seems to be very strongly aligned with conventional moral standards. He will follow strict rules and procedures, accepting 'the establishment' and what it represents in this sense; and he will want others to do the same. He is someone who can virtually always be relied upon to think very carefully about what constitutes the right and proper thing when making decisions.[19]

The other candidate – a woman – and I were sent to b interviewed by the National Undercover Selection Boar led by Scotland Yard's superintendent of covert operatio The interview itself was in Warwick, at a hotel that we we

to incognito. Afterwards, I received my feedback from the Metropolitan Police, informing me that I had been unsuccessful. During the interview, the board had spoken about how I should get some detective experience, and then reapply.[20] I had already tried to become a detective, and had my application blocked. The senior covert officers knew that.

In the new year, I officially submitted a request to transfer out of plain-clothes. I applied for a position in the new divisional key crime prisoner processing unit (KCPPU) at Collyhurst Police Station, the nearby station within the division, which investigated non-aggravated burglaries, vehicle crime and domestic violence offences. This unit came under the remit of the CID, the detective squad I had tried to join.

The plain-clothes inspector accepted my transfer request in the blink of an eye and made no attempt to persuade me to stay. But later he called me back into his office, to tell me that the prisoner processing unit had no vacancies, even though it did when I applied. Apparently the superintendent in charge of divisional performance, until recently head of the Criminal Intelligence Bureau (CIB), wanted me to work for him as his staff officer for a month. Staff officers were like personal assistants to police chiefs, and junior officers used the role as preparation for their next rank. If I took the staff officer role, he said, a vacancy in the prisoner processing unit would open up at the end of my stint. I wasn't being asked, but told.

In January 2005, I took up my role as the staff officer to the superintendent in the divisional performance management unit. In my new role, I answered directly to the superintendent, assisting in all aspects of his remit and gaining a strategic oversight of the division, which included the Race Equality Scheme (RES). Like most of these 'race initiatives' forced on the police by the government to meet its statutory duties required by the Commission for Racial Equality, they only worked if the police wanted them to. In order to get a

mandatory RES 'completion tick' on their personnel file, all officers had to answer a race questionnaire. It was my role to coordinate the implementation of the RES in the division and devise the actual questionnaire to gauge officers' understanding of race and equality.

Whilst doing this, I discovered officers were cheating the RES questionnaire by copying, and in some cases photocopying, other officers' answers. The number of photocopies of the same answers I saw was incredible. Whilst I was working on the scheme, the case of Charles Crichlow came to my attention. Charles was a constable at my Force and chairman of Manchester's BAPA. As reported by Black Information Link, Charles took GMP to an employment tribunal, stating that he was discriminated against on the grounds of his colour and that he had suffered four years of unfair treatment at the hands of his colleagues.[21] Charles, the only black race and diversity trainer at the time, told the court that he was removed from training duties to a desk job after complaining about racism. He had objected, amongst other things, to a 'slaves for sale' poster, which was pinned to a wall in Salford whilst he was carrying out race training. Senior officers ignored Charles's complaints and his suggestions about how to genuinely improve diversity. The Manchester employment tribunal ruled in Charles's favour, though they also ruled that Charles was not on the receiving end of racism per se. Ray Powell, chair of the BPA, welcomed the tribunal decision, stating: 'Until the police service sit up and start to take action we are going to have people who believe they can get away with blatant racist comments'. The officer responsible for the 'slaves' poster was 'spoken to'. The police's old, draconian, disciplinary system of 'speaking to' someone: 'Stop being racist, please.'

Like Gurpal Virdi's case, several of the officers named by Charles were promoted to more senior positions, including a sergeant who was described by the tribunal as not a 'wholly reliable witness', for evading and refusing to answer questions.[22]

When the Force was considering appealing Charles's win, the deputy chief constable, Alan Green, said: 'The findings of the tribunal relate to occurrences four years ago. We now have a Race Equality Scheme and training which emphasises the general and specific duties of our staff under the Race Relations (Amendment) Act 2000.'[23] This was the scheme I had just coordinated and implemented in my division, the Force's biggest, with its photocopied answers and lackadaisical response.

The week before Charles's judgment, a white police officer in GMP escaped with a slap on the wrist for sending a racist email featuring a black beauty queen with a monkey's head superimposed on her body. The tribunal also heard evidence about a message on GMP's intranet that poked fun at the tragedy of the fifty-eight Chinese refugees who had died whilst trying to enter Britain, in the back of a van loaded with tomatoes. The message, entitled 'Chinese Takeaway', read: 'I'll have a cold number 58 with tomatoes.' Another email referred to asylum seekers as 'parasites' who should be banned from Britain.[24] It also emerged that Special Branch officers had sent an email to officers asking for information on anyone intending to give evidence at the Manchester hearing of the Stephen Lawrence Inquiry. The fact that Special Branch, the arresting arm of MI5 which normally dealt with terrorism, was appealing for 'intelligence' seemed to suggest that giving evidence that might incriminate the police was somehow dangerous, and undermined public safety.

The Police Federation had refused to support Charles. Charles pointed out that the Police Federation supported officers involved in police custody deaths, but not his case. He said, 'I won my case. So what does that say about the Police Federation? It speaks volumes.'[25]

Charles also highlighted that those other officers remained on full pay whilst serious complaints against them were investigated, sometimes for years, yet he was threatened with a reduction to half-pay whilst he was off work sick with stress. In concluding the judgment in Charles's favour, the tribunal chair, Anna Woolley, said that the Force had discriminated against Charles by 'subjecting him to the detriment of not investigating his grievances and allegations properly or at all'.[26] The tribunal found that senior officers treated Charles like a 'troublemaker' and refused to investigate his complaints on seven occasions.

April came, and I received a letter from Justine Curran, congratulating me on my 100% attendance rate over the past year. I'd spent almost four years in the police force and I hadn't taken a single day of sickness. I also received a 'Recognition of good performance' memo from her staff officer,[27] in reference to my recent dealing with a robbery victim, who had been attacked in the city centre. When the victim, a young woman, returned home to Brazil, she wrote to the police telling them that I had provided her with a great service, and that 'the [level of the officer's] professionalism, attention and attitude was so high, it did not take long to restore my faith in Manchester being a safe city'. In that moment, I was proud to be a cop.

I did my best to keep going above and beyond the limited role into which I had been placed. During my time in plain-clothes, I had always been surprised by just how high the vehicle crime rate was. Despite the many hours we had sat in covert vans waiting for something to happen, peeing into plastic bottles, we could never get a handle on it. An area covered by my division, just outside Strangeways prison, had the highest vehicle crime rate in the Greater Manchester Force, and one of the highest in England and Wales. The number of vehicle-related thefts in England and Wales, as measured by the British Crime Survey (BCS) between 2003/04 and 2004/05 was 1,886,000.[28]

I decided to devise a project, which was submitted to the Force Suggestion Scheme, for a county-wide initiative to combat vehicle crime. I called it Operation Jackal. With the help of an old university friend, we designed a logo of a jackal for it, with a police slogan. Operation Jackal was to complement the already existing Operation Magpie for burglaries and Operation Hawk for robberies. Though the Force didn't implement my idea, as it wasn't big enough as a performance indicator, they did give me a monetary award for it, and in an email stated: 'Your idea has been thoroughly evaluated by the Crime Reduction advisors who note that you should be commended for the methodical and logical approach to the problem of car crime, [and] your suggested interventions are all very appropriate and realistic.'[29]

I learnt that the superintendent I was working for was to be promoted to chief superintendent and move jobs. I'd been a good staff officer for him and I knew he would help me, not as a favour but because I had worked hard. In my interim appraisal, he wrote that he had 'directly line managed' me, 'which is unusual for a Supt to PC relationship' and that he was 'very pleased' with my work.[30]

He asked me where I wanted to go after finishing with him, and I decided to apply for and join the divisional tutor and training unit at Collyhurst Police Station, the dark-looking building on the outskirts of the city centre. This was where the new recruits to my division went for their ten-week 'street duties' stage of their training, as I had done at Wigan. This time, I was going to be the one showing others the ropes. I was intent on helping shape new officers for their time on the front line.

6

Shock and Awe

I was due to take up my new role in the tutor unit in July 2005. The capital had won the 2012 Olympic bid on 6 July, and the terrorist threat level had been reduced from severe to substantial – level three of six.

On 7 July, three bombs were detonated in three London Underground stations, Aldgate, Edgware Road and King's Cross, and a fourth was detonated at the top of a double-decker bus at Tavistock Square. Fifty-two people were killed and more than seven hundred were injured. It was the most deadly attack on British soil since the Lockerbie bombing in 1988 (270 killed), and Britain's first Islamist suicide attack. In its immediate aftermath, people began to question whether this was a suicide bombing of the sort that had brought down the Twin Towers. Robert Mueller, the FBI head, visited London days later and was briefed by Scotland Yard.

I had begun working for the police three months after the New York attacks, and I knew that there would now be a backlash against black and brown people closer to home. For the police, it was a challenging time. Security was heightened throughout Britain, and Manchester, like everywhere else, was on high alert, particularly as it is a major city (it had been less than ten years since the IRA bomb). All available officers were sent out on high-visibility policing, the streets flooded with fluorescent yellow jackets. New aspects were introduced into our briefings and operational work with security upped, including the regular checking of important buildings and infrastructure, things that keep the country and economy running. Concrete barriers appeared around major landmarks and tourist attractions.

In times of crisis, the UK government's COBRA (Cabinet Office Briefing Room A) committee meets in the Cabinet Office buildings to plan a response. Terrorism stops under Section 44 of the Terrorism Act 2000 was one element. The Act was introduced to combat terrorism, and unlike the everyday stop and search, which requires officers to have grounds to suspect that an offence has been committed, Section 44 allowed us to stop any person and any vehicle, with no need to suspect the person of anything. Naturally, as with the general stop and search, black and Asian people were disproportionately targeted whilst out walking in the streets. The police said they wanted to create a hostile environment for terrorists, but what the Act actually did was create hostility towards the police amongst law-abiding people. In London alone, there was a twelvefold rise in searches, and the Met warned that it risked alienating minorities.[1]

On 21 July, fourteen days after the first attack, four more bombings were attempted in the capital. They were unconnected to the 7/7 bombings, but they only heightened the anxiety. In such a fraught atmosphere, panicked, knee-jerk reactions to perceived threats were inevitable. Operation Kratos, the Met's collective name for a range of anti-terrorism tactics, had recently come under review, particularly concerning the rules of engagement when using firearms. The very next day, at 10 a.m., Brazilian engineer Jean Charles de Menezes was shot dead by the police whilst he was on his way to work. The Met commander, Cressida Dick, was the Kratos-designated 'gold' senior officer on duty. (The police's command structure for major incidents and threats is divided into bronze (operational), silver (tactics) and gold (strategy)). Officers had mistaken De Menezes for one of the terrorists involved in the previous day's attempted attacks. His skin colour had been enough to mark him as a Muslim. But his skin colour wasn't the only reason that he was (wrongly) identified as a suspect.

In a press conference following the shooting, the Met Police commissioner, Ian Blair, said: 'The information I have available is that this shooting is directly linked to the ongoing and expanding anti-terrorist operation. Any death is deeply regrettable. I understand the man was challenged and refused to obey.'[2]

The shooting of an innocent person by the police is a tragedy that could, in time, be forgiven and understood, given the frightening circumstances. But Scotland Yard changed the narrative of what happened that Friday morning, either by mistake or by design. The police's press statement claimed that De Menezes had jumped the ticket barrier at Stockwell tube station, which he hadn't, and claimed that he had fled the police whilst wearing a bulky jacket with wires protruding from it, giving him the appearance of a bomber – none of which was true. CCTV showed that De Menezes had simply entered the station, picked up a copy of the *Metro*, tapped his Oyster card (the pre-payment travel card used in the capital) on the reader and descended the escalator. The Force also told the press that De Menezes's UK visa had expired and that traces of cocaine had been found in his body.[3]

As reported by the IPCC, surveillance officers involved in the operation falsified a log to minimise their culpability in the shooting after seven deadly bullets had entered De Menezes's head.[4] Scientific analysis revealed that the log had originally read: 'A split second view of his face. I believe it was NT.' 'NT' referred to Nettle Tip, the code name for the suspected terrorist Hussain Osman. However, the words 'and' and 'not' had been inserted and the entry read: 'A split second view of his face and I believe it was not NT.' The officer involved said he *may* have altered the log to correct an 'error'. He was given 'words of advice' – that minor disciplinary sanction the leadership used to give out – not to do it again. The IPCC said there was 'insufficient evidence' to prosecute the officer for attempting to pervert the course of justice.

The De Menezes family, grieving for Jean Charles, were forced to hear him denigrated, vilified and lied about. It was later discovered that officers had gathered 'intelligence' on these relatives, investigating them as if they really were terrorists. At an Old Bailey trial, the Metropolitan Police was fined £175,000 and had to pay £385,000 in legal costs over the shooting (for putting the public at risk – a health and safety issue). A jury in the health and safety criminal proceedings cleared Cressida Dick, as the gold commander in charge at the time, of blame.

Before the Met stood trial, most of Commissioner Blair's senior staff advised him to plead guilty, which meant the case would be brought to a swift conclusion and kept out of the public eye. He, however, disagreed, and staged an aggressive courtroom defence. After the Old Bailey jury found Scotland Yard guilty, Commissioner Blair said that the Met had made 'a serious mistake' by failing to correct the report that De Menezes behaved suspiciously. The subsequent IPCC report cleared 'everyone' in the Met apart from Andy Hayman, the assistant commissioner who led special operations and was ultimately in charge of the 7/7 investigation.[5] The IPCC accused him of misleading the public, covering up for some time that the police had shot the wrong man. Though the IPCC criticised Hayman, the MPA recommended that no disciplinary proceedings should be brought against him, and none were.

The IPCC criticism struck me in several ways: it blamed only one person, the man who neither fired nor gave the order. I also noted that Hayman had been the senior officer who helped to advise the so-called independent (from the police, that is) commission on its creation and introduction. Roy Clark, a former deputy assistant commissioner in the Met, became the IPCC's first director of investigations, a senior ex-cop in charge of investigating his former colleagues.

Six inquiries – one brought by the Health and Safety Executive, two by the IPCC, one by the MPA, one by the Met investigating itself, and the coroner's inquest into De Menezes's death (which returned an open verdict) – brought no justice to De Menezes's family. They believed there had been a cover-up.

After the 7/7 bombings, the structure of counter terrorism policing in the UK was changed. In London, the Anti-Terrorist Branch and Special Branch were combined into Counter Terrorism Command, also known as Special Operations 15 (SO15). This was the national command hub for all British terror operations, with the Met as the lead Force and other Forces around the country referred to as 'regional units'. For some purposes – like coordinating national response to major incidents, or the protection of the royal family and senior government ministers – the Met was a national Force, with the London commissioner at its helm. Despite the restructure, however, SO15 still ran as two separate and distinct operations: the Anti-Terrorist Branch dealt with investigating terrorists, whilst Special Branch dealt with gathering the intelligence. After John Reid became Home Secretary, a new Office for Security and Counter Terrorism was created, to establish how the UK government should deal with terrorism in the country; and the so-called CONTEST strategy was drafted, with its purpose to 'Prevent, Pursue, Protect, Prepare'. 'Prevent' involves investigating the factors behind radicalisation: what turns people to terrorism and extremism'; 'pursue' involves disrupting terrorism and bringing offenders to justice; 'protect' involves advising on how the country can protect itself against an attack, and 'prepare' involves compiling terrorism risk assessments and recommending measures following an attack.

The 9/11 attacks had had a significant impact on the kind

of policing I was to be introduced to: global terrorism was the
new threat to the world order, and the London bombings only
strengthened what had already been set in motion by the police
leadership. Although I had spent two decades living through
UK domestic terrorism, with the Northern Irish acts of terror
on mainland Britain – I'd started university in Manchester not
long after the devastating IRA bomb exploded in that city – I
knew that this new global kind of terrorism was going to have
a detrimental impact on policing. I had joined the police at the
start of the new century, and at the beginning of a new wave of
backlashes against immigration.

Prime Minister Tony Blair's Labour party had won the
general election in 1997, defeating John Major's Conservative
government, and many Britons, including my predominantly
white colleagues, believed their identity and way of life would
be eroded by this new era of 'multiculturalism'. I started to hear
more and more of this sort of sentiment from my colleagues. We
had reached our ethnic limit. We arrested two black men at the
back of the Midland Hotel in Manchester for allegedly selling
diamonds, and a colleague said, 'They should be sent back home.'
To where? I wondered. This same officer would often speak
about white officers being 'unable' to do or say certain things,
as if not being allowed to use racist language and discriminate
against minorities was somehow impacting his quality of life.
Another time, policing a football match on Manchester's Oxford
Road in a riot van, our driver saw two Asian males walking
across the road. They appeared to get in the way of the police
van and he nearly ran them over. He snapped that they were
probably 'illegal immigrants'.

Nevertheless, many colleagues said they were now voting
Labour (though the police is traditionally Conservative and right-
wing), because they had promised to be 'tough on crime' and its
causes. Despite being the party that introduced several progressive
laws protecting minorities, Labour ironically brought in the most

draconian police powers ever seen in peacetime Britain, creating over 3,000 new criminal offences. They attempted to extend the power to detain terror suspects without charge from fourteen days to ninety, something the Metropolitan Police commissioner, Ian Blair, supported and authorised his senior officers to lobby Members of Parliament for, politicising the Office of Constable. Assistant Commissioner Andy Hayman went to the House of Commons two days before the vote to champion the proposed law; but Labour lost the vote in Parliament, the first Commons defeat for Prime Minister Tony Blair. The *Independent* newspaper called the proposal 'dangerous, draconian, illiberal and unnecessary'.[6] Labour then failed to get the power extended to forty-two days, eventually settling on twenty-eight. The head of Scotland Yard also spoke out in favour of the government's proposals for a national identification card scheme, blurring the lines between police independence and party politics.

With a new kind of terrorism committed by a tiny minority of Muslims (or so-called Muslims, as true Muslims say that Islam is a religion of peace), together with mass immigration and new police powers granted by a pro-police party, a racialised recipe for disaster was on the horizon, more so in a police service that was already systemically and structurally racist towards non–white people. All of this was playing out under the guise of keeping crime under control and terrorism at bay.

So I started in the tutor unit, which also acted as the professional development unit for substantive constables. It had been created as a result of the divisional restructure, and was now the central location for the tutoring of all officers new to the division. I initially served as the deputy to the tutor sergeant. This hadn't been my plan, but my time in the press and public relations department, in the restructure team and in my role as a staff officer had prepared me for it. I was a cop who could do more than everyday operational policing. Besides, I reasoned that if the students were taught by a tutor who genuinely cared about equality and fairness in policing, we'd have a better class of police officer.

The sergeant was one of my old Bootle Street patrol supervisors who had tried to stop me from going on the press and publicity attachment, who had been accused of assaulting Delbo King. I deputised for the sergeant whenever he was on his own development courses, on annual leave and so on. For some ten weeks, whilst he was away, I answered directly to the divisional HR manager, reporting on any issues in the tutor unit.

I began to tutor the new student officers in their street duties, first guiding them in the application of the law they had recently learnt at the training school, then supervising them whilst they implemented it, in and around Manchester. It was fun and felt natural to be teaching. With the sergeant away more frequently, I had to take on the divisional transferees' course, and guide a transferee from London's Metropolitan Police (a substantive police constable) for five weeks as he struggled to settle into GMP, including compiling a report – both of which would ordinarily be the sergeant's job.

During my time tutoring, I was also the night 'silver' driver for the superintendent of operations. There was a rota, and every superintendent in the Force took turns covering the whole of Greater Manchester at night, attending any major incident. If it was serious enough, the chief on-call police officer (the assistant chief constable or above) would be woken up. I'd been the night silver driver for the performance superintendent when I was his staff officer, so I was familiar with the work. This time, I was driving the superintendent of operations, who was about to become the new chief superintendent of the division, taking over from Justine Curran.

All in all, I was doing quite a lot of work, and sometimes struggled with my ever-increasing workload. My tutor unit sergeant would often send me emails like: 'Kevin, I really need you back in here sooner rather than later – I am sinking! See you Thursday (morning if possible), loads of stuff needs to be done urgently.'[7]

At the time, I was tutoring a new student officer of mine, guiding him on how to deal with the 999 calls we received, and the subsequent incidents. But the sergeant still needed me to share his supervisory workload, checking stop-and-search forms and other paperwork filled out by the probationers and other tutors, in addition to my own normal operational duties and tutoring. It was a lot to handle, but he was, after all, the sergeant. During any downtime I had, I would clear his in-tray, which was always stacked high with paperwork from student officers and my fellow tutors. In my appraisal, I received five 'exceptional' and three 'fully competent' ratings.[8] I was earning every penny of my salary, and was rarely at home, which prompted my new boyfriend to come to the station to have a chat with me. He wanted to talk to me about our relationship, because he never saw me, and thought the station was the best place to discuss this, as I was guaranteed to be there. I was bothered by his actions, but I had to concede he had a point.

One day, the colleague who had collected the money for Macmillan Cancer after my mum's death asked me if I had heard about what happened to a female police officer at our old station, Bootle Street. 'No,' I responded, intrigued, 'what happened?' This officer was a white straight female and had applied for a post away from uniform patrol. She was not successful, having been accused of using threatening behaviour towards her supervisors. When they told her that she couldn't move, she said to her inspector: 'What if I say my name is "Kevin Maxwell, gay and black", will I get the job then?' Though she didn't know me personally, she nevertheless played me as a card, seemingly not realising that I'd been refused transfers myself. I brought this incredible story up whilst I was chatting with the divisional HR manager about the tutor unit, and she confirmed that it was true.

*

Another Christmas had come, and on 14 December 2005 I took part in my third carol service alongside Justine Curran, giving the second reading. The chief sent me a letter of thanks, saying that my reading 'was well delivered and impactive and was greatly appreciated by the congregation'.[9] A few days later, the tutor sergeant sent an email to the tutors about his further absence until February, letting them know that all issues and enquiries should be passed on to me.

At the beginning of 2006, I devised and produced a welcome book for the new officers coming into the division. It was a guide about who was who in my division, where to find places like the property store and the admin department, and how the Manchester Force and its systems differed from other Forces, designed to help officers who had recently transferred to us. It contained everything they needed to know about North Manchester and Greater Manchester on a practical level. Changing Forces wasn't easy, as I'd learnt from coaching the officer from the Met Police. It made me happy to be able to help colleagues like this. I was photographed for the divisional newsletter alongside the last seven North Manchester officers to be trained at Bruche, on their first day of their Stage 3A course.[10] I was now training the final intake from Bruche for their community engagement stage. Bruche, along with other police training centres, closed; all new officers to the service were to train within their respective Forces, and Centrex became the National Policing Improvement Agency (NPIA).

I had a productive and encouraging spring, and felt that I was really making a difference in the Force. Then, with summer upon us, the tutor sergeant took three weeks of annual leave. He asked that I cover his absence again, but this time I declined. I said I wanted to be out of the office, operationally, tutoring full time, not indoors covering the role of a sergeant whilst holding the rank of constable. There was a female officer in the office who wanted to be a sergeant, so I suggested that he ask her to do the role. He hesitated, but then agreed. There was, however, one last favour the sergeant wanted me to do: organise and run the North Manchester division 'transferees induction day', which included constables and sergeants new to Manchester from other Forces. I accepted and ran the course; it was a success. In the meantime, my female colleague covered the tutor sergeant office role. Things were finally looking up, I thought.

When the sergeant returned from his annual leave, he asked if he could have a chat. I thought it was going to be a catch-up, to see how things had been during his absence, as there were no issues to report. But this wasn't an informal catch-up. The sergeant wanted to talk to me because I had been accused of 'raising my voice'. I was completely taken aback. I racked my brain, trying to work out which situation he could be referring to, then remembered a conversation I had forgotten and which I thought had been resolved. I'd come in to work one day to find another tutor going over paperwork with the student officer I was tutoring in a back office. Apparently, the student officer had omitted some information. The tutor was correcting the officer in front of everyone else in the room, creating an uncomfortable environment. This was the same colleague I'd overheard giving the two new officers on the restructure team a dressing-down, and I'd stepped in then as well. I asked my colleague if I could speak with her privately in the next room. I told her that it was my responsibility as the officer's tutor to go over his 'omission' with him, and having her do it undermined my position and embarrassed him. Rather than lecture them in front of others, normal practice was for the tutor to speak to the trainee about any tutelage issues in the context of the Experimental Learning Cycle, using a SMART action plan ('specific', 'measurable', 'achievable', 'realistic' and 'timescale'). My tutor colleague originally did not concede that what she had done was wrong, but eventually she agreed she shouldn't have stepped in. After that, as far as I was concerned, the matter was closed.

Our conversation took place in front of two other female tutor constables, who were in a relationship with each other. Although it was against the rules, it was normal for couples to work alongside each other. One of the officers was the one I had recommended to the sergeant, to cover him during his annual leave. During my discussion with the other tutor, one of the constables said:

'You don't speak like us.'

'What do you mean?' I enquired. She said she hadn't meant it 'like that'.

She hesitated, then remarked that I was experienced beyond my rank. Her partner then commented that it was funny how some officers get 'some things' because of 'certain reasons'. I asked what she meant. She explained that she felt I'd been given certain experiences and tasks because of my colour, and referred to the 'positive action' internal affairs secondment I had been asked to go on over the spring (which I had turned down). My colleague also said that I hadn't been helping her whilst she was covering the sergeant's role. But, from my point of view, I had my own responsibilities, and was tutoring a student officer – and besides, I'd covered that role single-handedly before. During the disagreement, the female officer I had reproached for embarrassing the student I was tutoring told me to stop being 'aggressive'. I almost laughed. No one had ever called me aggressive. I told the sergeant about this, but he already knew all the details. He'd spoken with the other three tutors. There had been no shouting or anything of the like, I told him. It was just an adult conversation. I expected him to support me; after all, I'd worked for him dutifully, and he knew my character. But he told me I needed to apologise. I was angry and indignant, but nevertheless apologised to my colleague. She went on to tell my sergeant that I hadn't, perhaps annoyed that I hadn't seemed repentant for a crime I didn't believe I had committed. It was a ridiculous situation. We were at an impasse.

The sergeant made it clear that somebody had to leave the tutor unit, and that he would prefer it to be me. Overcome by confusion and disappointment, I told the sergeant that he wasn't handling the situation properly. I suggested that my filing a grievance would resolve the situation. With his next breath, he said, 'If you want to play the race card, go ahead.'

Stung by this accusation, I told the sergeant that I would transfer out of the main tutor unit at Collyhurst Police Station to the satellite one at Bootle Street, the police station I had just come from. I left immediately, taking the student officer with me. I never spoke to the sergeant in person again.

I was determined not to let my difficulties burden the student officer I was tutoring. He was white and straight, and I saw so much potential in him. But it was *he* who ended up trying to comfort and support me, his tutor, as we sat in the police van outside the station. I needed to get out of the tutor unit, so I applied for the second time to become a trainee detective at the CID – this time at the neighbouring Salford division. The tutor unit sergeant endorsed my application by internal post, because my performance had never been an issue and I had been consistently working above and beyond my rank of a constable.

I arrived for my trainee detective interview and met both the female detective inspector and that division's HR manager. Later that day, the inspector called to inform me that I had been unsuccessful. This was the second time I'd failed a Force-wide training programme. Frustrated and confused, I asked the inspector why I had not passed the interview.

'Some of your answers weren't snap,' she said. I had fully prepared for this interview and thought I'd been 'snappy' enough. I was fairly well educated, and was an officer with five years of service. I had been on an attachment at headquarters on a firearms amnesty, been seconded to a restructure team and also been a staff officer to a superintendent. I had been a tutor constable, deemed fit to guide and nurture student police officers. I was an officer trained in rape and sexual assault offences, had completed the Association of Chief Police Officers' Level 2 National Investigative Interviewing Course, and I had even completed the National Optical Evidence and Intelligence Gathering courses. Yet I couldn't even get myself on a *trainee* detectives' scheme.

Officers with just two years of experience in the police could successfully get themselves onto the detectives' course. I had helped several of them with their detectives' interview preparation. They were white. I was a minority officer with an excellent service record trying to get into the detectives' office on merit alone, contrary to the accusations made by others about my getting preferential treatment; but for some reason I could not pass the first stage.

The strain on my new relationship was becoming unbearable. My partner and I argued often. In a moment of total despair, I decided to do something I had resisted for so many years: I spoke with BAPA. After listening to their advice, I decided to submit an internal grievance. At least this might bring about a suitable and real resolution. I submitted an initial one-page document to the Force's equal opportunities unit.[11] Although the grievance was meant to be confidential, by now I had learnt that it wouldn't be. I was asked to go and see one of the new superintendents, who had featured in Charles Crichlow's tribunal and had been promoted twice since Charles's ordeal. The new chief superintendent – who was the senior officer I'd been driving around the Force area during his night silver duties (Justine Curran had moved into a GMP assistant chief constable role, and later became chief constable of both Tayside Police in Scotland and Humberside Police in Yorkshire) – was informed about the grievance. Out of the blue, I received an invitation from him to attend a ceremony for a divisional commander's award, relating to my time in the main tutor unit at Collyhurst. I was to receive a commendation for 'professionalism and commitment' in recognition of outstanding work,[12] for my role in a major violent disorder incident in which eighteen males had rampaged through the city centre. (The tutor unit had been tasked with investigating the aftermath and arrests, to allow us to teach new officers how to deal with major crime.) The divisional commander wanted to publicly congratulate me for my hard work. Sullen and exasperated, I thought: I don't want to play anymore. I wasn't going to stand there and have my photo taken with him in our uniforms, with fake smiles plastered across our faces. I was serious about the grievance, so I declined the invitation.

Part of the reason I had the confidence to submit my initial grievance was that I had been sent by my divisional command team to attend the International Black Police Association Conference. Since it was being held in Manchester – the first time in thirty-five years that it was held outside the US – my seniors asked me to attend and represent the division, then 'report' back on my experience. The event was attended by many American police forces and their black officers. Afterwards, hundreds of cops of colour from both sides of the Atlantic marched in 'solidarity' through Moss Side in Manchester, to cheers from the black community.[13] What struck a chord with me at the black officers' conference was that it was only the second time in my police career that I had actually felt comfortable in my own skin (the first time I had felt this way was on the personal leadership programme for ethnic minorities I'd attended in October 2003).

At the Manchester Conference Centre I heard Michael Todd, the chief constable of GMP, address the hundreds of delegates, along with Charles Crichlow, the chair of Manchester's BAPA. Charles's speech about the struggles faced by ethnic minority officers resonated deeply with me. Many in the audience had experienced the same thing, and I realised I wasn't alone. Retired

US cop Ron Hamilton, who spent twenty-four years with the District of Columbia Force, said that Moss Side was no different to Anacostia, the largely black area in Washington, D.C. He said that racism and 'agitation' by the police against the area were amongst the reasons he had retired at the same rank he'd joined.

Tarique Ghaffur, an assistant commissioner with the Metropolitan Police, spoke about how discrimination and prejudice had blighted his attempts to become a chief constable.[14] He had unsuccessfully applied for the post at Greater Manchester, West Yorkshire and West Midlands, and even for the deputy commissioner rank at the Met. Ghaffur said police selection panels lacked a 'true level of independence', and described being deliberately excluded from groups and shut out of key decision-making processes in his career. He had also experienced the sudden invisibility that minority officers sometimes face: coming up with ideas that were ignored or refused, only to see them come to fruition when white officers suggested the same thing. I knew how that invisibility worked, which was why I didn't turn to the Police Federation for help, the union to which I had paid subs since the day I joined the service. They'd refused to support Charles Crichlow, and had refused to back an appeal by an Asian ex-officer, Sultan Alam, who was also prosecuted after making a racism claim against his Force.[15] In 2006, the Police Federation was found guilty at an employment tribunal of having racially discriminated against Alam, by refusing to help him take legal action to clear his name. The employment tribunal ruling found that documents had been destroyed by a Federation official in an attempt to thwart Alam's case. Alam, who had served as a constable in Cleveland Police after making the racism claim, was then arrested for handling stolen goods. He was convicted, and jailed. A later investigation into corruption in Cleveland Police led to four officers involved in investigating Alam being charged with criminal offences for framing him. All were cleared, but one later admitted two offences concerning the investigation at a disciplinary hearing. Alam twice asked the Police Federation for help to clear his name after evidence for the framing came to light. The Federation refused, but paid the legal fees for the four officers charged with framing him.[16]

The employment tribunal heard that a document from the Metropolitan Police branch of the Federation referred to Alam as 'Paki', although the tribunal ruled that this wasn't racist, but 'insensitively' abbreviated. After leaving the Force, Alam said, 'I felt very wronged and that's why I took them to an [employment tribunal]. I feel vindication and relief, but there are no winners in an ET, we are all losers.' Alam was cleared by the Court of Appeal in 2007.[17]

As the weeks passed, GMP finally acknowledged my grievance. Now, it was up to the leadership to decide their next move. I remained focused on the job, to prevent any criticism of my performance.

Back at Bootle Street with my new student officer, I learnt that I was being left out of tutor emails, including emails from the tutor sergeant regarding available overtime. He didn't copy me into them anymore, which didn't entirely surprise me, given that I had just started the process of a grievance about racism within the police.

The equal opportunities unit contacted me to ask if I would take part in mediation to discuss the issues I had. After reflecting on the idea, I decided against it. It would involve sitting down, alone, with the tutor sergeant and the three female officers, the three people in direct disagreement with me. Besides, this solution missed the point of the grievance. It wasn't about those four people. It was about an institution that actively discriminated against black and Asian officers; it was an underlying, systemic problem.

As I was now tutoring at the Bootle Street satellite tutor unit and had raised a grievance, I was mindful that, since

I was no longer at the main tutor unit at Collyhurst, I would now be under immense, exhausting scrutiny, despite having an unblemished record. I began to update the sergeant daily, via email, on the work that I was doing with my tutees, as well as the times I started and finished work. I resolved to leave nothing to chance.

Usually, if the Force wanted to discipline an officer, it was over something petty, such as arriving late or not filling in a form correctly. Superintendent Martin Harding, former chair of BAPA, had raised many examples where ethnic minority officers (locally, nationally and internationally) had been dealt with more severely than white officers. Some were told action had been taken against them for 'underperforming'. Home Office research had found that, across the country, black officers are more likely to face disciplinary hearings, and punishments are more severe than those for other officers.[18]

I signed the student officer I was tutoring off as competent, and he was moved to independent patrol. With another new officer to tutor, I carried on with life. Eventually, an appointment was made for me to go and see the newly promoted chief superintendent, to speak about my grievance. During the meeting he listened but didn't hear me, then said he would 'look into things', and if the tutor sergeant or I were lying, he would deal with it. (He would later move to the command team of the Hillsborough Football Disaster Inquiry, which looked into the death of the ninety-six Liverpool fans from my home city.)

I returned to the tutor unit and checked my emails. There was an email from the tutor unit sergeant who was no longer speaking to me face to face, to congratulate me on my work as a tutor. He also informed me that one of the student officers who had not long left me had written a report saying that I was 'supportive, enthusiastic and went way beyond what you needed to do in order to assist his development and to complete the necessary policing actions'.[19]

I'd had another, even more surreal email: the Force headquarters career development unit wanted to recruit more minority officers into departments where they were under-represented, 'in an effort to ensure a diverse work force';[20] this included the CID – the detectives' office I'd twice failed to get into.

Six days after these two emails, I had a meeting with GMP's principal HR officer for equal opportunities, at Force headquarters. She was reassuring, and I felt good about the meeting. Two days later, the police constable from career development at headquarters alerted me to a problem with the detective trainee course and exam. Though they had emailed me about going on the detective training programme because they were keen to address under-representation in the CID, several senior detectives had objected to me being sent on it under the 'positive action' scheme. Unsurprisingly, these objecting officers were white and straight. This stance by old-school officers was the reason positive action schemes in the police did not work. They were implemented to appease people of colour, but were not supported by the majority. As far as white officers were concerned, they didn't need affirmative action, so it was 'unfair' that minority officers received it.

There was a standoff. A detective superintendent in the senior command team of the headquarters' CID had to get involved. To appease the senior detectives, the GMP wanted me to complete the detective training but remain a police constable. In other words, I'd be doing the same work as a detective, but not have the same status as everyone else.

In October 2006, whilst on duty with my newest student officer as well as another student I was looking after for a colleague, I started having chest pains, which became more severe as our shift went on. I asked another tutor constable to look after the trainees and a patrol sergeant took me to A&E at Manchester Royal Infirmary. A doctor identified an irregularity in my heart, something called 'left ventricular hypertrophy'. Though

I was discharged, I was referred to a cardiology specialist at the Manchester Heart Centre. There, after inconclusive investigations, the professor recommended that I have an angiogram.

At the beginning of the new year, I returned to the hospital with my partner. After further tests and consultations, I was told the results were negative, so there was nothing for me to worry about. I felt as if I'd been given a new lease of life. Then and there, I made the decision that I would no longer allow myself to be bullied or abused in the police. Not long afterwards, I submitted my official substantive grievance report to GMP.[21] I wrote about having to leave the tutor unit in circumstances that I believed were directly related to discrimination against me because of my race (like my sergeant's use of the term 'race card'), and that I'd been subject to discriminatory treatment since joining GMP because of my race and sexuality. The incident in the tutor unit had caused me great anxiety and distress, and my experiences had left me feeling isolated. I was keen to emphasise that my report went beyond individuals, to the body of people who made up the police – I didn't want to see individual officers sacked, because this would be like clipping weeds rather than pulling up the roots. I wrote that I enjoyed being an officer, and that I felt I had been loyal to the Force and that I strove to ensure that my integrity and conduct were beyond reproach, even during my negative experiences. I told the Force that I had believed they were keen to recruit and retain individuals like myself, but now felt that this wasn't the case.

I decided to apply immediately for a post outside the tutor unit, and tried again for the squad I had wanted to enter after plain–clothes: the key crime prisoner processing unit. They didn't want me in the CID, but I could think of no reason why they wouldn't want me in this one. I was mindful, too, that being in the prisoner processing unit would make it very hard for the CID to refuse any further applications to the detective trainee course, as the prisoner processing unit was a natural stepping stone.

Sure enough, I was accepted into the unit. Soon another Christmas came, and on 20 December 2006 I took part in my fourth divisional carol service, with the new chief superintendent. He thanked me for my contribution in a letter.[22]

Though I was focused on the future, I was worried about applying to the CID for a third time. I emailed my HR manager and asked whether it would be possible for constables such as myself to train as detectives in the prisoner processing unit, which did, after all, come under the CID. My suggestion was turned down by the new superintendent of performance. Unwilling to give up, a day later I again applied to become a detective. This time, I applied to the Bury CID, as this division was actively advertising vacancies at the time.

My new sergeant endorsed my application and I personally took it to Bury's HR unit. In support of my application, the prisoner processing unit sergeant wrote: 'He is respectful and professional at all times and presents a good image of GMP to everyone he meets. I can find no reason not to recommend him for this post and he would be a benefit to any office he joined.'

This time, I didn't even pass the paper-sift. I had used the same evidence to show that I met the criteria for the role as in my last two applications, but my new application was additionally strengthened by my time in the key crime prisoner processing unit. Nothing made sense. I had worked with some of the most senior officers at Manchester Police on strategy, including with the chief constable (on the national firearms amnesty), and had proven myself in many different roles; I had been graded as 'exceptional', and had tutored and guided police officers new to the Force and police service itself, but I had failed yet again.

Having submitted the grievance report, I received an email from the GMP's senior assistant HR director (the number two in HR).[23] My grievance had been passed up to her level under stage two of the procedure. We met three days later. She told me that she had spoken with a superintendent from internal affairs and had asked him to assess my grievance. She also told me that she had given the HR director, her boss, a copy of my grievance for his view, and that she had also asked a chief inspector from career development to come back to her with his thoughts regarding my progression.[24] With all of this going on, I continued to seek the reasonable opportunity of being trained as a detective and applied for the fourth time.

I was interviewed by a detective inspector at Grey Mare Lane Police Station, who had known me when I was a police constable at Bootle Street, and a detective sergeant. The inspector and sergeant told me they couldn't understand why I had not applied to the CID before.

Later, I received a phone call informing me I had come top in the interviews.

It was now up to me to pass the trainee detective course, and the national detectives' exam. The senior assistant director informed me that she had now had a response from internal affairs regarding the grievance, and that she had secured the recruitment papers from all my past failed CID applications. I met with her again, and she gave me a copy of the internal affairs report that had been produced by the chief inspector. She allowed me to take a copy away to read at my leisure, but told me not to 'share it with anyone',[25] especially not with Charles Crichlow or BAPA. Before I left her office, she informed me that the Force's recruitment manager, who had actually interviewed me to become a police officer, had reviewed my trainee detective applications. In short, HR agreed with the failed applications. Someone from HR had gone through my Bury division CID application, to see where I could have made a mistake. On the 'specialist knowledge, skills and abilities' page, the person reviewing my case noted that I'd written that the new Fraud Act was introduced in 2006. They corrected it to 2007. I went back to double-check. The Act had, in fact, been introduced in 2006.

They had made a mistake, not me. At that moment, I was sure that my grievance wasn't being taken seriously. In his memo to the superintendent of internal affairs, the internal affairs chief inspector stated that I may have been treated in a slightly 'clumsy' way at the beginning of my service, but that there did not appear to be evidence of racist behaviour by any member of GMP.[26]

I disagreed; in addition to my own experiences, I also knew that breaching my brother's data was in contravention of data protection law.

His responses to the points in my grievance were a step-by-step deconstruction of my time with the Force.

The internal affairs chief inspector acknowledged the 'coconut' incident at Bruche, saying that it was clear that the incident left me feeling more isolated and afraid to raise a complaint of racism. He described the advice of the superintendent who came to visit me during training as 'insensitive'. However, he did not think the incident could or should be revisited.

Regarding my time at Wigan, the chief inspector said he did not know if the homophobic comments were specifically directed at me or of a more general nature. I wasn't aware that my seniors had already known about the homophobia problem before I spoke with them, but internal affairs noted that my former chief superintendent 'had already considered the issue of a transfer because of concerns over victimisation resulting from PC Maxwell's sexual orientation'.

The superintendent's comments at Bootle Street, about my being on a crusade and flying the flags, was considered not to be overtly racist or homophobic, though potentially unnecessary. On the general conduct at Bootle Street, the internal affairs chief did say that 'these types of comments are highly offensive and would represent serious breaches of the code of conduct'. Unfortunately, given the passage of time, they would be extremely difficult to investigate.

Addressing the issue of my sergeant refusing to allow me

on the press and publicity attachment to keep me in my place, the chief inspector commented that this covered my general unhappiness in the police, rather than being specifically racist. Responding to the stand-up comedy bit at the Christmas party, he acknowledged that it was a 'clear allegation' of homophobic bullying by a colleague.

In response to my time in plain-clothes, he wrote that I painted a picture of feeling isolated and undervalued, but these were not experiences unique to a black and gay officer, though I had understandably interpreted my experiences negatively. The chief didn't understand my intersectionality: I knew of only one other mixed-race gay officer in the Force, which made two out of 8,000 (and he was not out). I did not live a single-issue life.

Finally, regarding having my secondment to the riot squad stopped, whilst my white colleague was allowed to join the Vehicle Crime Unit, the internal affairs chief inspector wrote: 'In isolation each decision may have been a fair and reasonable one, however, taken together, these decisions give rise to the suspicion that PC Maxwell was treated unfairly or discriminated against in some way.'

The response to the tutor unit incident was less promising. The chief inspector wrote that I became isolated and unpopular, but there was no apparent evidence of misconduct or discrimination on racial or sexual orientation grounds. He noted that any differences between staff in the unit were more to do with personalities than stereotyping or discriminatory behaviour. On the tutor sergeant using the expression 'playing the race card', the inspector felt that he should be 'advised' – once again, that famous police disciplinary procedure: 'Please stop being racist, thank you.' In reference to the officer who stated that she would have got a transfer if her name was 'Kevin Maxwell, gay and black' – more 'advice'.

Regarding my numerous applications to the CID, the chief inspector wrote that no obvious issue was highlighted, though it clearly raised questions about 'fairness and discrimination'. In conclusion, the internal affairs chief said he appreciated that I did not necessarily intend the incidents to be considered as separate episodes, because it was a pattern of treatment, rather than isolated problems, that I wished to see investigated.

After giving me a copy of the report, the senior assistant director never contacted me again. The Force had a statutory duty to resolve my grievance, but weren't going to unless I raised it. I had a decision to make. I was about to become a detective in Manchester. If I wanted the grievance progressed, I had to be ready for a battle. But I'd been offered a position I'd fought so hard for. I decided that the best thing for me to do was to keep my head down and mouth shut. I will pass the detectives course, I thought, then get as far away as possible from GMP.

7

Divide and Rule

I started as a trainee detective constable at Grey Mare Lane Police Station CID, an ugly building on the outskirts of Manchester city centre. Since the restructure, it was the main detective hub for North Manchester. This meant I'd now worked at all three main stations in my division.

I was apprehensive about joining the detectives' office. The detective work didn't bother me, but going into an office that had a notorious reputation did. It was a firm within a firm, with a reputation for heavy drinking and an unstructured culture.

I had to prepare myself to enter the lion's den.

Just as student police officers are assigned a uniformed tutor constable to guide them, trainee detectives were assigned a detective tutor. It was like going back to school and learning the ropes. Based on previous experience, and the lack of gay and black representation in the detectives' department, I thought I'd get the sort of gatekeeping, diversity-hostile tutor to which I'd become accustomed. I was, however, pleasantly surprised.

My tutor looked like someone out of the BBC television police programme *Life on Mars*, which was set in the bigoted and intolerant Britain of the 1970s, and he was certainly old-school in how he spoke and acted – we often sat in a car full of smoke with the windows closed as he puffed away – but he was a nice guy. I learnt a lot from him.

The goal of a detective is, as you might imagine, to detect crime.

In the CID, detectives were allocated a crime report, usually originating from uniform officers. It was their job to review the incident log, formulate a strategy, update the crime details on the system, read the witness statements, view the exhibits, and complete enquiries, which involved speaking with the aggrieved person (the 'a/p') and any other witnesses. Interviewing was the highlight of the job for me. I enjoyed talking to people, even the suspects.

As an advanced investigative interviewer, my style was consistent. In the interview room I'd be sitting on one side of the table and the suspect on the other, with his or her solicitor or appropriate adult (if they were a minor or vulnerable). I'd put the cassette tapes in and wait for the recording 'buzzer' sound to bleep before I began the introductions, stating the place of interview, time and date. I'd remind the suspect that they had a right to free independent legal advice even if their solicitor was sitting next to them.

Then came the caution, which I broke down into three parts. I'd explain the routine, the integrity of the tapes, how the suspect could obtain a copy, and that I'd be taking notes. The reason for their arrest and the interview would be laid out. I always set the expectations at the outset: no lies, no interruptions (by either of us), and speak clearly for the tapes. If the suspect had made a significant statement before or after arrest, like saying 'I did it', I'd put this to them. After I'd heard their recall of the events, without asking them any questions or pushing them in any direction, I would then summarise it, to make sure I had everything down correctly. That's when I'd start challenging any discrepancies. With a 'no comment' interview I'd carry out the same procedure as though they had talked, so that the court could hear that I had given them the opportunity to speak. I found the 'no commenters' the smartest. Many knew the police often needed more evidence, so they said nothing to incriminate themselves.

For an interview to be successful, an officer had to remember the 5WH and TED rules: 'Who, What, When, Where, Why and How', and 'Tell, Explain and Describe'.

When I joined the detectives' office ('the Office' or 'DO', as it was known) I was posted to a detectives' table, which had a detective sergeant and a handful of detective constables – eight of us in total. There were five tables like this in the office, which covered the division 24/7. The detective inspectors managed the tables, and answered to the detective chief inspector. There were about forty of us in the office, including support staff and the senior detectives. My division was the biggest in the Force, which also meant it was the busiest.

As I settled into the office, I quickly picked up on who was who. There was an officer who stood out: a female Asian detective sergeant, who was one of four brown faces (including mine) at the CID. No one had a good word to say about her, and her worst enemy was one of the officers of colour I had joined with. My colleagues were pretty direct in their criticisms of her, many of which centred around her weight and smell. I often heard them flatly stating, 'She stinks.' The bosses encouraged it by talking about her disparagingly in front of junior officers.

I soon realised that, though she could be annoying, there was no malice in her. It didn't take a genius to establish why she was despised. My colleagues believed that she should have been booted out of the police many years ago, but hadn't been because she was a woman and a person of colour – a special case. She was vocal about equality in the police, especially regarding race and gender, and an active member of BAPA. Her own run-ins with the Force were a bone of contention for many.

Once, on my way to an incident, she asked why I 'needed' to

go. It was part of a case that had been allocated to me by the detective inspector, so it was my call, as the investigating officer, whether I went to the crime scene or not. I couldn't think of a single reason a police officer would not want to go and visit the crime scene for a crime they were investigating. I didn't take it personally, having got used to her being nosy, so I just told her that I was going, and that if she wanted to, she could take it up with my sergeant or inspector.

When I returned to the office, a mini-celebration was taking place. I wasn't sure what had gone on. Was someone leaving, or had someone been promoted? No. The unpopular detective sergeant had gone home, and there were several people standing about, congratulating me for 'taking on the dragon and slaying her'. I'd become an instant hero.

The police force is dominated by white faces, but it is also dominated by men. Sexism and racism are a particularly potent pairing, and the unpopular detective sergeant was not an unusual case. I remember that one night I was covering the night detective duties and leaving the station, when I saw the acting superintendent, Karin Mulligan, a woman of colour who had risen to a high rank but who was struggling to break through the glass ceiling, coming towards me. Karin was covering the Force's night silver duties, driving herself (unlike the officers I have driven for). As she came closer and her face became clearer, I could see she looked exhausted. I had heard her name bandied about in a negative way, along with that of her brother, Superintendent Martin Harding. For years, Karin – at one point Britain's most senior black policewoman – had been battling with GMP. She had recently settled a race and sex discrimination case with the police in which she was reported to have 'explosive' evidence.[1] Karin had claimed that she had been overlooked for promotion, and furthermore that her personal life was investigated by the police because of her race and gender. The substantive chief inspector had agreed a deal with the Force before the employment tribunal, and the settlement included a clause preventing her from speaking about what happened. BAPA said: 'Regardless of the outcome of this case GMP still have a lot of issues that remain unresolved in regards to discrimination in the service.'

Similarly, in 2007, London–based police constable Senel Ismail was falsely accused of having a series of affairs with male recruits, leading to 'sex slurs' at the Hendon training school. She was wrongly alleged to have taken part in a police tradition known as 'Operation Rainbow', where women officers would try to sleep with as many of their male colleagues as possible. One senior officer pressed her for her phone number whilst at a police dinner, so that he could ring her for 'morning sex'. He allegedly stroked her leg and made inappropriately sexual comments about her body. Senel complained several times to her bosses, but no action was taken. Eventually, one officer was given 'words of advice', the lowest form of police discipline, about how to conduct himself. Senel received a five-figure payout as a result of the lies about her, but also signed a gagging clause. The male chauvinist pig was alive and kicking.[2]

Not long after I joined, we got a new detective sergeant. I couldn't believe my eyes when I saw him. It was my sergeant from plain–clothes who'd moved me off his team after two months. There was only one way to deal with it: only speak to or deal with one another when it was absolutely necessary. It was an unspoken agreement between us, and it worked. He didn't like me, and I didn't like him. He ignored me, so I ignored him. Given the process of the grievance procedure and the subsequent fallout, it seemed the best, and only, option.

As I progressed on my own detectives' table, an officer joined the office from uniform. He was white, and he was generally spoken of as gay. Back in uniform policing, when he'd taken a prisoner to the custody suite, the custody sergeant had asked him if he had 'shit' himself, saying he could smell 'cum', in front of some very amused officers and detainees. Another white gay officer in the detectives' office, who had a long-term partner, often went out with me and my closest ally at the DO, a gay officer who had been with me in plain-clothes. But the officer with the long-term partner dared not come out, believing it would lead the other detectives to question his integrity. For so many, coming out was not an option in the police. The majority of those who were out in the Force were still in office jobs, away from normal operational work.

The detective role covered all aspects of serious crime investigation, including intelligence-gathering, setting out forensic strategies, interviewing witnesses and suspects, and compiling the prosecution files for the serious offences. My workload particularly included rape offences (male and female), robbery, abduction, arson, aggravated burglary with a weapon, wounding, and night detective duties known as 'the Night Jack' – leaving a night detective log for the morning teams, of the incidents and crimes dealt with during the night. I was the crime scene manager for the division from 9 p.m. until 7 a.m., attending incidents and deciding how best to preserve evidence. I worked closely with the crime scene officers dealing with forensics: fingerprints, blood, hair and fibre. I completed the Police National Computer course (vehicles, property and names check), which was necessary for researching suspects, and helped my colleagues with criminal checks.

In the CID, we were issued with an A4-sized blue 'day book' to replace the police pocket notebook. This blue book signified our status to other cops. There was no such thing as a handover of case work in the CID, unlike in uniform policing, and I averaged eighteen-hour shifts, always willing to go the extra mile. I was glad to get recognition for this too – my detective inspector wrote to me and a colleague in an email: 'I just wanted to let you know how impressed I have been by the effort that both of you have put into your work in particular over the past few weeks. I know how difficult things can be when you are working excessive hours and dealing with complex and sensitive investigations. I will be putting you both forward for more formal recognition but in the meantime THANKS'.[3]

As I was being allocated a lot of male rape offences, I decided to volunteer for a role as a Force LGBT Liaison Officer, in addition to my detective duties. I'd been to incidents where officers didn't know how to deal with a man saying he'd been raped; and when the officer got awkward, it compounded the pain and humiliation of the victim. I thought that this volunteer role would give my colleagues the assistance they needed to provide the best support and gather the best evidence.

I still hadn't taken a single day's sickness in my by now more than six years on the Force – which added up to 2,303 days or 6 years, 3 months and 21 days of work – and in March 2008 I received a 5-year certificate of excellent attendance from my divisional commander for the period from April 2003.[4] Not long after, I also completed the detective training programme, which included the National Investigators' Examination. I was now a fully fledged detective. In my endorsement report for the substantive detective rank, my tutor wrote to senior detectives that 'Maxwell is a valued and well-respected officer within the North Manchester CID office. The quality of the evidential file produced to support this application is an example of the high standards he sets himself when undertaking any task during his day-to-day working.'[5]

Eighteen-hour days and a total focus on my career had its consequences. My second serious relationship fell apart soon after I became a substantive detective. I just couldn't have it all. It was a lesson I had to keep learning.

★

Life went on, bringing me a third new detective sergeant from Bury. He told our team he had already had a chat with his predecessor, and had been given the 'low-down' on who was who. I wondered what my previous sergeant – the former plain-clothes one – had said about me, but brushed the thought aside.

My seeming acceptance by my colleagues at the CID still wasn't total acceptance. One day, I returned to the office after attending a crime scene, and got to the top of the stairs to find my colleagues in the middle of a heated debate. When I walked in, their faces lit up like Christmas trees. They had been waiting for me to settle an argument. Whilst I was out, a detective on my table had had a disagreement with the sergeant. They were deciding what takeaway to get for dinner, when the sergeant suggested they have a 'Chinky'. The detective told the sergeant that the word was inappropriate. My team was waiting for me to rule on whether the word 'Chinky' was offensive to Chinese people, as I was the only ethnic minority on the table. It didn't matter that I wasn't Chinese. I seethed, not only because the word was definitely offensive, but also because I was tired of being singled out. When the gay jokes came out, mostly cracked by one sergeant who was particularly fond of them, I just laughed along, particularly when he called me 'gay boy', even making my own jokes. It was my new survival strategy. Self-deprecating and even self-derogatory humour meant I couldn't be made into a laughing stock – I was in on the joke. I went out of my way to make sure people liked me: I took over the tea kitty. I arranged a coffee morning for Macmillan Cancer, and collected money for the charity, and when I wasn't asking people if they wanted something from the local bakery or the chip shop, I was bringing in cakes and biscuits for the team. I had to make an effort, and that effort showed in my waistline. I had put on a lot of weight, going from twelve-and-a-half stone to fifteen stone, but I managed to turn that to my advantage, organising an office 'get fit' challenge to raise money for the British Heart Foundation, and getting my weight back down. But at the back of my mind, I knew I couldn't keep pushing my pain away to fit in. I had to move to a place that would accept me. At Manchester, I kept bumping into people from the past seven years who had made my life difficult or who had undermined or attacked me; I knew it to be a Force that hadn't taken my grievance seriously.

I applied for a detective's post at the Metropolitan Police, to work for SO15 (Counter Terrorism Command) at Heathrow Airport. The Met website said candidates for the post should have a good understanding of London's current affairs and the impact on its communities, the Terrorism Acts, the National Intelligence Model and the Regulation of Investigatory Powers Act 2000 (RIPA). Naturally, I'd studied all this intensively.

Bold letters on the Scotland Yard application form read: 'The Metropolitan Police Service is an Equal Opportunities Employer'. I declared that I was a male who was gay, mixed-race and a Christian. I ticked all the boxes, except the disability box. At Bruche, my glam colleague used to laugh that this was the only thing missing from my minorities bingo: a disability. We joked that I should pretend I had a wooden leg.

Whilst I had been off duty on the early May bank holiday, a huge public disorder incident had taken place outside the Bridgewater Hall, the home of Manchester's symphony orchestra.[6] GMP officers had stopped a motor vehicle outside the venue, just as the building was emptying after a children's talent show the Moss Side black community was holding. The driver and the passengers in the vehicle were all black youths. Some patrons of the show took issue with how the officers were conducting the stop, and an argument broke out. One of the officers pressed the emergency 'panic' button on his radio. This button would alert every officer in the city centre, overriding all other communication, and bring backup. Things escalated. Before long, a full scale public disorder was in swing, with over a hundred police officers from around the Force drafted in to deal with it. Officers indiscriminately used their batons on members of the public, including children, and arrested a lot of people. I didn't know about it until the next day, on my early detective shift, though it had made the news.

Back in the office, it became clear that the Force's handling of the situation had backfired and they were now in a damaging and embarrassing situation. Officers had arrested prominent members of the black community and members of the police's own Independent Advisory Group (IAG), many of whom had simply stepped in to try and calm things down. The IAG was the link between the police and the black community, something like local diplomats.

Internal affairs had initially carried out an investigation, but the black community was resistant and uncooperative. Mobile phone footage had been taken by the public: some of it was uploaded to the internet, and some of it was sent to solicitors to form part of civil suits against the Force. A London barrister had agreed to represent many complainants. I was approached a couple of days after the incident by my detective sergeant, who told me that I had been 'selected' to go on the new major enquiry team. I was, once again, the only black officer on it. I hadn't asked or applied for it, and I knew I was there because of my race, but I was keen to learn about major enquiries. The team was based in the North Manchester division's CID, and I was given the role of 'outside' enquiries detective. This meant taking many of the witness statements, both public and police. First, I was tasked with visiting the anti-gun campaigner Erinma Bell, to see if she would provide a statement, taking a trainee detective with me to show him the ropes. This was an especially difficult and loaded task. One of the arrested men, Raymond Bell, was an IAG member and Erinma's husband. On the night of the incident, my enquiry team were told that the silver (tactical) commander on duty had agreed to de-arrest him if he 'forgot' what took place. He refused. We had no idea if this was true, and there was no way of proving or disproving it, though Bell was arrested. Bell was going to lodge a formal complaint (civil action) against the police.

I was also tasked with interviewing the bronze (operational) commander on duty that night, an officer who was two ranks above me. Mrs Bell's contribution and the viewpoint of the initial officer in charge were vital to the investigation, so I had to get them right.

Mrs Bell was very cold to me when I arrived at her home in south Manchester. She had been in contact with senior command about the incident and raised issues of public confidence, so it's no wonder she didn't trust another police officer. She had refused to give a statement to several white officers. I told her that whatever she said to me would be recorded exactly the way she said it, which was true. For me, my job was simple: obtain her account and not twist it in anyway. However, I also had to be smart about the way I took her statement, as my police brothers would be expecting me to dilute what she said, if it was damaging to the police. To ensure transparency, I audio- and video-recorded her interview (which I conducted at Grey Mare Lane Police Station), and made comprehensive written notes to protect myself. I was leaving nothing to chance. I went about taking down her account like I was on a murder enquiry.

I persuaded Mrs Bell to tell me everything she had witnessed, then went back over it with her and probed her account further. I believed Mrs Bell was telling the truth about what she saw, although I didn't tell her this. I like talking to people, so interviewing came naturally to me. I wasn't threatening, and put people at ease. I remembered what one of my previous interviewees, a young white boy, had once said to me in the middle of a taped conversation: 'You're not like the others, are you?'

After the four-hour interview, I showed Mrs Bell out of the

station. She told me that she had just received notification from Buckingham Palace that she was to receive her MBE. Afterwards, I went straight to the detectives' office and looked her up on the internet. Prime Minister Gordon Brown had dedicated his 2007 book *Britain's Everyday Heroes* to her. Unwittingly, I had just interviewed a member of GMP's own advisory board, who was admired by the most powerful man in the country. And her husband, Raymond, had been kicked, punched and taken to the floor by police officers.

Word had got around the black community that I was a good officer who would treat people fairly and take a statement with integrity. Requests to be interviewed started to come in to the enquiry team, and I took the statements from many of the civilian witnesses. When I visited a community centre in Hulme, the local black pastor said he could tell I was a 'good one' and that he was 'proud' of the way I was conducting myself. A rush of emotion came over me with those words.

The senior detectives insisted that we keep digging for dirt on the members of the black community who were arrested. They believed the black community were lying and that it was our job to catch them out on inaccuracies. It wasn't the Moss Side community who weren't telling the truth, though. CCTV footage contradicted the witness statements made by some officers who had categorically denied being in a particular place – but the video footage placed them there, talking to other officers.

I was tasked to find out what I could about Mrs Bell to discredit her, checking if she contradicted herself during television interviews she had given. The leadership were keen to exonerate police officers and the Force. I was disturbed by this behaviour, but there was no way I was going to say anything. Soon I'd be out of Manchester and they could do what they wanted.

I just had to keep my mouth shut.

Manchester's black community reacted with anger when,

in September 2010, the police were cleared of any wrongful violence.[7] The internal affairs investigation, which was supervised by the IPCC, dismissed eighteen complaints of undue violence. The Force claimed the enquiry had been 'bedevilled' by a lack of cooperation, because most complainants had refused to speak directly to the Force's investigators. One of the senior internal affairs officers involved in my very recent grievance was the same officer in charge of the Bridgewater Hall incident. He stated: 'During the course of the investigation the majority of complainants have not been prepared to speak directly to us, causing significant delays and affecting our ability to gather evidence. After investigating all of the information available to us, we have not been able to substantiate any of the complaints.'[8]

This was patently untrue; they had spoken to me, I had taken their statements, and I'd spent four hours alone interviewing Erinma Bell.

In June 2008, I travelled to London for my interview with Special Branch. In preparation for it, had to study legislation relevant to national security, including the Terrorism Act 2000 and corresponding provisions – in particular Schedules 7 and 8, as well as Section 1 (which dealt with the question 'What is Terrorism?') and Section 40 (which asked 'What is a Terrorist?'). I was up through the night on my old university friend's couch in Balham, fitting in all the last-minute revision I could. I went over the country profiles of Afghanistan, Iraq and Iran, and the proscribed organisations under Section 3, such as al-Qaeda and the Real IRA.

I was assessed by two counter terrorism sergeants who tested the competencies required of the detective post. It was challenging, but I felt I'd prepped well and could only do my best. After the interview board, I went for a strong coffee and returned to the north. I was on a detectives' course at Sedgley Park, when I got a call from a woman at the Met's specialist operations recruitment. I left the police canteen and went outside into the courtyard to be able to hear properly what she had to say.

I'd been successful.

As with my last application to become a Manchester detective, I had come top of the interviewees. I was elated. I would be putting my experiences at GMP behind me and starting afresh with the Met at Scotland Yard. I'd be transferring to Britain's biggest Force, bigger than the Royal Navy and with the budget of a small country, and still had twenty-three years of service to complete and make my contribution.

I had a lot to offer London, and believed the Met had a lot to offer me. All I had left to do was pass the Met's vetting and security checks and fitness tests. I knew these wouldn't be a problem, as I had been a good officer and was relatively fit. I'd only just run a 10k in the Bupa Great Manchester Run to help raise money for the George House Trust charity, which supports those living with HIV, and completed it under an hour. I'd also met a new partner.

I passed the vetting, which gave me access to 'secret' and 'top secret' information. This was a requirement for individuals who were employed in a post that required them to have long-term, frequent and uncontrolled access to secret documents on suspected terrorists and terrorism plots. Individuals were also vetted before being granted access to certain levels of protectively marked materials originating from another country or international organisation, like the US.

The British government administered the clearances through Cabinet Office Mandates. My time came to leave GMP and all that I had experienced behind. I cleared out my drawers and returned my old uniform to the clothing store to be incinerated. I was allowed to keep the two police hats, as they couldn't be reissued for health and safety reasons. I donated the helmet to the police museum and arranged a leaving party at a city centre pub, the English Lounge.

I now had completed the rigorous process, with further security vetting, fitness testing, a check of my complaints and discipline history, a check of my last two personal development reviews (appraisals), and had obtained a health clearance.

I had never taken a sick day, had no complaint record or disciplinary actions against me, and had never been subjected to any performance-related issues.

On paper, I was the ideal cop. I was determined to prove just how good I could be. I was moving away from my home, my friends, my past and everything I knew.

I was now an officer of the Metropolitan Police.

8

Last-Ditch Attempt

I meant every word I said when, on joining the Met in October 2008, I re-swore my allegiance to the Queen at the Hendon attestation ceremony. I would, to the best of my ability, 'cause the peace to be kept . . . and prevent all offences'. I was serious about doing my duty and felt I had finally come to a place where my commitment would be recognised.

I had joined the secret arm of Britain's police, the one that worked with spies, a specialist intelligence unit with the responsibility of bringing to justice anyone engaged in terrorism or domestic extremism. Due to the nature of the work, most of the branch's intelligence came from the seaports and airports in the UK. I was sent to Heathrow Airport, the biggest in the UK and the busiest in the world. I would be interviewing terrorist subjects face to face. It would be a controlled environment, in that most people would be subjected to the standard airport security screening first. Along with interviewing, seizing exhibits from those stopped and so on, I was to work closely with the other governmental agencies, including MI5, and also with immigration and customs. Under UK legislation, SO15 counter terrorism command is one of the security services along with MI5 and MI6. My Heathrow identification badge read: 'Government Service, CSB (Central Special Branch).'

I began my first shift on an embarkation team, known as Ossianic: the majority of Special Branch officers at the airport were split into two groups – half would check passengers leaving the UK (embarkation) and the other half would check passengers coming into the country (disembarkation). My team's office at Terminal 3 was not much bigger than a toilet, located by the duty-free just after security.

There were seven members on my team, including me: four officers, my sergeant – all white – and one other black officer. He and I were the only two black officers out of the several hundred at Special Branch, who were known as detectives, although most were not 'detectives' in the CID sense, or had not been trained as such. As part of the reward for getting into the branch from uniform, police constables, sergeants and inspectors were allowed to use the 'detective' prefix before their rank. Whenever qualified detectives such as myself joined, they were distributed amongst the teams to add an investigative capability.

My day-to-day work involved interviewing persons and gathering intelligence on persons believed to be, or known to be, involved in terrorism under the relevant legislation; and submitting intelligence reports concerning individuals to other security service agencies. It came naturally to me, after my time as an investigator in the CID. I was a talker (a Liverpool trait), who put criminals on the back foot with my easy-going style. On one of my last cases in Manchester, I had called the suspect of a crime, to arrange for her to attend the police station for an interview regarding perverting the course of justice. After I said goodbye to her she forgot to put her handset down properly, and on the loudspeaker in the CID office my colleagues and I heard her describe me as 'nice' but, more importantly, heard her say that she'd actually committed the offence. At her subsequent interview she asked me: 'Am I the world's dumbest criminal?' I tactfully didn't answer.

Speaking to and gathering intelligence on terrorists didn't

faze me. I never felt consumed by nerves or fear when dealing with potential terrorists. After all, I'd always been able to do the job of policing (no one disputed this). Back when I was in uniform, and was called to a disturbance – in a pub, for example – and might be faced with a group of rowdy men who refused to leave, I'd concentrate on the biggest and loudest one as the others watched. Good officers needed that confidence, especially before backup arrived.

I enjoyed working with my black colleague at Terminal 3. He was a funny man. I saw him as an older, cooler version of myself, with a West Indian swagger. I admired how he spoke to people we 'did' together. He was never oppressive or domineering, but at the same time he got the job done. When he and I spoke to those black and brown people we stopped, many seemed taken aback that it was two officers of colour speaking to them about 'terrorism'.

One of the first things that was made clear to me at Special Branch was that, in part, my continued presence in special ops was dependent upon my performance, i.e. how many people I stopped. I would be measured not on how well I did my job in gathering intelligence, but how many figures (performance indicators) I had at the end of each month in comparison with the rest of my team.

My new sergeant was strangely hostile towards me. We'd only ever spoken over the phone, and when she first met me, she was cold. My black colleague was quick to notice her behaviour towards me, but advised me to ignore it. When the sergeant finally sat down with me to go through my performance development review,[1] I told her about my interest in the Home Office's High Potential Development Scheme, as I'd been identified as having high potential for leadership upon joining the Met.[2] She replied, 'Don't get above your station.'

When an officer joined Special Branch, they were meant, upon starting, to be taught how to access and use the different computer intelligence systems by an assigned mentor. I'd built a good rapport with my black colleague and requested him as my mentor. My sergeant denied my request on the grounds that he was not suitable, and said she would mentor me herself. Supervisors didn't normally take on this role, but she seemed no fonder of my black colleague than she was of me. I didn't understand why, because he was diligent and energetic, and interacted well with the public.

My sergeant's unfriendliness towards me continued as time progressed.

As mentioned, part of my role involving submitting intelligence reports on those members of the public who had been stopped by me under terror legislation. My sergeant took to reading out and changing these reports in front of my colleagues, much to their amusement. On one occasion, I submitted an annual leave form on the 'wrong' computer terminal. There were several computers, including one for general police business and another purely for special operations, containing secret and sensitive information. I had sent my annual leave request from the non-secret one, because as far as I was concerned it wasn't a secret (a holiday with my new partner). When my sergeant found out, she demanded to know why I had sent my leave using the wrong terminal. I replied that if I had known or been told not to, I wouldn't have done it. I had no mentor (she hadn't stepped up after giving herself the role) and I was trying to figure most things out for myself.

For example, she once instructed me: 'Turn the office alarm on before leaving.' But I had never been shown how to turn it on. 'Move. I'll do it,' she snapped, nudging me aside.

Or: 'Unlock the safe,' she demanded.

'I don't know how. I don't know the code.'

'For God's sake,' she muttered.

It wasn't really what I was hoping for in a mentor.

I noticed that others on my team were being offered the support that I wanted. One of my colleagues wanted to return to the tactical support group (TSG, the Met's full-time riot squad), where my sergeant had once worked. She had also been a sergeant at professional standards (the new name for internal affairs). In the weeks I had been on the team, my colleague had applied to return to the TSG, changed his mind (his old team was being investigated for misconduct), and then applied for a post of prison intelligence officer (those who bug cells and prison visits). Throughout it all, the sergeant aided him with each application, in a friendly manner that she reserved for everyone except me and my black colleague. She even phoned her line manager, the detective inspector, to ask for his endorsement on behalf of my white colleague.

I began struggling to sleep and eat, and needed to force myself to go to work. I wasn't sure what was happening to me. I spoke to the black officer in confidence about our situation. I told him I was gay. He was fine with it.

'Keep your chin up,' he encouraged me.

I had made much effort to settle into London. I really wanted it to work. It should have been an exciting time for a black gay detective in one of the world's most diverse cities, and I had arrived fully prepared to succeed and thrive. But the disillusionment was setting in. My sergeant's behaviour brought back memories of Manchester. I was always battling in the police, and wasn't sure what I was doing wrong. After a few months, I came out to the youngest officer on my team. Soon after, the two older officers became more distant, so much so that on some shifts only a single sentence would be spoken between us. I heard a 'poof' comment, and the sergeant started to pick on me for even more insignificant things. My new partner was the only person I could share my frustration with.

One day, in mid-November 2008, I arrived for my shift, entered the office and then immediately left again. I would sometimes walk from the office to the toilets, sitting on the closed seat to think, waiting for the time to drag on. That day, I found a private place away from my colleagues and made a phone call to a woman at Scotland Yard special operations recruitment. I remembered her from my open day as the one who had informed me that I had been successful in my transfer application. I told her what was going on. She suggested that I contact SO15 HR, and so I emailed the manager there.[3] She too wasn't helpful and told me to 'speak to your line manager',[4] the very same sergeant I wanted to speak to them about. She also forwarded my email to another HR manager, asking: 'Have you been made aware of any issues?'[5]

Finally, I visited the National Ports Office at the airport to find my sergeant's line manager, the detective inspector, who I had never met. I approached the inspector's office, but couldn't find him. Another officer spoke with me and introduced himself as the detective chief inspector. I told him that I was trying to find my inspector.

'Is there a problem?' he enquired.

Not wanting to break the protocol of rank, I said no.

But as he prepared to turn away, I corrected myself: 'Yes, actually. There is.'

I told the chief about the problems. He suggested I transfer from my team at Christmas, along with other officers who were moving and joining Special Branch. He said that he was already aware of problems in my team.

The woman I'd contacted at special operations recruitment told me that she had found a detective inspector from terrorism investigations (the Anti-Terrorist Branch) who was willing to talk things through with me. I met this Asian inspector at Tintagel House, next to MI6's headquarters, and told him how my sergeant was treating me. He knew her, he said. He thought it might be good for me to 'get away' from intelligence and join him in investigations, taking into account the fact I was a substantive detective. The inspector said he would speak with the Special Branch superintendent at Heathrow.

The sergeant's behaviour towards me got worse, and I found

it impossible to do anything without being criticised. On one shift, I was at the immigration controls, where passports are checked before passengers' outbound journeys. The sergeant approached an Asian man who was leaving the UK and asked for his passport. She then forcibly brought him over to me and, in front of other members of the public, said: 'This man is leaving the country, here is his passport.' The impact of her actions were twofold. Firstly, she ignored my power to choose who I stopped and spoke to, something I never saw her do to anyone else. We both had equal powers when it came to the Office of Constable (every police officer from the commissioner and chief constables down is a 'constable' in law). The sergeant could not force or instruct me to use specific powers if I didn't consider their use justified. Secondly, she had implied that an Asian man was somehow suspect, and I was somehow refusing to see it. There was no basis for her stop him, other than the colour of his skin and the demands of the performance indicators.

The general view at the airport was that we could stop who we wanted to under terrorism legislation, for whatever reason we wanted. My colleagues' behaviour followed suit. Black and Asian people were deliberately targeted on grounds of their race and colour. There was not much the passengers could say in return, although I witnessed some trying to argue their point and object to the 'random' stop.

The behaviour some of my colleagues showed towards black and brown people was not reasonable, and neither did it comply with the police's own 'community strategy', as it did not engender confidence; the random stops were designed to help people feel safer in the face of anonymous dangers, but their execution was less than ideal. Even talking to airport security staff was frowned upon. A large number of Asian people worked at Heathrow, living and commuting in from the immediately surrounding areas, and we were told not to socialise with them because they might have links to terrorism.

Aware of the divide between intention and action, senior management organised an Islamic Awareness Day at a Mosque for the officers. Some officers, huddled in groups, having whispered conversations, were angry that the event was compulsory. Why, they demanded, should they be lectured to by imams, who were doing 'nothing' to stop terrorist attacks? One officer from my team refused to eat the food the staff had made, saying, 'They will have spat in it.' Another officer refused to take her shoes off, stating it wasn't her religion or rules.

The year I joined counter terrorism, more than 100,000 people were stopped by the police under terror legislation (Section 44 of the Terrorism Act), yet there wasn't a single arrest for terror offences. This power, like others, could not be kept if it wasn't justified. The police had to show the public that they were not just targeting people with the wrong colour skin, so people started being targeted for other offences, like illegal immigration, and deported by the UK Border Agency.

In 2010, the Home Office admitted the scale of the problem: between April 2009 and April 2010, 101,248 people had been stopped and searched under these powers, without even one arrest.[6] For many, the official statistics heightened the concern that terror legislation was being used to target people who posed no terrorism threat at all to the UK and her allies. Eventually, Section 47A (stop and search) of the Terrorism Act would replace Section 44, a power used regularly by the British Transport Police.

At the time, Schedule 7 of the Terrorism Act 2000 allowed examining officers to stop someone and examine them through basic questioning, a search of property and/or a period of detention up to nine hours. Any person could be examined at an airport, passengers and crew. The power to stop, question and detain under the terrorism law was to be used when a person at a port (like Heathrow) fell under Section 40(1)(b) of the Terrorism Act. Officers were meant to stop a person to determine whether he or she 'is or has been concerned in the commission, preparation or instigation of acts of terrorism'. 'Terrorism' means the use or threat of action, such as trying to influence the government or advancing a political cause. Under the terrorism code of practice, we were known as 'examining officers'. However, 'the powers . . . should not be exercised in a way which unfairly discriminates against a person on the grounds of race, colour, religion, creed, gender or sexual orientation'.[7]

Most members of the public did not know that Special Branch officers (those examining 'ports officers') had these powers in addition to their everyday police ones, which derived from Schedules 7 (Port and Border Controls) and 8 (Detention) of the Terrorism Act 2000. Counter terrorism legislation superseded PACE, the 'everyday' Police and Criminal Evidence Act, and the code of practice stated that 'when deciding whether to question a person the examining officer should bear in mind that the primary reason for doing so is to maximise disruption of terrorist movements into and out of the United Kingdom'.[8] Although examining officers did not need 'to have any grounds for suspicion', the Home Office issued clear guidelines stating that the powers 'must be used . . . reasonably' and 'not be used arbitrarily'.[9] The police used the 'no suspicion needed' wording of the code, simply ignoring the accompanying 'guidelines'. Critics of the Terrorism Act, like the civil rights group Liberty, claimed that police were using the exceptional circumstance of the terrorism powers as 'another tool in the kit of day-to-day policing'.[10]

The 'examination clock' (the maximum time you could examine someone without arrest), was meant to start when a person was stopped, and when more than brief screening questions were asked, or when that person was directed to another place for examination, or when they were searched. When an examination reached a duration of one hour, or a person was detained, the National Joint Unit (NJU) at Scotland Yard was to be notified, as there was a UK database for government statistics and a requirement to keep a record beyond this time. A TACT (Terrorism Act) Form 1 (Notice of Examination) must be served at one hour, or at any time before. A person has to be formally detained if they refuse to cooperate or try to leave, if biometrics or a strip-search are required, if they are held incommunicado or their rights are delayed, or they are taken to a police station for further examination. A TACT Form 2 (Notice of Detention) must then be served.[11]

However, during all stops my colleagues routinely examined ethnic minorities for more than an hour (with no intention of arrest), and without informing the NJU for the purposes of recording the stop on the database. Special Branch officers would pretend the examination took less than an hour, so that they didn't have to inform the NJU and create unnecessary paperwork.

According to Home Office statistics, more than 97% of examinations lasted less than one hour, and the majority less than 15 minutes.[12] Once, I was with one of my colleagues at Terminal 3 when we stopped some Iranian men; he interviewed them for considerably more than an hour, yet the examination did not reflect this because he served no notice and did not inform the NJU. I could not remember being present at the examination of any white person in similar circumstances, though Russian espionage and Irish republicanism were still significant threats to the UK, and police officers in Northern Ireland are still targeted and injured by those fighting for a united Ireland.

I was not naive about the counter terrorism environment. I had joined to protect my country from those who posed a threat. Those images of 9/11 remain ingrained in my brain. However, I started to think that this kind of oppression was what created terrorists and extremists in the first place. My colleagues' actions had consequences. Asian and black people, minding their own business, were constantly being stopped by the law who saw them as 'troublesome' citizens. In turn, they began to view themselves as enemies of the state, unwanted by a society that persisted in treating them differently. I often asked myself why those four young British men caused such tragedy and harm to their country of birth during the London bombings of 7 July. Three came from West Yorkshire and the fourth was Jamaican-born, who came to the UK with his mum aged one and later converted to Islam (which many say accepts them as they are, unlike conventional society, which has appeared to reject them). Why did these men terrorise their own country? What makes a young British man or woman turn to al-Qaeda and its ideologies? Those already on the margins of society turn from good to bad when all their interactions with the state teach them that they are intrinsically suspicious and not worthy of society.

Just before Christmas, I received a phone call from the Special Branch detective superintendent and visited her office. At first, she asked why I wanted to see her, which I thought would have been obvious after she'd spoken with the Asian inspector, whom I had told that I felt 'unsupported and unwelcomed' in the Met. I felt like I was bothering her. I told her I thought my sergeant was not treating me well, and that I had discussed with the Asian inspector the possibility of moving away from the airport. Special ops were advertising for twenty substantive detectives within investigations in the same command, and it seemed like this would be a good move for me.[13] The superintendent told me that leaving Heathrow was not an option, and to give it six months on another team at the airport, after which things might be reviewed. She suggested that my sense of discomfort might be linked to the problems of living in a big city and at Gilmour Section House in Kennington, the police accommodation allocated to single officers until they found a permanent home. I told her that I was born and grew up in inner-city Liverpool, and spent ten years in inner-city Manchester. I was no different to the hundreds of other officers who lived at Section House. These weren't my problems.

The superintendent then spoke about the problems with the two older officers on my team, and strangely added that she felt my sergeant wasn't up to scratch. She asked me to rate my sergeant, and I said 'zero', but knew that this appeared not to answer the question, so changed my response to a more measured 'one'. I explained that my sergeant had made my life hell since joining the Met and was the worst supervisor I had been under.

Shortly after my meeting with the superintendent I was placed on the airport's internal transfer list, along with others. I was to be moved from Terminal 3 to Terminal 5. To make it look 'normal' – as per the usual process – my sergeant had to tell me about my transfer, even though I already knew about it. The only other black officer at the airport, the one on my team, was also being moved to another terminal, although he hadn't requested it. The sergeant herself was also being transferred. She didn't have much to say to me about my transfer, only expressing confusion as to why they were moving her.

After announcing my transfer in December, my sergeant sat down with me and said that we should go through my mentor forms to see if we could 'tick off' some things. She couldn't send me to a new team with no mentor papers, as this would reflect badly on her, so she went about ticking what she thought I had covered, and backdated them. I had no energy to challenge her. I wanted to get away from her and her team.

Ten days before Christmas, I transferred ahead of all the other moves. Terminal 5, the disembarkation team, was seen as the best office at Heathrow. The office in the new airport building was modern, surrounded by trendy restaurants and coffee shops where officers could receive a discount both on and off duty (using that 'gold' warrant card), and it was away from senior management, who were based at Terminal 2, at the National Ports Office.

My new team was supervised by a male sergeant. Again, there were seven of us in total, including me. There were five other constables, three men and two women, but all white and heterosexual. Four of them had partners who were also officers in the Met.

At Terminal 5, gathering intelligence on those people believed to be involved in acts of terrorism covered a significant part of my role. Those suspected of terrorism are, like most people, creatures of habit. People might imagine them sneaking into the UK under the cover of darkness, but they arrive on scheduled flights and eat the same airline food as regular folk, with the accompanying trolley service.

It was no secret that my colleagues' main focus was on Pakistan, which the police said posed the most significant threat to the UK, with an estimated 75% of plots against Britain originating there.[14] Visits to Pakistan, they said, fitted the profile of the 'modern terrorist'. However, the police was blind to the fact that, although many suspected of terrorism came from Pakistan, not every Pakistani person was a terrorist.

My job was to continue stopping people, which I believed needed to be done as a result of the intelligence we'd received and not based on someone's appearance. Intelligence came from many sources, but particularly from the other security services, like MI5. Special Branch officers were meant to use their own intelligence-gathering skills too, like observing a person's behaviour when entering the UK. That said, just because a person *acts* 'suspicious' at an airport it does not mean that he or she is necessarily up to no good. Many law-abiding people find immigration controls intimidating even when re-entering the country of their birth.

Many people of colour have spoken out about their everyday experiences of being viewed as suspicious, for example when out shopping, with store security watching, and in some cases following them around: shopping whilst black. When I was working uniform patrol at Bootle Street, I was stopped by security at a store half an hour before my night shift was due to start at 9 p.m. After going to the gym, I popped to the small Sainsbury's on Manchester's Oxford Street to pick up a sandwich, bag of crisps and drink from the fridge near the main entrance and the tills, to have on my refreshment break in the early hours. As I went to leave the store the security guard blocked my path. He said he wanted to search my bag. I asked why. He said people 'like me' had been stealing in the past. I had to assume he didn't mean gym-goers. By now the store manager and a small crowd of customers had joined us. I asked the manager why the security guard wanted to check my bag, which only had my gym gear in, and those three items I had just bought. The manager reiterated what the security guard had told me – because of thefts 'in the past', not that they'd seen me do anything untoward. I identified myself as a police officer, showing my warrant card, and asked for the third time what their actual grounds for carrying out a search were. Red-faced, the manager now said that a search wasn't needed and it was all a misunderstanding. The security guard moved slowly out of my path. I told the manager she could search me and emptied the contents of my bag on the shop floor. The other customers, all white, broke into applause.

I went to work and told my colleagues about what had happened (the store was on our beat), and they found it hilarious. Nothing of the sort had ever happened to them. Why would it?

Sainsbury's head office later sent me an apology and said the staff at the store would be sent on 'diversity training'. But security in stores is one thing; with the Force, one expected a more informed and intelligence-led form of policing.

Those stopped by me and my colleagues would be taken to a secure interview room and we'd 'discuss' the purpose of their visit to the UK and, more importantly, their past life – intelligence vital to protecting the country. My communication style as a police officer was noted in my performance development review (annual appraisal) by my new supervisor: 'He is a good communicator with a laconic yet professional approach that breeds confidence amongst the less experienced.'[15]

My approach to interviewing terrorists was for them to do the talking and for me to do the listening. I tried to be fair and observant too, which also came up in my review:

> *DC Maxwell's reports are concise and well written. He is able to portray his point in a clear and well-argued manner as evidenced by his file submissions and reports on subjects . . . He displays high standards of diplomacy, fairness when dealing with people regardless of their race, religion, [and] gender and will focus on the issue at hand without stereotyping subjects.*

Although I was performing well and had personally made a good impression, senior management insisted that officers' performance development reviews required officers to take 'personal responsibility' for doing more. My appraisal stated that I needed to: (1) conduct at least two port stops per tour [of duty] (i.e. shift), (2) submit 'at least' two intelligence reports per month, (3) identify one potential CHIS [covert human intelligence source] (police informer) referral each month, (4) have one cash seizure, (5) have one facilitation each month (escorting VIPs through the airport – Ronald Noble the secretary-general of Interpol being my latest) and (6) collect as many biometric details (fingerprints and such) as possible.

In his email to our seniors, my new inspector called these targets 'minimum workrate'.[16] In the Terminal 5 back office, which senior management also used, the performance targets were pinned to the wall. These were some heavy and serious pressures on officers. We had to go out and literally find terrorists – as if they would be waltzing through the airport. To ensure management knew they were performing, my colleagues regularly targeted ethnic minority passengers to keep to their quota. At the airport, there was a database that management controlled, which kept track of all the stops. Each terminal was allowed to view each team's – their competitors' – indicators. My team was ahead of the race.

My colleagues would sometimes spend much of the day sitting about talking, reading the newspapers and so forth in the Terminal 5 front office directly behind the immigration controls (as you enter the UK), with one-way-mirror windows. Management, inspectors and above rarely visited this office. Towards the end of the shift, my colleagues would go out and find their targets to put in the two stops required. There would be planned targeting by announcement in the office. As long as management saw that we had two stops that day, we'd played our part in keeping Britain safe.

This practice became more disturbing when it came to landing cards, the personal details many passengers complete when arriving in the UK. In order to keep up their stop figures, my colleagues would attend the immigration desks, mainly when they were unstaffed, and take a handful of landing cards that had been filled in by passengers who had long gone. They would sift through the cards, looking for what they considered non-white names. These passengers would then be processed, using the information from the cards, and put onto a police database as if they had been stopped. If the individual's details were already known to police in matters unrelated to terrorism (like domestic violence), this was a bonus and a 'just' entry – though the individual had never been stopped and spoken to. This is why thousands upon thousands of people had been stopped without any arrests.

Once, I heard one sergeant talking to another in the main office, about a presentation counter terrorism were putting on for Lord Carlile, the UK's independent reviewer of terrorism legislation.

'It's about telling and showing the lord what he needs to know,' he explained. 'It's about people being correctly stopped within the law, and making sure the legislation isn't being misused.'

In front of immigration controls, my colleagues would point out an ethnic minority person in the queue and advise me to stop them. The trick was to stop the white person in front of the Asian person as well, so that the latter didn't think he was being stopped for the colour of his skin. When the officer then spoke with the Asian person, their details would be taken and entered onto the terrorism database, whilst the white person's would not be. It was a strategy to distract the intended target and obfuscate the officer's true intentions. As I was waited with my team to check incoming passengers, they joked that I should stop the black or Asian people first, as a 'buffer', before handing them over to my colleagues: 'Blacks don't complain about blacks.' This conduct happened frequently, and was part of the general culture. The police believed there was always a reason to stop black and Asian people.

I was finding it hard to concentrate at work, but put on the same face I'd put on for the past eight years. I was tired, had low self-esteem and no energy, and wasn't sleeping or eating properly. I lost a lot of weight. I was starting to worry about the severe headaches and stomach pains I was getting.

One day, I was asked by colleagues what I thought about Brian Paddick and Ali Dizaei, both former senior officers. I'd never met either of them but knew one was gay and the other was an ethnic minority. I was told that both had 'screwed' the Met. The year before, in 2007, Dizaei had published his book *Not One of Us*, about how he spent two and a half years trying to clear his name after he was taken to court by the police commissioner, accused of drug and sex worker use, taking bribes and being a threat to 'national security'. The Iranian-born superintendent was acquitted twice at the Old Bailey, after a multi–million-pound investigation. Paddick had also just written a book, *Line of Fire*, about his time in the police as a gay officer. He explained that he had it all because he had not come out yet and was a white man, and had breezed through policing, all whilst being helped by those like him. He wrote: 'I found my success incredibly bizarre.' Then he finally came out after fifteen years, and reality hit home. From then on, he suffered 'a campaign of "monstering" or "othering"' against him by the press,[17] where he was portrayed as some kind of dangerous, destabilising demon. He was described as being one of those people who, 'while thankfully rare and probably mentally ill, are a dangerous breed so entirely different from "normal people" that they must be isolated, attacked and, if possible, eliminated'. Paddick was also notable for instructing his officers not to arrest and charge people found with cannabis so that they could focus on crimes that affected quality of life in the London borough of Lambeth, where he was police commander (the London rank equivalent to the assistant chief constable) between 2000 and 2002. Black people, especially young black men, are disproportionally stopped and searched for cannabis-related crimes, despite being less likely to use drugs.[18] Unsurprisingly, Paddick's instruction generated a huge amount of controversy.

In the spring, ready to move out of Section House and wanting to find my own space after having worked and lived with other officers for a while, I started looking for accommodation in London, and asked some colleagues for advice. One officer told me to make sure that I didn't live in south London, below the river, with 'the scum'. He and another officer went on to discuss the Met's Operation Trident, which had been set up to tackle gun crime and homicide in London's Afro-Caribbean communities after a series of shootings in the south London boroughs of Lambeth and Brent. I mentioned that Trident was looking for experienced substantive detectives to join its command.

They told me not to apply, as I would be dealing with 'shit' all day – meaning the predominantly black victims and witnesses.

One day, whilst I was using a computer terminal, an officer came in and began talking about gay men 'taking it up the arse'. He continued his rant about homosexual sex until a female officer interrupted him.

'Enough,' she snapped. He stopped.

Wanting to be alone, I went to the toilet to sit on the closed lid and gather myself. When I returned to the office, there was silence and the ranting officer had gone. On a later shift, he came back, having since been informed that I was gay. He attempted to apologise, but the damage had been done.

Shortly afterwards, I stopped an Asian man who had just got off a flight. I believed he was frustrating my lawful conversation with him; in fact, he was blockading me to such an extent that I became frustrated and my tone changed. I was sharp, angry. I was so upset with things at work that I took my frustration out on him. I was disgusted with myself, having always striven to speak to others as I would like to be spoken to. On this occasion, I had let myself down, terribly. But my sergeant congratulated me on my 'firmness', and what he called 'a more authoritative manner'.

On what would have been my mother's seventy-third birthday, 24 June 2009, I attended day two of a terrorism forensics awareness course at Paddington Police Station (this was the second day of two different short courses I was having that week), where those suspected of terrorist acts were initially held. We were to be given a briefing by one of the only two trained Met custody officers for terrorism, and I was one of fourteen students. The presentation sergeant, a white man in his fifties with a shaved head, opened his briefing by stating, 'I am not politically correct.' He went on to tell us that it was the Met that needed him, not the other way round. He had completed his thirty years' service, got his pension, and came back on the so-called 30-plus scheme. He was giving a presentation on how to preserve evidence when arresting suspected terrorists. The first slide of his PowerPoint was of a man at a fairground surrounded by children. He told the class the man on the screen was 'as gay as a gay in a gay teashop', and everyone laughed.

When the day was over, I went to the Globe pub on Marylebone Road with a detective and two other colleagues from the course, and admitted how I felt. My colleagues said the sergeant was stupid and unprofessional. A valid point, I thought, yet no one had stood up to him. Because everyone, including myself, stayed silent, the behaviour was sanctioned, acceptable. Once again, I found myself part of the problem.

My headaches and stomach pains started getting more severe and on the second day of a Ports course at Heathrow (one of the two-day courses that week) I asked a trainer if I could step out of the class as I wasn't feeling well. I felt like I was going to faint. The next day, I turned up for my normal afternoon shift at 1 p.m. An hour in, I was walking along the public concourse at Terminal 5 when I suddenly became intensely aware of the bright lights above. They were shining down hard, blinding me. I doubled over, buckled by a sense of acute pressure in my stomach and head. I threw my hands up to cover my eyes from the brightness. I stumbled, managing to catch myself, and panic set in. As sweat quickly beaded all over my body, I staggered over to the duty sergeant and asked if I could go to hospital. He said yes and I went alone, refusing an ambulance. I arrived at the NHS walk-in centre in Soho and sat in reception, petrified. I knew something was wrong. I'd never been ill like this, never had to take a sick day. I had letter after letter of congratulations for my perfect attendance record over eight years. What was happening to me now?

After a short time of watching people come and go, I was called to the consultation room. Lucy, the nurse practitioner, was a short woman in a dark blue uniform. Her smile was warm and comforting. After some brief screening questions, Lucy started to carry out an examination. I tensed up as she poked and prodded, but I knew she needed to know the reason for my sudden illness. She checked my urine, blood and joints, but still said nothing. A few quiet moments passed, and then she finally spoke:

'How are things in your life? Are you happy?'

Taken aback by the personal nature of the questions, I couldn't speak. Suddenly, I became aware of a wetness on my face. I reached up to touch it. Not the sweat of panic, but tears. I was crying. Lucy put me at ease, and I began to tell her about how unhappy I was.

Like a dam breaking, everything I had bottled up over the many years in the police burst out. I was a mess. Lucy told me that she needed to leave the room for a moment, but that she'd be back. As she closed the door gently behind her, I sat at the end of the bed, sobbing in my formerly immaculate detective's suit. I buried my face in my hands and miserably thought about my mum. I needed her by my side, comforting me. I was all alone. The door handle turned, jerking me away from my thoughts. Lucy sat beside me and gently took my hand in hers.

'You're suffering from depression,' she said.

I was stunned. Depression didn't happen to people like me, I thought. I wasn't weak. I didn't even understand what it was, so how could I have it? I had coped for the past eight years in the police, despite the negative experiences, so why had it happened now? But here I was. I was defeated, after a lifetime of denial on the Force, and betrayed by a body that had finally had enough and given up.

PART TWO

9

Fight or Flight

That same weekend, I travelled to Manchester to see my GP (with whom I was still registered), and told her about my experiences and the extent to which I dreaded going to work. I pleaded with her not to diagnose me with depression, but she said I should make an appointment with the surgery's mental health nurse – a cognitive behavioural therapist – and then come back to see her. I was given a sickness certificate for two weeks, for the severe headaches and stomach pains, pending further evaluation.

After two weeks away from work, I attended a national counter terrorism course at MI5, at Thames House. Besides combating terrorism, the British Security Service (formerly known as Section 5 of the UK's Military Intelligence), was charged with protecting Britain's domestic secrets, i.e. counter intelligence, and to prevent sabotage, subversion and the theft of those secrets. After the course, I returned to my normal shifts and discovered that I had been placed on Operation Minstead, a Force-wide police operation to catch the serial burglar and rapist Delroy Easton Grant. I had been volunteered for this even though I had only just returned to work and was recuperating, and although I was meant to attend the next stage, Stage 3, of my MI5 course. I'd have to work a week-long set of seven nights after two weeks of illness.

I returned to Manchester to visit my GP and spoke with the surgery's mental health nurse, Charlie. In his assessment, he gave me a score of 32 on the Beck Depression Inventory – an indication of the most severe level of depression – and a score of 17 (rising to 24) on my PHQ (Patient Health Questionnaire). I was certified unfit for work, suffering from severe reactive depression due to my 'prolonged exposure to the situations at work'. I was issued another sickness certificate – this time for four weeks.

I was at a loss about what to do. I telephoned the acting superintendent about my diagnosis; he had been the person I'd spoken to about my bitter experiences in Terminal 3, and I thought he might be able to suggest a good direction forward. He didn't want to know, saying he was 'busy', and that I should contact my sergeant.[1]

I went back to see Charlie and he asked me what I wanted to do: fight or flee? Would I take on the Force, or run away from my troubles? I didn't want to fight with the police about the job I'd wanted to do all of my life, but the Force had damaged me.

I telephoned my sergeant and explained why I'd be off for four weeks. He just asked for my sick note. He submitted an occupational health form, which was completed without my input and contained a number of errors and inaccuracies. He got my age and my year of transfer wrong, as well as the date I'd joined his team. He wrote he was 'not aware' of any issues relating to my having to be off sick. Not surprisingly, he made no mention of discrimination. He wrote: 'I have not yet spoken to Kevin directly and am at this point unsure as to the nature or cause of Kevin's stress/depression' – when we had literally just spoken.[2]

He finished the form by stating that 'caution' should be exercised.

I sent my sergeant a text asking to be referred to occupational health. A few days later, he sent an email about me to Nigel

Quantrell, our inspector, and to another inspector. It read: 'Firstly welcome back . . . Secondly this is for your information' – referring to an attached document about me – 'John will fill you on the minutia[e], read with a large malt in hand.'[3]

Quantrell replied, 'Hmm, yes . . . will discuss over a latte next week.'[4]

Whilst I was on my way to my doctor's, I received a call from Quantrell. He asked me what I was up to and why I was going to my doctor. I thought it had been fairly obvious and explicit: I was off sick with depression. I told the inspector about the issues and that I was waiting for occupational health to get in contact about seeing a Met counsellor.

'A counsellor can't help you. All they can do is listen, so just forget about occupational health,' he said.

Flatly, I said, 'It's not easy being black and gay in the police.'

'That's life,' he replied

Quantrell asked where I was staying in Manchester, and told me that I had to call him regularly. For some reason, I had two welfare and sickness managers (my sergeant and Quantrell), and both were calling me regularly, against the Force's own sickness policy, which stated that they should only contact me once every two weeks.[5] In September, Quantrell told me during a call that in future, if he called me and I didn't answer, I would be treated as missing; he would phone my next of kin, and officers in Manchester would come to my partner's address (where I was staying at the time).

Knowing I was under obligation to meet Quantrell, even though I was sick, I travelled down from Manchester to London. It would be my opportunity to talk about the situation face to face. But he cancelled our meeting half an hour before it was due to start. On 17 September, I sent him an email instead, giving him an update on my health and writing that I believed my depression had been caused by the racism and homophobia I had experienced at work: 'Since finally admitting [to] my doctor the feelings and experiences I have been bottling up as a result of my experiences at work, I am now seeking ways to address how I go about dealing with them and getting myself back to full health.' I mentioned that I was apprehensive about taking anti-depressants, but my doctor had described me in his notes as 'very flat, tearful and distressed with fleeting suicidal ideation'. I explained that I found it hard to concentrate. If I slept at all, my sleep was erratic and broken. I was irritable and my self-esteem had plummeted. I had lost a considerable amount of weight and I was not eating properly due to a loss of appetite and drained energy. I said I had good and bad days; on the bad days, I couldn't bring myself to even wash.

The inspector sent me a curt reply the same day, saying my email was inappropriate. Regarding his cancellation of our meeting, he wrote: 'As you say I had work commitments and I need to prioritise my commitments . . . I have no knowledge of colleagues treating you any differently or making you feel uncomfortable. If this is the case I need to know immediately in order that I can take action . . . Unless absolutely necessary, Kevin, I will not be contacting you by email.'[6] I telephoned Quantrell to apologise for my email.

In his contact log for a later call, he wrote: 'I said staff would be wary if they thought [Maxwell] would get them into trouble with the organisation. By this I meant if [Maxwell] had a personal agenda to progress his career or sue the organisation based solely on his race or sexuality.'[7]

I eventually met Quantrell in a coffee shop at St Pancras station. We spoke for two and a half hours. I told him exactly what had happened to me, mentioning some of the incidents in Manchester. I didn't want to be obstructive, or be described as obstructive by the Met; I wanted to be open and honest about my experiences.

Quantrell said the Met had let me down, and that I should write a book about my treatment in Manchester and London.

He said that, before the meeting, he had researched me to see if I was an 'okay' person and not a 'troublemaker'. In his notes of this meeting he wrote that I spoke 'openly' and 'fluently'.[8] I later became aware that he had attempted to access my personal file at GMP without my consent.[9]

I felt that the union representative allocated to me by the Police Federation after I made them aware of my illness – who, when I met him at Scotland Yard, told me he was a friend of Quantrell's – was not the best person to support me. He told me that in his thirty years as an officer, he had never encountered derogatory comments in relation to race or sexuality. He went on to say that I could have *any* job I wanted in the Met. All he had to do was to go next door, where the counter terrorism commander, Shaun Sawyer, was based and it could be sorted – just like that. He wrote me a follow-up email after the meeting:

> *I really do believe the organisation have [sic] taken great steps towards achieving equality in gender, sexuality and race but that doesn't mean that there aren't a few bad apples left in the barrel. All I was trying to say is that I haven't encountered them. I really do wish you well and hope that your experiences don't lead you to take the decision to leave the organisation because from what I know of you, they would be losing an asset.[10]*

That same day, I attended a case conference concerning my ill-health absence, which was held at Scotland Yard.[11] The occupational health nurse I had been in contact with was present, along with another nurse, Quantrell, my sergeant, and the counter terrorism HR manager representing the Met. An administrator took the minutes. I had made some notes so I wouldn't forget what I wanted to say. I told them I was feeling better and making progress. I said I had been working with my doctor, had a prescription for anti-depressants that I found helpful, and was being assessed regularly. I mentioned the various therapies I was undertaking, trying to keep my mind active.

I told them my doctor had referred me to external counselling at the Kath Locke Centre, which specialises in supporting people with depression and mental illnesses, and that I felt positive about my counsellor, Sonia, a black woman (I thought she might understand me better). I stressed that all the professionals I had seen – my doctor, the mental health nurse and the counsellor – agreed that I should not return to work until I had made a full recovery, to prevent a relapse. My working environment had, in their eyes, been the catalyst for this collapse.

I took a breath. The SO15 HR manager approached me and handed me a letter, which I opened right then and there.[12] It was a notice saying that my pay would be reduced. They were going to take half my salary off me for being ill.

Whilst my complaints and treatment were discussed at the case conference, Quantrell incorrectly told the others I had been called a 'queer' and a 'faggot' in the Met (a note of his, which predated this, said 'faggot, nigger and coon'),[13] and I said this was not true. I had no desire to make false complaints, as they would only undermine my real ones. The HR manager stated that counter terrorism were devising a training package for managers regarding all strands of diversity, which would also deal with the impact on individuals of unacceptable behaviour. This sounded promising, but I was also concerned that the managers, who set the tone and led by example, might resist the training package and encourage those below them to do the same. I told the conference that racism and discrimination were a cultural issue within the police, and that I didn't think a simple training package would solve the problems. I'd seen how colleagues completed the new online NCALT [National Centre for Applied Learning Technologies] diversity packages run nationally by the Metropolitan Police. Officers had to complete questionnaires individually but colleagues collected the usernames and passwords of peers and completed them on their behalf.

Six days after the conference, I received another call from Quantrell. He asked about my counsellors and wanted to know how many sessions I had completed. Though I'd repeatedly told him that I was based in London, he still asked where I was. 'Your family and friends are in the north. Why do you keep coming back to London? What for?' he pressed. I told him that my job, my home, my life were in London. Three days later during another call from him, Quantrell said that Detective Chief Inspector Raffaele D'Orsi, as a member of senior management, wanted to speak with me.[14] The inspector later recorded in his contact log that I 'sounded drowsy and slightly slurred'. I was heavily medicated, but the wording could easily be read as a symptom of day drinking.

One morning in October, I got up later than I normally did, as I wasn't feeling too good. I had two answerphone messages from Quantrell. The inspector's first message asked me to call him, as D'Orsi wanted to meet up with me in London the next day. The second message repeated the same thing; D'Orsi wanted to meet me sooner rather than later. I called Quantrell back.

'I've already told you everything, so you should be able to tell the chief.'

'D'Orsi wants to see you personally,' he replied.

'I can see the chief inspector next week when I see the medical officer,' I said. 'I'm not feeling too good.'

'Not feeling too good? Why? What's up?'

Incredulous, I replied, 'I'm depressed.'

Quantrell said I had to make myself 'available' to management. It looked like I didn't have a choice, so I made myself available to the management of the workplace for which I was signed off sick.

The next day, on 27 October, I met Quantrell and D'Orsi at the Place Hotel in Piccadilly, in Manchester. The meeting was, rather strangely, held in a hotel room. D'Orsi said that I shouldn't worry, that I wasn't under investigation. Quantrell had said the same thing in the phone call. I didn't understand why they kept saying it. Of course I wasn't under investigation. I hadn't done anything wrong. I was signed off sick. I told them again of the problems at work, but they kept pushing me to return to work. The detective chief inspector said I had not been looked after properly and had been let down by the Met (the second senior to say this), but his priority was to get me back to work. The chief inspector said I would be suited to a borough (the new name London used for police divisions, to fall in line with the local 'borough' councils) like CID or local policing (roles I'd already done), but not a specialist department, when or if I returned. He explained that the officers in those departments were closer to my age and that the teams were often more diverse, and I wouldn't face the issues I had at Scotland Yard's Special Branch. They both said Special Branch had an older median age, which I took to mean white, straight, older men. The black and brown people I saw around Scotland Yard were cleaners, canteen staff and security. D'Orsi commented that I had 'broken the mould' in counter terrorism. I could now tell others in the borough, and they too could join. Somehow, my illness was the cure for everything. I'd leave the counter terrorism unit (where I had really wanted to work) and get out of everyone's hair, but my mould-breaking would constitute a step forward for diversity and inclusivity.

At the end of the meeting, they gave me a list of phone numbers for other senior officers, ten in total, whom I didn't know, and with whom I was expected to share my circumstances.[15] One name was highlighted – Chief Inspector Bailey, who was the 'diversity lead' for counter terrorism. She had already been 'briefed' by Quantrell.[16] On the bottom of the piece of paper was the number for the Samaritans! As they wrapped the meeting up, they added that they wanted to hear directly from my GP about my condition.

A few days after the meeting, Quantrell wrote a memo to the Force's medical officer, Dr Celia Palmer. Under 'Facts', he wrote: 'Kevin alleges that his illness is as a direct result of his treatment on duty, although to date the MPS [Metropolitan Police Service] have not classified this as such.' He said the fact that my GP had prescribed anti–depressants had not been 'corroborated'.[17]

I wrote to the Met about the decision to put me on half-pay, explaining why I was off and asking that discretion be exercised in my case (which was allowed), to continue me on full pay whilst I recovered. This was essential for me to keep up with my financial commitments and not suffer any further. Later, I woke to two phone calls: one from the police union and one from Quantrell. Quantrell said that in my letter to the deputy HR manager about the half-pay, I had mentioned a lack of support from the Met, and demanded to know what I meant by this.

'Nobody seems to care and all the tell-tale signs are there,' I said, frustrated.

He scoffed. 'What are you talking about? People are queuing up to help you.'

'No they aren't. And you're an example of this.'

I had thought my letter would be treated as confidential and would go directly to the commander from HR, and then to the assistant commissioner, as it was meant to. Quantrell should never have known about the contents, but he was made aware, as was another inspector and the professional standards (the new internal affairs) department. The HR manager wrote to Quantrell: 'We discussed the contents and I specifically asked you not to share them with anyone'.[18] Unhappy with my private letter being shared around the police, I sent an email to the deputy HR manager.

Quantrell wrote to the directorate of professional standards: 'It is clear from the signed letter that he is making allegations of wrongdoing and lack of support.'[19] D'Orsi also wrote to the heads of SO15 intelligence and Special Branch about the letter to 'protect the interests of the MPS now and in the future'.[20]

My sergeant sent me a letter saying that the level of contact from the Met had a detrimental effect on my recovery. He said I had been 'over-contacted', which was in breach of the Met's own attendance management policy.[21] Whilst I was sick in bed, I would receive numerous calls and messages in one day. Instead of being contacted once a fortnight, I was contacted forty times.

Despite this on-the-record letter to me, my sergeant also wrote secretly to Superintendent Terry O'Connor (the new Special Branch head in charge of ports) and chief inspector D'Orsi, saying that if I didn't reply to a further letter he was sending me 'there's always the three man overhead option [a tactic the police used to forcibly enter a property] left to gain entry should all else fail!'.[22]

My partner suggested I start to look for lawyers, to see if the police had broken the law, but I just wanted to get better with the right help and support. Besides, I was worried about the consequences of telling people about my experiences in the police.

I was afraid for my career, afraid of being discredited (which I'd seen happen to others) and dismissed (which I'd seen happen to others), or even arrested (which I'd seen happen to others). I remembered the Met deputy commissioner, Paul Stephenson, telling Tarique Ghaffur during a news conference to 'shut up and get on with the job', after he challenged the racism in the Force.[23] When I spoke to Tarique on the phone in April 2019, I asked him what his take was on this, and he explained that before Stephenson had made his comment he, Tarique, had raised the issue of racism with him. Tarique believed Stephenson's comments were a 'pitch for his own leadership bid' for the commissioner post, 'without any regard for me or the community at large'. After the comments by Stephenson, Tarique said he was subjected to a 'structural campaign' of hate.

Nevertheless, my partner looked for a solicitor and found Arpita Dutt online. I had no idea at the time that Arpita was already on the official books of the Police Federation, representing officers. Her employment-law firm, Russell Jones & Walker, where she was a partner, was frequently used by the police union. On 10 November, I sent her a long email about my predicament. A mere nine minutes passed before she replied. She thanked me for my 'heartfelt' email, and said she was sorry to hear of my experiences and the ill health that had been caused over many years, despite my diligent work for the police. She told me she would very much like to assist me, if she could, and asked if we could speak on the phone later that day. My spirits lifted slightly.

One of the things she instructed me to do immediately after our call was to phone the police union again and demand that they support me, as there was no reason for them not to. I called the local Met Federation again and insisted that I speak with someone new in the union, face to face. They arranged for me to see a new Federation representative. An employment tribunal was now looking likely, but I really did not want to fight the organisation I had dreamt about working for as a boy in the courts.

The police leaders sent me to see the occupational health psychiatrist, Dr Robert Oxlade. He was a white man in his fifties. I told the doctor about my experiences. He asked how many hours of sleep I got, and I said about four each night.

'Sometimes not sleeping is what causes depression,' he noted. 'Are you a sensitive person? Your other colleagues – the ones like you – do they integrate better?' He added: 'Look, most organisations like the Met have their problems. But if you have a good fighter pilot and he says an inappropriate word, does that mean he can't fly anymore? He's still a good pilot, right?'

I'd come across this attitude before. I wasn't talking about individual racist slurs against me. I was talking about a detrimental culture. If the police was a business, it would have been shut down a long time ago, but there was no incentive to stop the bad behaviour, because officers are rewarded for being bad – it was 'firm', it showed 'authority'. After giving the doctor examples of what I had experienced, Dr Oxlade told me that African and Caribbean people had integrated well into Britain, but that Asians had not and did not want to: 'You can understand police officers not knowing if the next Asian they meet is going to want to blow them up.'

This man was a police psychiatrist. I had to stay calm, no matter how offended I was, no matter how unprofessional I found his comments. He had the power to write what he wanted about me and I worried about what he might say if I showed a negative reaction.

This idea of 'integration', and the correct way for a person of colour to integrate, comes up in numerous walks of life, and the police are no exception. Take the case of the Police Community Support Officer (PCSO) Asad Saeed, reported in *The Guardian*[24]: PCSOs were introduced in England and Wales by the Home Secretary, David Blunkett, in 2002. They were to be the 'eyes and ears' of the police in the community. PCSOs are not sworn officers, i.e. actual 'ranks', but civilian staff. They are part of the police family, but with no powers of arrest. Like other citizens, they can apply through the usual channels to become constables. They were meant to be a reassuring uniformed presence on the streets, whilst sworn officers dealt with crime. PCSOs are part of Safer Neighbourhood Teams, consisting of a sergeant, two constables, and three PCSOs. They mainly deal with antisocial behaviour. However, many sworn officers despised them. They said PCSOs were introduced to replace them. Removing the middle words 'community support' left the words 'police officer', they complained, which, as far as they were concerned, the PCSOs were not. The PCSOs are often people of colour; they can help Forces swell the number of ethnic minority employees, presenting a diverse face to the public. Unfortunately, this difference, combined with a general resentment about the role of PCSO in the police force, was a red rag to white police officers.

In his employment tribunal against the Met, Saeed said officers were given a 'licence to bully' and that bosses turned a blind eye to threats of violence and a culture of apartheid. He was sacked from the Force, but later reinstated on appeal, with CCTV evidence disproving a claim from one of his police accusers that Saeed had assaulted a vagrant whilst on duty. In support of Saeed, PCSO Peter Campbell said that an inspector at the station drew up a hit list of black officers to get rid of, and shared this with white officers. Things were so bad at that Belgravia station, that white officers rode in a separate van from ethnic minority colleagues, barring entry to any black officer who tried to get in, and refused requests to pick them up. The canteen and television rooms were also subject to 'apartheid', with white and black officers sitting separately.

In his witness statement, Campbell said that black officers were 'treated like dogs'. He added, 'When we were on the beat after dark we would often notice a police car following us. Eventually one of the constables told me that they were playing a game called "spot the PCSO". We would look over and see two white police officers gawping at us from the vehicle. The joke was that all PCSOs had black or brown skin, so they were very hard to see in the dark.' Saeed lost his claim of racial discrimination.

The representative from my union, the Police Federation, sent me some forms to fill in to get legal help, but I told him I would fill them in once I was feeling better. I had been suffering acute stomach pains and headaches for several days. Not long afterwards, I received an email from my rep, telling me that the detective chief superintendent, head of counter terrorism intelligence, would be sending me a letter. Apparently the chief wanted to meet: 'She appreciates that you are instigating employment proceedings against the MPS and she in no way wishes to influence your decision or interfere with that process.'[25] I didn't know until this moment that my rep and management were in contact with each other about me. In fact, I was mentioned in an internal document that listed me as part of 'Significant People Issues'.[26] The police union was informing the Force of my next moves.

When the detective chief superintendent called me, it was purportedly about my career. She felt I hadn't been given the right opportunities in the Met.

'My police career is over,' I said flatly.

'I wish there were more officers with integrity like you,' she said. 'You've been let down [she was the third senior to say this] and I want you to give me the benefit of the doubt by meeting with me. I have twenty-four years of experience.'

What did I have to lose? 'Okay. We can meet.'

The chief and I decided to meet in the London Transport cafe in St James's Tube station, across the street from Scotland Yard. I walked over there with my partner. We met the chief superintendent outside the tube station and walked to the transport cafe. The short walk was awkward for everyone. It was obvious she was meeting me to nip things in the bud. This all happened on her watch, and somehow or some way, it had to be stopped. After choosing a table, I gave her a summary of my treatment at Heathrow, much of which she knew, having formerly been the Special Branch head there (before being promoted). The chief said that, even though I was considering taking the Met to a tribunal, they still wanted me to work for them. My departure would mean they, and she, had failed, she said. She spoke of restitution, something I hadn't heard of before, saying that it was another way to resolve the matter. She said the commissioner might be fined 'say, two million pounds', but those who had let me down still wouldn't be answerable. She said I could speak with those individuals face to face and explain how their behaviour had affected me. I told her the female sergeant from Terminal 3 would never do that, and if she did, it would be through gritted teeth.

'You might be surprised,' the chief said.

'I *would* be surprised,' I retorted. 'You would have to wheel a lot of officers into your office.'

'So be it,' she said.

She went on to say I could have *any* job in the Met I wanted. I said I didn't want *any* job. I already had a job. I wanted to be able to do that job.

Regarding this meeting with the chief superintendent, my sergeant wrote to D'Orsi: 'The plot thickens still.'[27]

Later that day, I had an appointment with the Met's medical officer, Dr Palmer, as a follow-up to my appointment with Dr Oxlade, the Force's psychiatrist. During the consultation, Dr Palmer had a medical report from Dr Oxlade in front of her, accompanied by handwritten notes. I was not allowed to view the contents, and Palmer later said that she didn't disclose them because the report was in draft form. Based on Dr Oxlade's report, Dr Palmer told me her determination was that I was 'fit for full operational duties', contrary to the opinion of my GP and my counsellor. She told me that I wasn't a danger to the public – a grossly obvious and rather insulting observation.[28]

Upon being notified that I was fit to return, the detective chief superintendent telephoned me and said that I should consider working for her in the interim, so that my pay would not be affected, and then decide what I wanted to do. I told her that my GP and counsellor's opinion was that I wasn't ready to return because I was sick, and that I shouldn't have to go back to being accountable to a chief superintendent (being supervised by someone five ranks above me would be like a pupil being looked after on their own by the head teacher). She said she would contact me in a week's time, when she returned from work in the US.

I was promised the reports from Dr Oxlade and Dr Palmer

within two weeks, but after not hearing anything I sent another email to the Met, asking for the reports as a matter of urgency. Dr Palmer had deemed me fit for work based on Dr Oxlade's report, but I, the patient, had not been allowed to see it. The occupational health nurse told me that I now had to apply under the Data Protection Act to get copies of my medical reports, in spite of signing *two* access forms after both consultations one and two.[29] Each form stated: 'Important [in bold]: due to new guidance recently issued by [the] General Medical Council (GMC), occupational health is now required to provide you and then your manager with a copy of the medical officer's recommendations regarding your fitness for work.' I also still hadn't received the final decision on whether my pay was to be halved.

I eventually received an email, with a letter from my sergeant attached: 'There is no easy way to convey this but we have now been advised that following consultation your pay is to be reduced by half.'[30] It felt as if they considered my illness a crime that needed to be punished, rather than a consequence of impossible working conditions. I had no time to fight the weight of the depression, as I had to fight my employer.

In his letter, my sergeant wrote that careful consideration had been taken in reducing my pay and that the reason would be explained in an official letter. He acknowledged the devastating impact it would have on me, but reassured me that if I returned to work, I'd be kept on full pay. My union rep wrote to D'Orsi about the decision,[31] as he had not had the opportunity to liaise with the (temporary) assistant commissioner, Rose Fitzpatrick, who had taken the decision to reduce my pay.[32] She later became the deputy chief constable of Police Scotland, and later retired after it emerged that she had received taxpayer-funded relocation expenses worth nearly £70,000 from the Scottish Police Authority – years after moving from the Met to take up her post. There was no suggestion that she did anything wrong receiving the money.[33]

I was so concerned by the way in which the decision was made that I wrote to my union rep, detailing the breaches of the Regulation 28 policy regarding sick pay,[34] including an email I discovered from HR5 to the deputy HR manager, which said: 'I will add the attached memo as requested and confirm the ET [employment tribunal] action in our summary for the AC [assistant commissioner].'[35] The Met had breached its own policy under clause 8.1.7., since the regulation did not allow the assistant commissioner or any other person involved in my 'full pay' representation to be influenced by or concerned with the issue of an employment tribunal. I later learnt the police could never have continued my pay: to do so would have been an admission of liability, i.e. that my illness had indeed been a direct result of discrimination.

Around the same time, I received a phone call from the detective chief superintendent. She spoke, again, about me going to work for her in her private office. The chief told me she had just chaired a recent 'gold' (i.e. strategy) meeting. Gold groups are set up and led by the most senior police officers and staff when something serious goes wrong in the Force, a major incident or subject that threatens the very fabric of policing, for example the London bombings or the fatal shooting of Jean Charles de Menezes. The commissioner had initiated the gold command structure around me as an 'internal critical incident'. Most gold groups received an operational name, but I was referred to as 'him' or 'KM'. The purpose of the group was to 'preserve the reputation of the Metropolitan Police Service'. The chief superintendent told me that the decision to reduce my pay was partly based on the opinions of Dr Oxlade and Dr Palmer. I told her my GP and counsellor disagreed with the reports. She replied that the Met doctors worked to different criteria.

Two days after I was notified of the reduction in pay, the Met sent me the two medical reports written by Dr Oxlade and Dr Palmer.

The medical report from Oxlade was disturbing and hurtful. Although I was concerned about many inaccurate points in the report, some things stood out: he stated I was 'reasonably cheerful' when with him. But I was depressed and intensely worried about my job. Prior to meeting with him, I had left a meeting with my union rep, crying. At the same time, my GP noted in my medical records: 'There has been no significant improvement.' I was still on anti-depressants, still seeing a counsellor. It was a strange definition of 'cheerful'. Oxlade also described me as 'self-reflective' and 'thoughtful', but a sensitive man with high standards – as if sensitivity to racism and homophobia spoke to unusually high standards, instead of a baseline for decency. He wrote: 'Management should be advised to be extremely careful.' He went on to add that they 'should also be careful to pursue the education and training around equality and diversity. Complaints about inappropriate management or offences should be taken seriously by senior managers.' Oxlade considered that being upset by people's words was 'inevitable' in large organisations like the Met. His report questioned whether I could 'lighten up' and 'make some effort' to be 'less sensitive'. He finished by saying I was a 'likeable' and 'intelligent' man.[36]

I emailed the deputy HR manager about my intention to challenge the assistant commissioner's decision on my pay. I asked HR for copies of the Force's grievance procedure[37] and the procedure for dealing with employees who were absent from work because of sickness.[38] I also asked for a copy of the criteria the police's doctors worked to in establishing fitness for duty. I was going to have to fight at every step, cover every corner.

Exhausted and ill, I reconsidered resigning with immediate effect, but didn't know where that would leave me, especially how it would affect the assistance with legal fees I received from the Police Federation – the union I had been paying into for some eight years. In any event, a colleague of Arpita's, the lawyer whom my partner had found online, strongly advised me against resigning until I had received advice from a lawyer. Resigning would significantly limit my options in challenging the police, I was told.

The Met were trying to silence my voice and close ranks around the problem of the discriminatory culture. I wasn't making myself heard, so I decided to raise the issues of discrimination and wrongdoing with those responsible for the service, externally. There were people who had a legal obligation to ensure that we had a Force fit for purpose, and that institutions like the police were carrying out their statutory duties. I was determined to ensure that none of these public bodies misunderstood the extent of racism in the police and its surrounding culture, which impacted the very communities they were sworn to protect.

In November 2009, I had sent an email to London's then mayor, Boris Johnson, informing him that I wanted to contribute to his inquiry into 'race and faith issues in the Met',[39] which had been announced the month I joined Scotland Yard, when Johnson was chair of the MPA. It was to examine the way in which these issues were managed in the police, whether all staff were confident in the process and felt that their opinions regarding equalities and diversity issues were valued. I was too late.[40] I also sent an email to Nick Hardwick, Chair of the IPCC.[41] The IPPC's response was: 'A serving police officer or a former police officer or police staff cannot make a complaint against another officer(s) in relation to an incident that happened during the time they worked for that force.'[42] Section 29 (4) of the Police Reform Act 2002 forbade police officers from challenging racism and homophobia externally. We had to go to professional standards, even though this just meant asking the dragons in the dragon's lair about the behaviour of other dragons. I sent an email to the Home Secretary, Alan Johnson, about the problems in the police, and copied in Keith Vaz, Chairman of the Home Affairs Committee.[43] In their reply to me, the Home Office said: 'The Independent Police Complaints Commission (IPCC) is the statutory guardian of the police complaints system. Any serving member of police staff or officer wishing to report any concerns of wrongdoing or malpractice within their workplace can do so by contacting the IPCC's Report Line.'[44] I was being told to make contact with the organisation that had just stated I could not report discrimination or wrongdoing because I was a serving officer. A month had passed and I still hadn't received a response from the Equality and Human Rights Commission. I had sent a letter to its legal casework department at the end of October.[45] Although I was disappointed in the lack of response, I wasn't surprised. I was asking for support, advice and guidance from an equality organisation, whose own Chair, Trevor Phillips, had earlier in the year publicly claimed that there was no longer such a thing as institutional racism: 'Is the accusation still valid? I don't think so.'[46] In the Race and Faith Inquiry report that was published the same day as the anniversary of the 7 July bombings, Boris Johnson praised his inquiry chair, Cindy Butts (a member of the police authority) for doing the same: 'I welcome Cindy Butts's finding that the Met is not institutionally racist.'[47]

With the new year upon me, I was mindful not to send Arpita information about the police by email or post until I had met with her and established that I could trust her to find the best resolution to the situation. I also wanted to ensure that I remained within the law with what I told her. The last thing I needed was to breach the Official Secrets Act. I sent her several documents, including a copy of the diary of my contact with the Force – all those overwhelming phone calls, texts, emails and letters. I also sent her a copy of my health diary and my 'thoughts and feelings' diary that my partner had advised me to keep.

All my emails to the Force about my case had to go to the detective chief superintendent. I requested a copy of everything the Metropolitan Police Service currently held on me or referred to me in.[48] By law, I was entitled to this information, and I was asking for it under the Data Protection Act, which gave them forty days to comply. The Act specifically placed an obligation on the police, when holding personal information about any person, to provide a copy of that information (unless an exemption applied) to the individual concerned. In response to my email, the chief stated that all requests for information had to go through the directorate of legal services (the police's internal law firm), to which she had now referred my dispute about discrimination.[49]

My union rep sent an email to me about this, in which he failed to mention that he was at the recent two gold groups (and that a third one was scheduled). He was keen to tell me about the chief superintendent: 'Sadly matters have now been taken out of her hands, as a result of the recent MPS medical disclosure [Dr Oxlade's report], which have now placed us in the current arena.'[50] Although I knew the Police Federation was working with the Force, I still appreciated the time and support of my new rep. I knew that having to work with me placed him in an awkward position as an officer and member of counter terrorism.

I was at home when I received a bundle of documents (personal file, HR record and sickness file) from the Met in response to my request for information under the Data Protection Act. I wasn't surprised to notice that many were incomplete or withheld, including an incomplete copy of the file that reviewed the decision to reduce my pay. I asked to see the complete information and was told it could only be disclosed after harm-testing.[51] A public authority like the police can withhold the disclosure of documents by stating that this would threaten to cause harm to them. The police were going to give me nothing that would support my case, because it could harm them and their reputation.

An email from the inspector, Nathan Crinyion, who had been given responsibility for handling the disclosure to the police lawyers, revealed why: some of the documents 'would imply to some readers a tacit acceptance by the MPS of their guilt'.[52]

Amongst the documents provided, I saw that Dee Caryl from the Met's diversity directorate had written to Quantrell to say that the Force could receive confidential updates from the occupational health counsellor they had appointed for me – a disturbing fact, which explained why my GP had wanted me to see an external counsellor (i.e. not a police counsellor).[53] Even more alarming were the incomplete minutes from the gold meetings held to determine what to do about this threat to the very fabric of policing, Kevin Maxwell. At the first gold group, with the 'strategic overarching' intention of 'safeguarding the current and future interests of the MPS', the detective chief superintendent had discussed how the Met could defend itself at an employment tribunal. She informed the group that I had told her in confidence I was being 'bullied by his line manager' (my Terminal 3 sergeant).[54] Caryl told the group that homophobic behaviour was more difficult to address. She pointed out that I could raise it with the press and, in particular, the 'pink media'. She finished by saying that the police needed to prepare lines for the directorate of public affairs (the Met's media machine), i.e. to refute anything I said about discrimination against homosexuals in the Force. Chief inspector D'Orsi said that the Met needed to close my allegations once and for all.

My police union rep told the meeting: 'If Kevin wants to make allegations, then so be it. He needs to be clear as to what his intentions are. It may well be that the Police Service is not for him any more. There is a lot of emphasis here on doing everything right. Sometimes we should accept we can only do so much.' My Fed rep went on to state that after my meeting with him (the next day) the MPS would be 'better sighted' and that they had done as much as they could.

My rep's comments disturbed me the most. The union was the body that was supposed to represent my best interests and work towards an equal workplace for all its members. To see them suggest that my problem was best dealt with by removing me was a terrible blow. I was wounded by the knowledge that he had been reporting our conversations back to the gold groups.

At the second gold meeting, two weeks later, Dr Palmer told the group about the issues I had raised with her (my consultation with her was meant to be confidential and I did not give my consent for my medical details to be disclosed).[55] She said that Dr Oxlade had confirmed my GP's diagnosis of depression, but she had deemed me 'fit for duty' according to the Force's criteria. Dr Palmer said that, in addition to the medical issues, they should take account of my 'personality', which she said was 'sensitive, reflective, thoughtful and perhaps more vulnerable to off-the-cuff remarks'. She brought up a 'lack of resilience' on my part, and the 'organisational culture'. She did, however, note I had 'no physical or psychological problems in relation to policing'. Dr Palmer finished with: 'He must take responsibility for himself.' D'Orsi discussed my contact with the solicitor Arpita, so it seemed the senior management knew about my confidential meetings. He added: 'The Federation have also met with her.' The next gold meeting was scheduled for January.

I wrote to the commissioner's office to request a new welfare officer outside of counter terrorism, someone of colour, who therefore might be better able to empathise with my situation. Separate to the police union, a welfare officer is a line manager who keeps in regular contact with you whilst you are away from the workplace. For obvious reasons, my sergeant was not suitable, and Quantrell no longer made contact with me after letting me know he had seen the contents of the confidential sick pay letter I had sent to HR. I was given a new officer, an Asian detective inspector, based in the crime academy at Hendon. He was the same staff officer who had worked for the former commander Ali Dizaei prior to his suspension, whilst the Met were re-investigating him over a dispute outside an Iranian restaurant in West Kensington. Following his previous fallout with the police,

Dizaei was finally sentenced and imprisoned for misconduct in public office and perverting the course of justice. He was found guilty of trying to frame the web designer Waad al-Baghdadi; after helping Scotland Yard convict Dizaei, al-Baghdadi told the press: 'They used me. They held a gun against Ali Dizaei and I was the bullet.'[56] *The Guardian* stated that the new guilty verdict in relation to Dizaei would do little to quell suspicions amongst black and Asian officers that the former commander was not the subject of a witch-hunt.[57]

In January 2010, I met with Dr Eileen Cahill-Canning, the chief medical officer for the Metropolitan Police. She was Scotland Yard's top doctor and one of the four highest-paid civilian staff in the Force, paid more than the British prime minister.[58] We discussed Oxlade's conduct during the consultation and his subsequent report. Dr Cahill-Canning apologised for his behaviour in a letter: 'I am aware that this apology does not change the embarrassment and upset you experienced during your OH [occupational health] assessment, but I am hopeful that the learning points that emerge from this matter may go some way towards making life less difficult for individuals from minority groups in the future.'[59] This made her the first (and to this day the only) person to acknowledge any wrongdoing at the Met. On two occasions, Oxlade was to be sent on diversity training, despite having initially refused to accept that he had done any wrong. Dr Cahill-Canning wrote to the police's lawyers: 'Dr Oxlade has since received training in diversity on two separate occasions.'[60]

After seeing Dr Cahill-Canning, I was sent next door to see her junior, Dr Palmer, despite my request for someone else, because she had declared me fit for work when I was unwell, and had made unauthorised disclosures about my health at the gold group. Completely reversing her previous decision, Palmer now determined that I was unfit for work. She did, however, tell me there were now only three options available: (1) the MPS could sack me; (2) I could resign; or (3) I could apply for ill-health retirement. It was a destabilising moment.

The reality that I could no longer be a police officer suddenly hit me.

I prepared to attend the February appeal hearing concerning the reduction in my pay, along with my Fed rep. Standing in the corridor outside the inner office, which was peopled with officers and administration staff and led to Yates's grand, boardroom-like office at the top of the Scotland Yard building, my nose began to bleed. I had never had a nosebleed before. I had recently been grinding my teeth at night, a problem which eventually resulted in my having to have surgery to remove one tooth, and procedures on others. My body and my career were both disintegrating.

Assistant Commissioner John Yates, who had taken charge of the decision from Rose Fitzpatrick, dismissed the appeal after five minutes. The decision to reduce my pay was sustained. My new welfare contact phoned me to tell me that an employment tribunal might throw out my discrimination claim, because I had not taken up the Met's offer of returning to work at any other job, in any other department. Their proposal would show the tribunal that they had made some effort to correct things, he explained.

At the third gold group,[61] the police leaders discussed whether the Met could overturn my GP's position as my primary doctor, and thus overturn the diagnosis that I was unwell (with depression). They were having trouble getting rid of me, because current employment law was meant to protect my rights: you cannot just fire your employees because they are sick. But now I didn't want to be there any more than they wanted me there. I began looking for an exit. I told D'Orsi and my seniors that, unless legally obliged, I wanted no more meetings, as they had become detrimental to my health and recovery.[62] Despite this, D'Orsi requested that I meet with him.

Arpita emailed me about the case. Her email read: 'I have not, in recent times, seen anything change by bringing race ET proceedings against the MPS. Recently the most high-profile race claims against the MPS have failed, yet I have no doubt that all the claimants brought those cases with equal conviction.'[63] Although Arpita said she was trying to be realistic, as opposed to dissuasive, I was deeply discouraged. No wonder so many officers with real grievances opted to settle out of court. Even lawyers were put off by the challenge of taking on the police. But I could not accept or believe that the Force or its leaders were beyond reproach. The more people told me to give up the fight, the more I became determined not to. I could not become just another statistic. Arpita reminded me that if I lost, my loss might come into the public domain, and the response wouldn't necessarily be sympathetic. I might, in fact, be in for a kicking. She wrote, 'You will have to live with adverse findings against you. Bear in mind that you are presently untainted in your career.' Like officers who had brought racism claims to employment tribunals before me, I might be countered with excoriating interpretations of my behaviour – regardless of my spotless record until now.

I mulled it over, steeled myself and replied that I understood her concerns, but that people like me bringing these matters to the courts – which were meant to adjudicate on behalf of a democratic society – was the best path towards progress, and for the Metropolitan Police Service and GMP to be held accountable in some way. I knew the tribunal would be hostile. I knew the magistrates and judges worked closely with the police. Freemasonry was as prolific in the judiciary as it was in the police. But I didn't think I would gain anything if I backed down now.[64]

I had to choose fight over flight. My conscience demanded it.

Arpita said she would send her advice to the Police Federation, about the merits of my case against the police. As Russell Jones &

Walker's 'funding' client, her first loyalty was to the English and Welsh police union. The Federation sent me her advice.[65] She said it would be difficult to fight the GMP under equality law, given the passage of time. It would also, in her opinion, be too difficult to fight the Met, given the passage of time. However, there was the possibility of action under the Protection from Harassment Act 1997. I wanted to fight the police under equality law, even if that meant that I could only fight the Met. We had to at least try.

Arpita went on leave and Chris Haan, another lawyer assisting her, took over. Simon Cuthbert, another lawyer, was to oversee the case.

In May, I read about the senior black officer in the Met who was suing the Force over claims that other seniors covered up a damaging report into racism in the ranks.[66] Superintendent Paul Wilson alleged race discrimination, and was sidelined from further promotion. I knew if black and Asian officers, including those who were senior like Wilson, kept their mouths shut, they could get promoted for not rocking the boat. For 'lightening up', as Oxlade would have it. What senior black police officer wanted to speak out about racism within the police, if this carried the very real risk of losing his or her career and livelihood? Wilson said of his case, 'It is a sad indictment of how the organisation has consistently failed to embrace the learning process in the 10 years since the Stephen Lawrence case inquiry.'

Wilson, like so many before him, had settled with the police without going to court. The police gave out its usual statement about resolving its dispute with Wilson, without 'any admission of liability whatsoever', following the withdrawal of his claim. It was a line familiar from the many previous settlements. I didn't want to be another one of those officers, settling out of court. I wasn't sure how I could escape being crushed by the wheels of so-called justice, but surely I had to try?

To start my fight, I commenced proceedings against the

Metropolitan Police commissioner, Britain's most senior police officer, for direct racial discrimination, direct sexual orientation discrimination, racial harassment, sexual orientation harassment, racial victimisation and sexual orientation victimisation.[67] The police wasn't my employer, but the commissioner himself was, as its chief officer.[68] I was the claimant and the commissioner was the respondent.[69] I had to register my claim with the employment tribunal at Reading in Berkshire, because of where my workplace, Heathrow Airport, was located.

My last days with the Force had begun.

10

Dirty Tricks Campaign

The employment tribunal wrote to inform me that it had accepted my claim,[1] and a copy of my claim was sent to the commissioner, giving him twenty-eight days to respond. I was sure that Scotland Yard would do everything in its power to stop me getting to tribunal and speaking out. I had been due to meet my welfare officer, but as soon as we had arranged a date, he cancelled.[2] However, D'Orsi did want to meet, again. I had just named him in my claim, and he was to be a potential witness at the tribunal.

I met D'Orsi at the Novotel London St Pancras for another welfare meeting and two days later received a letter: it was a notice from the commissioner that I was to go from half-pay to no pay.[3] My head swam. How I was going to afford rent for the new home I'd moved into with my partner, on Wilmington Square in Clerkenwell? How was I to pay for the part-time distance-learning writing course I'd recently been accepted onto? To rub salt into the wound, the letter acknowledged that my pay being stopped would 'cause [me] domestic and financial problems'.

The police commissioner appointed a solicitor, Jacqueline Morris, from his in-house law firm, under the leadership of the director of legal services, Edward Solomons. Morris was quick to defend the Force. First, she wrote to the tribunal to ask for a five-week extension before providing the commissioner's response to my claim.[4] My lawyers advised me not to challenge this. Morris then sought my authorisation for her to disclose my occupational health file,[5] the medical file they had illegally tried to obtain without my permission. There was no reason for me not to disclose it, as long as it was lawful, so I gave my consent, because I wanted to be transparent during this process.

Nathan Crinyion, the inspector appointed by the commissioner to handle the disclosure, wrote, 'Various documents have not been disclosed to you as I believe they [i.e. the communications between the police lawyers and police chiefs] may be subject to professional legal privilege.'[6] He later informed me that a fourth gold group had taken place, chaired by Commander Stephen Kavanagh.[7] This too was subject to legal privilege.[8] Kavanagh had now taken over counter terrorism and the leadership on my case from Commander Shaun Sawyer, who later became the chief constable of Devon and Cornwall Police.

In her briefing report she wrote about me for Kavanagh, the detective chief superintendent (the Met's head of counter terrorism intelligence) shared her concerns about the 'escalation towards ET' after Dr Oxlade's inappropriate and insensitive medical report, together with Assistant Commissioner John Yates's decision to continue to stop my pay. She wrote that this combination 'has had a devastating affect on Kevin's perception [of], confidence and trust [in] the MPS'.[9] This acknowledgement was all the more disturbing for the fact that the combination had been allowed to go ahead.

In the briefing, the detective chief was clear to the commander about the 'risks to the MPS' I posed:

1. Unless the officer can be facilitated back to work, the loss of an experienced detective, who has stated that his life-long ambition was to be a police officer
2. The potential impact on the recruitment of black and

minority officers/staff in the field of CT [counter
terrorism] work through the negative publicity
anticipated from an ET would be detrimental to the
SO15/MPS drive to increase minority representation in
this specialist area of work

3. The ET is likely to also raise allegations of homophobic
   behaviour by MPS officers, adversely impacting on
   recruitment within and into the service
4. Detriment to the reputation of the MPS as a fair and
   equitable employer, dedicated to developing a diverse
   workforce
5. An ET may expose sensitive CT area of business (ports)
   to MPA, media and public scrutiny
6. MPA concerned that the SO15/MPS has not embraced
   the learning from the Morris Enquiry [sic; i.e. the
   report by Sir Bill Morris about racism in the Met] and
   integrated it into their working practices
7. Timing of any tribunal hearing in the wake of other
   public cases likely to result in adverse publicity

I took a stroll into central London – as I did most nights because I
couldn't sleep – to help clear my head. I found these early-hours
walks therapeutic, and little else was comforting during these
times. As I was walking towards Oxford Street, quiet at this hour,
I spotted my previous boyfriend from Manchester.

'What are you doing in London?' I asked, surprised to see him.

'Stopping blacks,' he said drily, and laughed.

He had joined the Lancashire Constabulary, and had since
transferred from the north to the Met, like I had. He was on
plain-clothes duty from uniform policing in Camden. We were
civil with each other, and he gave me his new phone number,
jotting it down on the back of a Crimestoppers leaflet.

As I headed off, I recalled a comment I'd seen posted on the
Gay Police Association page on Facebook: 'Joining the Met from

Lancashire in November, glad to read the above comments about the Met NOT being homophobic, reassuring.'[10]

I realised that he had been the author of the comment. Despite there being prejudice against both sexual orientation and race, there was still a vast difference between a gay white man and a gay black man. As long as I had been on the gay scene, there had been anti-black sentiment in the LGBT community, masquerading as 'preference'. Gay dating profiles often read things like, 'No fats, no femmes, no blacks and no Asians.' It is not surprising that more than seven out of ten black men have experienced racism on the scene. In a survey for the gay health charity GMFA's magazine *FS*, 80% of black men said they had experienced racism in the gay community. One contributor commented that 'the only approach I've had at a gay bar was when I was asked if I supplied drugs.'[11]

There were hierarchies of tolerance in the police. Gay white men who toed the party line could do well, because they looked 'right'. People of colour, and women, struggled much more. In June 2010, a Met officer, Lara Goldie, hanged herself and left a four-page letter blaming homophobic bullies for her suicide. She wrote that staff at the Hendon training school treated her differently because she was a gay woman. Her body was found at her home in Hackney, East London. Her letter detailed problems in her personal life, but one paragraph singled out her colleagues for their mistreatment of her. Scotland Yard gave its official statement to *The Sun*, vehemently denying any homophobic behaviour towards Goldie. One officer even told the tabloid, 'Once the police had a reputation for being homophobic and racist. But we have moved on a lot since then ...The Met has been in the forefront of promoting equal opportunities and cracking down on prejudice . . . If anything, the main complaint we have these days is that we are too focused on minority rights.'[12]

At the same time as my dispute with Heathrow, armed officers at Gatwick airport – part of the Sussex Police force – were using their radios to point out and rate women by level of attractiveness. They also ran a forfeit system, where they had to buy each other doughnuts as a punishment for leaving their guns lying around. Constable Barbara Lynford, nicknamed 'Lipstick' and 'Whoopsy' by male colleagues, was the only woman on the Sussex Police firearms team, and brought a case to tribunal. She won, and was awarded damages after successfully claiming that she was forced out of her job because of sexual discrimination.[13] She described colleagues regularly making remarks about her breasts and covering the walls of their office with pictures of topless women. She said her colleagues routinely faked anti-terrorism patrol reports, which lined up with my own experiences at Heathrow. At Gatwick, officers watched porn, slept on duty and left their guns unattended.

Following a meeting with Arpita and Chris Hann, who had taken on the case whilst she was on leave, I wrote to Arpita, seeking their opinion on a few things.[14] My motivation in challenging the police had been about justice and equality, and I'd been ready for the fight, but the challenge looked insurmountable and I knew it was impacting my relationship with my partner, whom I'd recently married. It was meant to be a new start for me. I was also starting to feel shaken and sad about the fact that I couldn't have justice *and* a marriage, and was wondering if I should choose the latter.

I asked them whether I should continue with my challenge. Arpita responded: 'I find employment tribunal claims unsatisfactory as vehicles for change for many reasons and so it is important to understand the limitations of the system. History tells us that there is quite a price to pay for freedom. Freedom has never been free.'[15] Having digested her response, I decided to call it a day, thanking her.[16] She was another ethnic minority, and a woman; she knew how challenging it could be to succeed in a system stacked against her.

I no longer had a salary, and I couldn't live on fresh air. Like so many before me, I had to give up fighting for my job. I typed up my resignation and prepared to hand it over at my next welfare meeting.

In July, D'Orsi wrote to me again.[17] I felt that this level of contact was excessive and harassing, like that from Quantrell before him. I wrote back, saying that I met with him in May, and that my sickness reporting obligations were restricted to my welfare officer (the Asian inspector), who was meant to be my sole point of contact. I told D'Orsi that 'I find these requests for meetings intimidating, not knowing what they are for.'[18]

I called my welfare officer to seek his advice about D'Orsi, telling him I was fed up. He advised me to meet with the detective chief inspector to see what he had to say now, since the most recent gold group chaired by Commander Kavanagh.

D'Orsi emailed me again the same day,[19] saying this email's purpose was to remove any feeling of intimidation. He then sent me *another* email with an attached letter that set out all the things the Force had tried to do for me.[20] I suspected that this had been written for the tribunal. My suspicion was confirmed when, through disclosure, I later discovered an email from Superintendent Terry O'Connor to D'Orsi: 'The Cmdr has now suggested that tied into the letter / contact with Kevin we should set out all the opportunities we have offered to date against a timeline.'[21] This followed a meeting between the terrorism commander, chief superintendent, Jacqueline Morris, someone called Esme (who I later found out was Esme Crowther, head of the Met's employment tribunal unit), and Martin Tiplady, the Force's director of HR, 'to discuss the claim and the MPS response'. The woman whose name was highlighted by D'Orsi and Quantrell when I met them at the Place Hotel in Manchester, Chief Inspector Melanie Bailey, was copied into this email about the meeting.[22]

D'Orsi finished his letter by saying: 'In respect of your recent emails suggesting [my welfare officer] be the sole person to contact you, I would like to stress, as I have in our meetings, it is my responsibility as your SMT [senior management team] line manager to maintain clarity as to your welfare . . . and I will not abrogate this responsibility.'

Exhausted, I replied: 'I know that I am getting better, but when I receive contact from the MPS[,] in particular having to respond to your letter today, it makes me go further into depression, whilst I am fighting to get myself out of it.'[23]

On 24 July, a bright, sunny day, preoccupied with negative thoughts and wanting to work on my relationship with my husband, I went for a walk with him in Regent's Park to relax. As we were walking along, I glanced at my phone and saw notifications of a voicemail and an email from my welfare officer.[24] The *Sun* newspaper was running a story about me. My welfare officer had forwarded me an email from D'Orsi from the day before, letting him know that he might 'wish to' inform me of the leak.[25]

Further down the email chain, below D'Orsi's, was an email sent to D'Orsi by the Met's press officer, Alex Fedorcio: 'I attach the media support letter, which is offered to officers and staff who may be the subject of adverse media attention.'[26] They had sat on the story until the weekend. Deeply upset with the breach of my data, I called D'Orsi from the park to share my anger with him. I then contacted the Met's press bureau. I was dismayed to learn that the bureau had confirmed my details to the *Sun*. The press officer told me the reporter's name, which was Anthony France. When I googled him, I discovered that, ironically, France is black. Following my call to the bureau, the officer detailed our conversation in an email to D'Orsi.[27]

The *Sun* planned to out my mental health status and sexual orientation, and falsely report that I had a history of submitting unsuccessful claims to tribunals against the police throughout Britain. Prior to this (one) claim against London's commissioner, I had never made a claim or set foot inside a tribunal. In an email to Martin Tiplady and many others, Fedorcio wrote that the reporter for *The Sun* had 'very detailed information about the claim, and it appears he has spoken to colleagues of Maxwell'. The reporter was focusing on what was described as 'dodgy' proposed evidence of racism.[28]

I rushed home with my partner, shaken, trying to work out what we could do to stop any article from being published in Britain's biggest daily newspaper. I wasn't worried about the lies that were going to be told about claims and employment tribunals, as I had expected nothing less. But the idea that my depression and sexual orientation would become public knowledge in such a large-scale and sensationalist way made me feel utterly violated. We spent the weekend in despair, fearful for our safety, unsure if my counter terrorism status and our address would be published.

Counter terrorism officers never identified themselves by name, to ensure their safety. During a stop and search, the police must provide certain information, including their name and the station they work at, unless the search is being carried out under the terrorism law, or if giving his or her name may place the officer in danger. In these cases, they give an identification number. As a matter of course, counter terror officers always give warrant numbers. My airport ID had no name. But *The Sun* had been given all of my personal details.

As the leak was a gross invasion of my privacy, I contacted Scott Langham at the Press Complaints Commission (PCC).[29] Ironically, that same day *The Sun* published an article criticising those who had leaked information that put British soldiers at risk in the Afghan war.

I wrote to D'Orsi, copying in the commissioner and other seniors: 'My safety and identification as a current counter terrorism officer has been put at risk and my forthcoming employment tribunal claim has been prejudiced.'[30] I tore up my resignation letter. I wasn't going to let them get away with this breach by giving them the excuse that I was no longer with counter terrorism. I knew this meant that it was the beginning of the end for my marriage, but I couldn't back down now. My Fed rep wrote to me to assure me he hadn't been the leak: 'You will be away [sic] that Ian Blair, Andy Hayman, Ali Dizaei and Tarique Ghaffur all alleged that someone within the MPS was engaged in a dirty tricks campaign by leaking stuff to the media at a time they all had cases running.'[31]

The PCC passed a brief statement from me on to the *Sun*'s editor, Dominic Mohan, to try and halt the story.[32] Because it was a weekend, I wrote it on my own, without being able to consult my legal team. The leak had been timed impeccably. Whilst I understood the right of the free press in the UK, the ramifications of placing my security role in the public domain with an as yet unlisted tribunal case were a serious threat to my life. Still, *The Sun* continued to push forward with the story, and made contact with Arpita.[33]

The unknown persons within the MPS (because *The Sun* never reveals its sources) had fed the newspaper limited information about the claim, before the commissioner's tribunal response was filed. Amongst the allegations listed was that a colleague refused to eat food because he said the staff at the mosque would have spat in it; the reporter, Anthony France, told my lawyer that the officer who had refused to eat the curry did so because he was on a low cholesterol diet due to illness. How curious that France knew such private details about my colleague's health, and about the commissioner's defence! But the fact that France specifically knew to call Arpita was something that could only have resulted from him seeing the initial tribunal claim form, where her name and number were listed under my legal representation. Indeed, in an undisclosed email to D'Orsi, the acting superintendent of Special Branch said it was 'likely that [France] has seen detail of the claim'.[34] That weekend, I understood that the Force would do everything in its power to harm me and my reputation.

My mood deteriorated rapidly. I was tearful and any confidence I had built up was gone. My anti–depressant dose was increased to the highest daily amount allowed.

The leak's ramifications not only put my life in danger, but also my husband's. Furious, he sent the commissioner an email and copied in the relevant police authorities. Martin Tiplady (who held a rank equivalent to assistant commissioner) said that they would launch an investigation. A detective inspector, Mike Sunman from professional standards, was to carry it out. Tiplady said that he had spoken with the *Sun*'s journalist, Anthony France, whom he knew, and reassured us that 'he will not now be running the story'.[35] In an internal email, Tiplady wrote: 'I have known France previously and found him to be helpful.'[36] How did the police leadership have so much influence over Britain's biggest tabloid?

On 27 July, Sunman took my partner's statement at Islington police station under the supervision of a detective chief inspector, Chris Le Pere. During the interview, Le Pere told my partner that the Met sometimes release details of counter terrorism officers to the press, which was preposterous. He told my partner that he had also spoken with France, having dealt with him 'many times' as they had a 'relatively frank relationship'.[37] I had no reason to believe Le Pere was responsible for the leak.

Not taking the police at its word, my legal team's defamation department sent a letter to Dominic Mohan, objecting to the publication of the article.[38] When there was no response, my lawyers sent a second letter to Mohan.[39] For days, the editor and his top team didn't know whether to publish or not, but after much editorial wrangling, the tabloid didn't publish the article about my claim, even though France had drafted it. But the leak had still happened, and I lived in fear that it would somehow be made public.

To reclaim my narrative, I created a blog called Max News: View From the Bottom. I wanted to establish who I was and share the whole truth about myself with the world, in case a tabloid ever tried to present a distorted version of me. The Force, of course, was furious, but it gave me some stability of mind to know I had a medium through which I could speak.

After I started the blog, D'Orsi sent me a letter about the police's Unsatisfactory Police Performance and Attendance procedure (UPP/A).[40] In the police, if someone was off work for a long time, usually because of sickness, the Force could initiate the UPP/A procedure and issue an Improvement Notice, setting out conditions that have to be complied with. This includes setting a date by which the person in question would need to return to work. At Stage One, you are given a written warning to return to work. Stage Two is the final written warning, if you haven't complied. Stage Three is the dismissal meeting. There are twenty-five cases of UPP/A procedures nationally each year. In my case performance wasn't an issue, but my absence through sickness was. Even if someone is very unwell, 'It is expected that the specified period for improvement would not normally exceed 3 months.' I had three months to rid myself of severe reactive depression, or else.[41]

My Fed rep waded in and wrote to D'Orsi:

> Kevin has not been asked to see any medical practitioners from the MPS since that appointment eight months ago. Given that medical advice from both the MPS and his own GP has stated that Kevin is unfit to return to work, I would ask that you seek assistance from OH [occupational health] before undertaking such a course of action.[42]

The commissioner finally sent his 'Grounds of Resistance' to my first claim.[43] He stated that he had not treated me differently because of my race and/or sexuality. He did not acknowledge any mistreatment towards me, or apologise. He denied everything. He would be fighting the claim. The tribunal listed my claim for a case management discussion,[44] to ascertain what matters should be considered going forward.

My partner then received a letter from Inspector Sunman about the leak investigation. Sunman said an investigation would be disproportionate and that the Force had no case to answer.[45] My partner got another letter from the IPCC[46] stating that the Met was correct and his appeal would not be upheld. The Force was closing in fast.

In September 2010, another gold group was held with eleven of my seniors at Scotland Yard, to discuss what to do about my illness. It was agreed that 'the situation will need to be brought to a conclusion – this cannot go on indefinitely'. Dee Caryl of the diversity directorate said that 'stress levels could leave him open to more erratic behaviour. Do we have the appropriate press lines?'[47] The next gold group was scheduled for November.

Despite my illness and my union rep's concerns about my not having seen a police doctor for some eight months, D'Orsi pushed ahead with dismissing me for unsatisfactory attendance.[48] He said I had to return to work immediately, invoking Stage One of the UPP/A. He held a meeting with me in Room 1502 at Scotland Yard.[49]

At the same time, I began further proceedings against the commissioner in the Reading employment tribunal.[50] This was my second claim, and it focused on the leak of my personal data to the tabloid newspaper. The claim was accepted. As with claim one, I was permitted to send a questionnaire to the commissioner.[51] I asked the police chief if he agreed that I'd been subject to victimisation, and if so, if he accepted the unlawfulness of such discrimination in relation to *The Sun*. Again, he was allowed eight weeks to respond. He replied seven months later, denying any victimisation.[52]

The leak, and the fact that *The Sun* wouldn't confirm to my lawyers that it would not publish a sensational story about me, drove me once again to take control of my own narrative. I was ready to 'out' myself as a gay man with depression. This took place in *Outnorthwest*, the magazine of the UK-wide LGF, based in Manchester. I used to take the student police officers to the LGF for their community engagement input when I was a tutor constable. In the 100th issue of the magazine, I featured on its front cover above the banner 'Being LGB (Liverpudlian, Gay and Black)'. Leaving out specific police information so as not to jeopardise the tribunal case, I shared my thoughts on issues that were important to me, especially on bullying and blackmail. Bullying left many isolated, having feelings of self-loathing, and depressed. I described battling the black dog of depression whilst fighting for my rights: 'There comes a point in your life when you have to stand up and be counted...Bullies only bully if you let them.'[53]

Sixteen months after I was first diagnosed with depression, the commissioner finally wrote to my GP requesting further information about my condition. Given the seriousness of my illness and the gravity of my experiences, I was now under the care of one of the practice partners at my GP's office. In his letter to Dr Palmer, my GP wrote that I had been registered with the surgery for just under six years and that he held all of my medical records since birth in Liverpool. He stated: 'Prior to Kevin registering with this medical practice, he had no known long-term health conditions and no past history of psychiatric or psychological problems.' He mentioned that I had been treated for acid reflux in the past and that I had once seen a cardiologist for the chest pains I had whilst in the Manchester tutor unit. He also reported the experiences that I had recounted to him.[54]

With my pay stopped entirely, I was sent to a Jobcentre Plus medical assessment by the Department for Work and Pensions (DWP), to see if I could claim a weekly state benefit through the contributions I had made since starting work at sixteen. It was embarrassing, but I had bills to pay. My partner sat alongside me as the Atos Healthcare (as it was known then) doctor, Paul Obiamiwe, assessed me at the Marylebone medical examination centre. Dr Obiamiwe saw me for all of twenty-three minutes before declaring that my depression was a 'moderate disability and not severe'. My partner of several years was also my legal spouse, but the doctor refused to acknowledge him as my partner, preferring to call him my 'friend' in person, and throughout his subsequent report.[55]

I sent a letter to my MP, Emily Thornberry, sharing my concerns about Dr Obiamiwe and his conclusion.[56] She wrote to the DWP, asking for an explanation, and invited me to meet in person at St Luke's Community Centre. Emily was different to many of the other establishment figures I had dealt with – I was struck by her warmth and empathy. She was a rare kindred spirit with a genuine commitment to equality and I liked her a lot.

Emily received a letter about the DWP assessment, which upheld my complaint. The DWP ruled that 'Mr Maxwell's medical assessment was flawed' and that Dr Obiamiwe's medical report was 'not medically reasonable or appropriately justified'.[57] Though this was a dark time in my life, I was pleased to see that there were people in positions of power who had equality and fair dealing at the heart of their work. There could, I hoped, still be a way forward.

After this, an appointment was made by my lawyers for me to go and see a consultant psychiatrist who I believed would be impartial and not be linked to the police force. In cases of psychiatric injury both parties are allowed to put forward a medical report as to what might have caused the depression; however, we hadn't even had a liability hearing for the two claims to see if there had been discrimination under the law in the first place. I met Dr Charles Hindler at Guy's Hospital on 12 November 2010, and spent an hour with him at the Munro Centre. I spent much of the hour crying, as I relayed my life experience as a gay black man. Before we began, I asked

Hindler whether he had worked for the police. I knew that, if he said yes, I would have walked out of that consultation; but his response satisfied me that he had not, and I stayed. I had seen so many different doctors by now (GPs, as well as police and DWP doctors) that I no longer expected anything good or bad from them. But I made a couple of fatal mistakes. Firstly, I criticised Dr Oxlade, a fellow psychiatrist (Hindler did not mention in the consultation that he knew Oxlade, though I brought him up); secondly, I said that I felt 'persecuted' by the police. This was a trigger word. Black people often use it to describe their experiences with white authority figures; white authority figures understand it to be paranoia, a persecution *complex* rather than true persecution, and will summarily dismiss such claims.

A few weeks passed before I received an email from Chris, the lawyer, who warned me that I would be very upset by Hindler's attached report.[58] I opened the report. Struggling to catch my breath, I began to cry. Hindler made Oxlade look like a saint. Worse still, Hindler had provided, along with the report, a copy of his curriculum vitae, which included the line: 'Dr Hindler was also employed by the Metropolitan Police Service for 2½ years to undertake Occupational Health Psychiatry until December 2006.'[59] He'd definitely worked for the police – and at the same time as Oxlade. Oxlade joined the occupational health unit in 2004, two years before Hindler left.

In the report, Hindler said my experiences were 'inferential' rather than direct. He criticised me for bringing the claim against the Met and for the grievance about GMP. He wrote about the 'general police officer attitudes towards gays and black people', saying: 'They appear to be accepted as benign or innocuous by police officers generally, i.e. an accepted part of "police culture or banter".' He said he concurred with Dr Oxlade's comment that I was likely to 'encounter people saying things which would upset [me] in large organisations such as the MPS'. Hindler claimed it was only my 'view' and 'assumption' that the police had leaked my details to *The Sun*, and that 'This matter could be viewed as part of Mr Maxwell's belief that others are intent on harming or exploiting him.' He went on: 'Taking an overview of the memos from the doctors in the MPS occupational health department, it appears that Mr Maxwell's complaints were heard and recommendations for change and adjustments to his workplace suggested to best manage the complaints.' Hindler concluded his report by saying that it was his opinion, taking into account the statement by the police commissioner disputing my depression, that I was *not* depressed. Even Oxlade had acknowledged this medical fact, for which I was receiving medication and treatment.

Hindler's professional opinion was that I considered myself to be depressed and was therefore paranoid about discrimination and wrongdoing. He claimed that my mum's death from cancer had brought on my paranoia, and ultimately concluded that I had a personality disorder.

I was badly shaken by the report. I emailed my counsellor about Hindler, expressing my horror and dismay at the discovery that he had worked for the police, and then took myself to the mental health centre at St Charles Hospital[60] and asked to see another psychiatrist. I was seen at about 5 a.m. A mental health nurse was also there. I told this third psychiatrist – an Asian doctor – about my experiences with Hindler and Oxlade, about how desperately I wanted someone to understand me. He told me to take no notice of them and that the best thing to do would be to figure out why they had said what they had. The NHS was rife with racism, he said, having experienced it himself. He had no time for those who said racism was just in the minds of black and brown people. After nearly two hours with him, my spirits had lifted somewhat. It was cathartic just to be heard and acknowledged. These oases of solidarity are what keep other black and brown people going. When we really listen to one another, we take the first steps towards empathising with and protecting one another.

I went online to research Hindler. The Priory Group website read: '[Hindler] has worked in the occupational health department of a large organisation [i.e. the police] for 2½ years', without mentioning which organisation. On the BMI Healthcare website, Hindler listed the places he had worked but excluded the Metropolitan Police. On LinkedIn, Hindler listed all the places he had worked, going back some eighteen years to 1992, with no mention of the police. The fact remains omitted from his online profiles.[61] For the first time, fury drove out my overwhelming despair. A fire had been lit somewhere within me. As I was not in direct contact with Hindler – the report had come through my lawyers – I sent my lawyers a forceful email, expressing my anger that no one had disclosed to me that Hindler had worked for the police; I pointed out the relevant part of the CV, and added, 'So, you sent me to see a psychiatrist who was employed by the Metropolitan Police Service not so long ago and no doubt still has contacts there, to get a psychiatric report on me. How is he independent?'[62] My relationship with the lawyers was never the same afterwards. After I wrote to them, I never heard from Hindler again. I don't know if he was ever informed of the shocking distress he had caused me with his report, or my anger that he had not disclosed his links to the police.

Later, I wrote to the General Medical Council (GMC) to share my concerns about Hindler. Though I felt that Hindler had caused me harm, the GMC disagreed. It stated: 'As psychiatry is not an exact science, opinions and diagnoses would rely on the doctor's perception of the patient's mental state.' It added there was no 'evidence' that he intended to be 'harmful' to me. Responding to the fact that Hindler had not disclosed that he had worked for the police, they said: 'In relation to declaring possible conflicts of interest our medical advice is that it is not the responsibility of the doctors to declare this at the time of appointments.'[63]

My next obligation was to attend the tribunal's case management discussion on 17 December 2010. It was my first time seeing the police's barrister, Philip Mead, and solicitor Jacqueline Morris. Mead took his seat in one of the two chairs facing the judge on the left-hand side of the room. My appointed counsel, Mo Sethi of Devereux Chambers, and I did the same on the right-hand side of the room. I was sitting in the claimant's chair, gazing at the respondent's chair opposite me. It was occupied by a black woman. Jacqueline Morris, a black solicitor, was to fight me over racism in the police. Anthony France was a black journalist about to out me. Out of all the internal lawyers, the commissioner had chosen a black woman as his representative to fight a black man. It was a smart and bold move.

Mead, speaking on behalf of the commissioner, stood up and told the tribunal that I needed to decide if I was black or mixed-race, as if being mixed-race might have meant that racism didn't count. Did they insist on calling Barack Obama the first mixed-race president of the US, or was he black? I had been racialised as black, though I was mixed-race.

The judge ruled that we were to go straight to a full six-week hearing in the next year. The tribunal order that followed confirmed the application by the commissioner to strike out my two claims (the discrimination and leak) 'as having no reasonable prospect of success'.[64]

With my claims now going to public hearing, Scotland Yard issued a statement which D'Orsi sent to my welfare officer, who sent it on to me: 'IF ASKED: Can confirm the MPS has received two employment tribunal claims (now consolidated) from DC Kevin Maxwell alleging harassment, victimisation and discrimination on grounds of race and sexual orientation. Not Prepared To Discuss Further.'[65]

11

War of Attrition

My intention had been to go on the record about my experiences, to say to others: you are not alone. However, my lawyers were still keen for me to mediate and settle with the commissioner without going to tribunal – take whatever money might be offered and run. The police had destroyed everything I valued and I struggled with the idea of quietly settling, but even my legal team didn't think pursuing justice in the courts was a good idea. After thinking about it for a long time, and through gritted teeth, I told Arpita that we should try and mediate/resolve this within the next two months, so that everybody could move on.

The tribunal wrote to both parties about resolving the dispute through judicial mediation,[1] which a senior judge would chair. The commissioner declined.[2]

D'Orsi was still pursuing my dismissal on behalf of the commissioner[3] before the employment tribunal started. My Fed rep wrote to him:

> *Kevin, as you have alluded to, is currently certified sick by his General Practitioner. In addition to this Kevin has also been seen by the Metropolitan Police Service chief medical officer, who has also concluded that Kevin is medically unfit to return to work. Kevin cannot return to work whilst certified sick.*

Any instruction to do so is both unlawful and in contravention of health and safety legislation. To imply that the illness is not related to the absence is factually incorrect and insensitive.[4]

He concluded: 'If the same amount of effort that is being used against Kevin [wa]s used in trying to engage in meaningful dialogue to resolve these matters, then those affected would be able to get on with their lives.'

I had not always found the Police Federation especially supportive, but I was impressed by the bite in this message.

The Police Federation were so concerned about the way the leadership was going after me that they considered taking action against the Force under the Public Interest Disclosure Act 1998. The Act was designed to give people greater protection whilst challenging an organisation as powerful as Scotland Yard. Nevertheless, the intensity of the campaign against me was exhausting. Rallied against me were some of the most senior officers in the Force, coordinating their attacks from those high-level gold groups. Further disclosure demonstrated that the chiefs strategically planned numerous ways to dismiss me before the hearing. They had documented how I spoke to them in emails, on the phone and in person at meetings, to see if I could be dismissed because of my tone – professional standards concluded that 'He has not yet breached the Codes of Discipline.' They also created a file on me, protected from disclosure, called the 'Maxwell Journal'. I had also been placed on the Met criminal intelligence database (Crimint) under the number TLRT00126498, for cycling on a pavement whilst crossing a junction in Islington on the way to counselling.[5] I wondered how many white middle-class London cyclists featured on this 'criminal' list for doing the same. I just wanted acknowledgement of wrongdoing, yet they were going after me as though I had the codes to a nuclear device.

I attended Scotland Yard with my rep, for D'Orsi to formally begin dismissal proceedings under 'attendance management'. My rep reminded him about the 'appropriateness of using UPP/A' and that 'credence [needed] to be given to the uniqueness of [my] situation'. He also told D'Orsi that if he continued with the UPP/A against me, the Police Federation would progress to taking action under the Public Interest Disclosure Act. D'Orsi responded, copying the Federation rep: 'Having considered the above . . . I have adjourned my decision on the appropriateness or not of the Stage One in these circumstances until I have been able to take stock and seek the relevant advice and clarification.'[6]

As I was mounting my claim, *The Guardian* reported that Asian people were '42 times more likely to be held under terror law' than white people.[7] People from ethnic minorities were more likely to be stopped under Schedule 7 of the Terrorism Act, the one my colleagues and I mainly used. This schedule allowed the stopping and searching of the innocent, and granted them fewer rights than suspected criminals. There was no need for reasonable suspicion that they were involved in any terrorism. Those stopped had no right to maintain their silence, as a failure to answer questions could lead to being charged with an offence. Questioning would begin without a lawyer present, and those interviewed had to pay for one themselves if they wanted legal representation.

The claims the paper made matched my own experiences. It said the figures had led to accusations that police had resorted to 'ethnic profiling', a claim which the Force denied in its grounds of resistance to my claim. They denied everything, including the 'buffering' I said I was involved in – officers pretending to stop white people just to get to people of colour.

One of those stopped under Schedule 7, Asif Ahmed, described what had happened to him after landing at Edinburgh airport: 'He was separated from his wife and taken to a room and told he must answer questions about his beliefs and faith. Then, incredibly, he was asked if he would spy on his community. "They asked if

I would like to work with Special Branch, to keep an eye on the Muslim community in Edinburgh. They asked me three times. They said do it covertly,"' he said.

Asif Ahmed was only one of 85,000 people that year who went, in the eyes of the police, 'from model citizen to terror suspect',[8] and after London was attacked by actual terrorists Ahmed worked for the city's mayor to improve relations between Muslims and the rest of the population. Ahmed told journalists that when he asked my colleagues why he had been stopped, one officer replied, 'No reason, it is just a random stop.' Not surprisingly, Ahmed also noted that he was one of only two people on his flight who appeared to be Muslim.

I came across an op-ed in *The Guardian* from October 2008, by my local councillor Claudia Webbe. In it, Claudia said it was 'business as usual for police racists' after the notable lack of progress since the Lawrence inquiry. She asked her readers who would really want 'to join an organisation with racist tendencies and policies and repressive practices limiting progress and ambition? ... Black police staff, both officers and personnel, describe to me a police service that is designed to break you physically, mentally and spiritually.'[9] These words – coming as they did from a chair of a major police operation – resonated with me. I was not alone in seeing what I was seeing. I was not paranoid.

The BBC *Panorama* documentary 'The Secret Policeman Returns' had been aired a few days before Webbe's op-ed, five years after the original. It confirmed my experiences.[10] Reporter Mark Daly found 'a bleak story of officers and staff who feel sidelined and victimised' and heard 'disturbing allegations that police officers who speak out over race feel victimised by their own forces'. In surveying BPA members, the *Panorama* programme found that 72% had experienced racism at work, 60% felt their career had been hindered by their ethnicity, and 61% said things had stayed the same or got worse.

★

June began with the Met finally beginning dismissal proceedings to oust me for unsatisfactory attendance. My brother wrote to me, saying, 'Better to fight on your feet rather than your knees – don't let them stop you getting natural justice.' This was a boost I had so desperately needed. My Police Federation representative sent me an email about the dismissal proceedings that were now in full force against me: 'I appreciate that all of this is having a serious detrimental effect on your focus and well-being and as you may recall I said to you at the outset that the MPS would engage in a war of attrition against you, to wear you down.'[11] It wasn't good news, but I appreciated that someone else could see what was happening to me.

My appeal against stage one UPP/A was held at Scotland Yard in July. I sat in front of Superintendent Terry O'Connor (head of Special Branch in charge of ports) and a white woman I'd never seen before. The woman scribbled a note and passed it to O'Connor, evidently wanting to communicate secretly. The meeting was adjourned. 'I'll be back in five minutes,' O'Connor announced. When he returned, he said that he would be giving the room his decision about my appeal then and there: I was still to be dismissed for being unwell. O'Connor confirmed the failure of my appeal in a formal follow-up letter.[12] He felt that everything that had happened in the aftermath of my illness was 'reasonable'. In his minutes of the meeting, he included the name of the woman who had written that note to him: Lesleyanne Ellis.[13] I had seen her name amongst those present at one of the gold groups,[14] for which I received no minutes (just the agenda), and in emails and other correspondence concerning me.

O'Connor confirmed that she was part of counter terrorism's professional standards team. In the circumstances I could not help suspecting she was only at the meeting to see if the Force could successfully dismiss me.

★

After rejecting my appeal against Stage One, O'Connor heard Stage Two of the UPP/A process in September 2011 – my final written warning, because I had not returned to work because I was so unwell.[15] Ellis was present again, but was this time joined by Nigel Foster, advisor to the deputy police commissioner, Craig Mackey. The proceedings didn't go smoothly. I had to relive my experiences – again. The day-to-day misery of the process hit me all in one go. I got upset and was reduced to tears. I didn't have the strength to hold it together and asked to leave the room to use the bathroom. I stood in front of the mirror, crying, in my suit. I knew what was going to happen. The Force could not condone my absence from work. The discrimination I had suffered, and the fact that it had made me unwell enough to be signed off work by doctors outside and inside the police, was irrelevant.

I was repeatedly asked by O'Connor why I 'wouldn't' return to work. I explained I was unwell and all the doctors, including their own, said I shouldn't. They refused to listen to or understand my anguish. My Fed rep wrote to me following the meeting, about the fact that the Force was refusing to suspend the proceedings until after the employment tribunal, and that the UPP/A process was to continue. He said: 'You are free to appeal this decision, however I would urge caution',[16] because the next stage (third and final) would be heard by detective chief superintendent John Prunty. And he was no fan of mine.

Back in July 2011, *The Guardian* had run an exposé on the relationship between the police and the media.[17] Senior officers at the Met (the number one, two and three: Commissioner Ian Blair, Deputy Commissioner – later Commissioner – Paul Stephenson and Assistant Commissioner John Yates) had been having regular meetings – lunches and dinners – with senior News International staff. Data obtained by Baroness Doocey, a Liberal Democrat member of the London Assembly and Police

Authority, showed that there had been many meetings between media mogul Rupert Murdoch's editors and executives, and Scotland Yard's leaders. Yates had been responsible for reviewing the evidence into phone hacking. He was now responsible for counter terrorism. In a call for him to quit (Yates refused), Baroness Doocey said, 'It is shameful that John Yates found time to have five lunches with the *News of the World* and News International, but after just a few hours decided there was no additional evidence to justify a further investigation into phone hacking.' Commissioner Stephenson backed Yates, saying, 'John . . . has an excellent record.' Having been called before Parliament for his failure to reopen the hacking inquiry, Keith Vaz, chairman of the Home Affairs Committee, told Yates he found his evidence 'unconvincing'.[18]

The exposé caused a chain reaction, and the press started to dig deeper. It was revealed that Chamy Media, owned by Neil Wallis, a former Executive Editor of the *News of the World*, had been appointed to provide strategic communication advice and support to the Met, including advice on speech-writing and public relations, whilst the Force's deputy director of public affairs was on extended sick leave recovering from a serious illness. Even the *Daily Telegraph*, the right-leaning broadsheet that normally came out in favour of the police, went after the commissioner, with the headline: 'The Met commissioner and the Wolfman of Fleet Street' (Wallis's nickname because of his fiery temper and grizzled grey beard). It revealed that Wallis had been paid a £1,000 day rate by the Force for consultancy services; the funds came, of course, from the public purse.[19] Yates faced more calls for his resignation, particularly as Wallis was a suspect in the hacking scandal Yates refused to reopen. Worse still, Yates helped secure a job in the Met for Wallis's daughter, telling his staff Wallis had been a 'great friend' of the Force. Yates also reminded staff Wallis had been a close adviser to the commissioner, Sir Paul Stephenson.

Whilst the IPCC found no evidence that Yates directly influenced the Met's decision to offer Miss Wallis a job, it concluded that he had shown 'poor judgment' in passing on her CV. Contrary to Scotland Yard's recruitment policy, she was hired without a formal interview and apparently without any references being taken up.[20]

Regarding Stephenson, the London Assembly Chair Jeanette Arnold, also a member of the MPA which supervised the Force, said she was flabbergasted: 'Yesterday the confidence was low, today my confidence in him is completely shattered.'[21] The Labour MP Chris Bryant tweeted: 'I am firmly convinced now that the Metropolitan Police was corrupted to its core by NI [News International]. [Paul] Stephenson and [John] Yates have to go.'[22]

After this, Stephenson finally resigned, though Yates initially refused to go — the BBC reported that 'Mr Yates's resignation came after he was informed he would be suspended pending an inquiry into his relationship with Mr Wallis'.[23]

The Met's number one and number three weren't the only scalps taken. It was becoming known that the Force's head of public affairs, Dick Fedorcio, had met with Dominic Mohan, the editor of *The Sun*, for drinks during the month following my claim against the Met for leaking my information. Mohan was the one to whom my lawyers had sent those defamation letters. Alex Fedorcio, the Met PR officer who informed D'Orsi and others that *The Sun* was running the negative story about me, was not only Dick's son, but had also worked at *The Sun*. The relationship between News International and Scotland Yard ran deep. After disciplinary proceedings were announced against him regarding an investigation of a contract which was awarded to the ex-*News of the World* executive Neil Wallis, Dick Fedorcio went on long-term leave and then resigned. This was the end of his career with the Met.[24]

The IPCC contacted me about the 'emerging evidence in relation to phone hacking and media leaks',[25] finally interested in my complaint now that the scandal was cresting. However, as I remained a serving officer, they still couldn't allow me to personally pursue the complaint. The IPCC said that 'if [my] partner would like to make a new complaint based on the emerging evidence about relationships between the MPS and the media, then he [could]'. They finished by saying they could only apologise that I felt 'let down'.

My lawyer sent me a statement from the Asian detective inspector I had gone to see at the beginning of my troubles when at Heathrow. He'd written a letter in support of me, and provided some backup documentation I wasn't aware of, including the emails between the female chief superintendent (head of intelligence) and other seniors that had not been disclosed through the disclosure process, like the email she sent to Commander Shaun Sawyer after she had 'briefed' him about me, after speaking with 'the Fed rep dealing with the officer'. Regarding my seeking redress through an employment tribunal, she wrote: 'Clearly, this would potentially be very damaging to the MPS and its drive to encourage a greater diversity of staff within the CT [counter terrorism] command in particular'[26] – but my heart sank when I realised the full truth of the situation: Simon, my solicitor, told me that the Asian inspector had recently been fired, so his support as a witness was not worth anything anymore. Another officer of colour – a Pakistani Muslim – sacked. I learnt he had gone for a promotion interview and was so concerned that he wasn't going to be given a fair hearing that he recorded it on tape. He was caught in the process of doing so and dismissed.

Amongst the documentation the Asian inspector had provided was a seriously shocking discovery. My colleagues in counter terrorism, unbeknownst to me, had been producing an internal newsletter called *The Ports Monkey Times*. Its subtitle read:

'Published in connection with Mainstream paranoia.'[27] Written and edited by Special Branch officers, issues of this publication depicted apes in police uniform, as well as pictures of Al Jolson in blackface, with big white lips and 'jazz' hands; amongst its stellar works of reportage, it featured a poster for the imaginary film *Bully* by Al Jolson, which mocked bullying in the workplace. Another poster, entitled 'R.T.S – Repetitive Tasking Syndrome' depicted an ape-like man with a big nose, big lips and big teeth. The strap-line read, 'Don't suffer in silence – call Dr Al Jolson today'. One edition had a warning poster with a picture of an ape screaming, with a thought-bubble featuring Osama bin Laden above its head. Another ape held up a mocking 'Fairness at work' placard.

Although the Asian inspector told my lawyers that what had happened to me was 'unforgivable', they were not keen to use him as a witness because he had been dismissed for reasons relating to his honesty, despite mitigating circumstances. Putting him on the witness stand would just give the police another weapon against me. I insisted that we use the documents even if we couldn't use him, and instructed my lawyers to obtain copies of these from the police. Morris, the police's lawyer, refused the request. I gave her several days to reconsider before I began proceedings under a tribunal order.[28] Once her hand was forced, she officially disclosed them, but my counsel then decided that these newsletters would undermine my case. I wasn't allowed to raise the issue of widespread (institutional) racism, only racism directed at me. *The Ports Monkey Times*, though discovered, and now, fortunately, in the public domain, was treated as another dirty police secret.

Commander Stephen Kavanagh had been promoted to deputy assistant commissioner at the Met, so a new commander, Richard Walton, had taken over counter terrorism and was to chair the gold groups that discussed the threat I posed to the Force.

I had been sent two boxes of files by the Force, containing the evidence they would be relying on in the tribunal hearing. As I settled down to go through them, my lawyers sent me an email to let me know that the Force had sent me the 'wrong' files, that I should ignore what was in front of me, and wait for the 'correct files'.

One morning, in the early hours, I sat on the floor of the flat with the old and new files next to one another. I started going through the thousands of pages one by one, side by side, to see if anything was different or missing. I'm legally not allowed to share the contents of the emails and documents that were included within the disclosed files, which I was never meant to see and which would have advanced my case or for public discussion, because they were (and remain) subject to professional legal privilege. In any other circumstances this would be collusion. I still don't know if somebody deliberately sent me the wrong (truthful) files so I could see what was happening behind the scenes – an ally inside the Force – or if it was just pure clumsiness.

In the documents that I could legally use, I spotted some alarming changes. In the second version of the minutes from a gold group held at Scotland Yard on 5 July 2010,[29] whole passages that might have assisted me had been deleted and other sentences changed. The original copy recorded that Commander Stephen Kavanagh chaired the meeting. He sat at the top of the table with the press office representative, the head of intelligence, the Special Branch chief, my welfare officer, the counter terrorism HR manager, professional standards, Dee Caryl from the diversity directorate, the lawyer Jacqueline Morris, the police's employment tribunal unit and a representative from the Police Federation representing the people I alleged had been discriminatory. Their rep was the sergeant whose permission I'd asked for when I needed to go to the hospital after I first collapsed. In the version of the document the police wanted the tribunal to see, the newly promoted Kavanagh had now been removed, deleted from the gold group as if he hadn't been there at all. Unlike in the first version of the same meeting, now no one was listed as the chair (the chair of the meeting was merely 'missing'), as if the meeting had chaired itself. His name didn't appear on the attendees list, although those numerous senior officers present would have witnessed him there. Unfortunately for whoever doctored the document, they'd forgotten to remove the minuting of a comment he made later in the meeting. Emails showing his presence at the meeting were no longer in the bundle either. In the first version of the minutes, it stated that Dr Palmer had found me unfit for work. In the new version, the line had been removed and rewritten to suggest that I had been the one to declare myself unfit for duty. The second version of the same meeting recorded what Kavanagh told his subordinates: 'If all offers are rejected' – to accommodate my return to work, in spite of my ill health – 'then we can go for unsatisfactory performance with a view to dismissal.' O'Connor was also at this meeting (he told me later – and put it in writing following the UPP/A appeal – that 'the MPS is not instigating dismissal proceedings against you'[30]).

The minutes recorded that my challenging them had created 'a lot of fear', but that my colleagues were supporting each other and 'support has been put in place for them' by management. They recorded that some were worried about the employment tribunal because 'they [were] worried about potential embarrassment'. Caryl suggested the Gay Police Association could assist them. The meeting finished with my most senior colleagues saying that 'publicity could be huge and negative' and Kavanagh wanting to 'be informed of any significant developments'.[31]

This wasn't the only document in which Kavanagh's chairing of a gold group had been deleted. The agenda for a gold group chaired by him nine days before the leak to *The Sun* had been removed entirely.

There was also a note about a gold group meeting for which

I had never received any notes and of which I had not been aware. Even the my welfare officer's contact log notes had been changed. One version had a record of contact with me (about my upset with the leak), in the other version it had been deleted.[32]

I had to write a statement for the tribunal in preparation for the hearing, and received a copy of the police's statements in return. There were over thirty statements in total for the Force. More than thirty officers and staff were going to speak against me to say that discrimination and wrongdoing did not exist in the police. Like my lawyers Arpita and Chris had done several times, Simon warned me about the employment judges. He explained that tribunals were there to resolve 'factual disputes'. As I had suspected, the tribunal was not concerned with the changing or fabricating of public documents (like the gold-group minutes), although it signalled corruption, and raised questions of contempt, perjury, etc. I couldn't mention any of these words. I had to argue any claim of lying in a 'measured way'.[33]

After hours of reading, I looked over the last statement in a Caffè Nero across the road from police barrister Mead's chambers in Holborn. Though the last seven hours had been sobering, I had a tiny glimmer of hope. I had a feeling that I might be able to put a crack in the police's armour – however small.

The next day, after years of silence and pain, I was going on the record to officially tell the police that I'd had enough. I knew I was about to be punished severely, but I also knew that, whatever the outcome, I had at least had the guts to speak out.

I had to hang on to that.

12

Trial and Retribution

On 7 October 2011, the UK press descended on the employment tribunal at Reading. I was interested to note that two conservative, pro-police outlets covered the hearing fairly – perhaps the scandal around the press leaks had really hit home. The *Daily Telegraph* reported on my statement that my colleagues regularly put passengers with Arabic names on a security database to make it appear as though they had been busy – just as PC Lynford had alleged at Gatwick.[1] Surprisingly, the *Daily Mail*, the most right-wing national paper, did not sensationalise my race or sexuality whilst I was in a vulnerable state,[2] though the tabloid did later report the police's side too, saying that 'Detective Constable Maxwell was offered any job he liked (in the Met)[3].'

As I was about to give evidence, my Police Federation rep emailed to say he had fallen ill and wouldn't be able to attend the six-week hearing at all.[4] My colleagues had their representatives in the packed tribunal, and I was disappointed not to have my own representative to support me. But by this point I was accustomed to being on my own. I also had new counsel now. Mo Sethi had asked for more money than the police union would grant, so I had to find cheaper representation.[5] Kweku Aggrey-Orleans of 12 King's Bench Walk was appointed to me.

I always knew that giving evidence was going to be traumatic, especially whilst battling depression, but I knew I had to do it. I was to tell an all-white judiciary that the police officers and Special Branch detectives who kept them safe at night, and the psychiatrists who kept mad men off the streets, were racist and homophobic. I was going to tell them things they didn't want to hear. I'd seen first hand as an officer how the justice system looked down on black people who had no power or wealth. Even more so since juries had gone from civil courts. I wasn't naive, and my legal counsel had given me fair warning of employment tribunals' attitudes to similar claims.

I would be asked to provide evidence of racism, as if officers gave out receipts for their behaviour the way they gave receipts for confiscated property. My hope was that the police would trip themselves up and the tribunal would contradict itself.

At 11.10 a.m. I was sworn in at Tribunal Room 4 to be cross-examined by Mead, the police's barrister. I was in the witness box over a three-week period, whilst considered too sick to work by my GP and the police's own doctors. The tribunal heard evidence from the police's witnesses, and were directed to some 2,300 pages of documents in the bundle of folders (the disclosure). During the hearing I saw my colleagues packed together in the respondent's waiting room, some giving each other high-fives whilst I sat alone next door in the claimant's room.

John Yates was the Force's star witness, as my most senior direct line manager. Yates had previously had overall responsibility for investigating misconduct in the Met, and had been forced to resign over allegations about his own conduct during the hacking scandal. When Jean Charles de Menezes was shot dead at Stockwell tube station, Yates was one of the seniors in charge. The then deputy assistant commissioner travelled to Brazil to visit the De Menezes family, to offer them £15,000 compensation for their son's death at the hands of the police. They refused, and said they felt 'pressurised' by the visit to their home.[6]

Whilst he was giving evidence in my case, the BBC had reported that, although he had publicly resigned, Yates was still very much employed as a police officer.[7] He had announced in public his intention to resign, but had never stated when. Yates didn't step down immediately following the hacking scandal, presumably because he still had several months to go before he could claim his police pension. Scotland Yard appeared to allow him to give notice of his intention to resign, so that his benefits would not be affected. He wasn't alone. Andy Hayman, another assistant commissioner, had resigned after allegations about his conduct over expenses. He took four months of unpaid leave to officially qualify for his pension, as he described in a book he wrote after his retirement.[8] But when I became unwell, Yates had continued the stoppage of my pay.

Mead, who spoke on behalf of the commissioner, started off by saying I had brought the claims against the Force because I did not like white people. *I* was the one who was racist, he said. My problem, he claimed, was that I had a 'chip on [my] shoulder'. I almost laughed. I had to remind the tribunal that my mother was white and that my husband was also white.

In total, the commissioner sent thirty-three witnesses to give evidence against me, each denying that they had treated me any differently to other colleagues. The three leaders (consecutive chairs) of the gold groups held against me at Scotland Yard, commanders Shaun Sawyer, Stephen Kavanagh and Richard Walton, provided no statement and did not appear at the tribunal to explain their high-level meetings.

I told the tribunal that the police deliberately targeted black and brown people with stops, and about the 'buffer' system at Heathrow. Every white officer denied this. Then came the turn of the Asian officer from Terminal 5, who my colleagues didn't think highly of but who was to speak against me. He explained that he was regularly sent out to stop people of colour, but that he was 'okay' with it. This appeared to be an own goal. He seemed to have confirmed my account of the 'buffer' system. Despite myself, I felt sorry for him.

My Terminal 3 sergeant denied treating me differently. Addressing the issue of the Asian passenger she had brought over to me as he was leaving the UK, she said she would expect someone of 'DC Maxwell's calibre to be able to deal with this comfortably'. That wasn't my point – my point was that she had undermined my powers. On her transferral after my experiences at the terminal, she said it now made sense why she was moved. The tribunal noted the document from Inspector Quantrell: 'K disclosed to D/Superintendent . . . This is what resulted in K being moved from Embarks to T5 and was a factor in DS moving to St Pancras (though it may not have been overtly badged as such).'[9]

My Terminal 5 sergeant said his email to Quantrell suggesting that he should read about my experiences 'with a large malt in hand' was meant in a 'light-hearted way . . . DI Quantrell does like malt'. His correspondence about 'the three man overhead option left to gain entry' was also 'light-hearted'. On the subject of seeing if I was an 'okay' person and not a 'troublemaker', Quantrell told the tribunal, 'I was a little confused whether [Maxwell] was a genuine case or not, whether he was genuinely suffering from depression or had other motives.' While Quantrell did attempt to access my personal file at GMP without my consent, he didn't know consent was needed, which the tribunal accepted. On scoffing at the contents of my Regulation 28 sick pay letter, and wrongly passing it on to others even when expressly directed not to do so by the SO15 HR manager, Quantrell said he did so because I was 'damaging [the police's] good name'. He said he was 'angry and disappointed' with me for what I had written (about racism and homophobia).

It was clear from his witness statement and what he said in evidence, that Dr Oxlade was not happy with my challenging his comments at our consultation and his subsequent medical report. However, he accepted what I had said about his views on ethnic minorities needing to integrate. He said the observations he made to me were 'frequently reported by social scientists and commentators in this country and as such I did not regard them as controversial'. Speaking of his recollection of our consultation, he said: 'One should understand that his colleagues at Heathrow might be very anxious about jihadist extremists wanting to blow themselves up.' I remembered that he hadn't used the word 'jihadist' in the consultation, but 'Asian'; he used a different word in the tribunal hearing.

After Dr Oxlade gave his evidence, the employment tribunal judge Richard Byrne held a case management discussion. There was a debate at the tribunal between the lawyers and the judge as to whether or not Dr Oxlade was in fact an employee of the police. If he wasn't, he couldn't be held accountable for the comments he had made about race and racism during our consultation and his subsequent report. I was asked by the judge to agree that he wasn't an employee of the commissioner's, which I refused to do. He had seen me in his role as a police doctor in a police building, and sent his report about me on his police-issued letter-headed paper. In Dr Cahill-Canning's letter dated 29 January 2010, she had referred to Oxlade as 'the MPS psychiatrist'. The tribunal said that Oxlade was not an employee of the police. As far as Dr Hindler was concerned – in his report about me, he had stated that he himself was 'employed by the Metropolitan Police', but Dr Hindler's prior employment status was not issue before the employment tribunal.

The tribunal against the commissioner ended the way my dispute had begun, with Mead using the Police Federation as a battering ram against me. Mead argued that my rep, who had been at the first gold group, had been representing me, regardless of whether or not I'd been aware of this. Kweku countered by demanding how I could be said to have been represented by him, when I hadn't yet met with my rep to discuss the issues.

But Mead pushed on relentlessly, arguing the opposite so intently that the judge appeared to agree with him. D'Orsi, who sat at the back of the room for the entire six-week hearing, was the last to give evidence. He denied that I 'had not been looked after properly and had been let down by the MPS'. He called me 'ungrateful' with regard to the police's 'support'.

In the middle of my hearing, the *Sun* journalist Jamie Pyatt was arrested over alleged payments to the police.[10] He was the sixth person arrested under Operation Elveden, which was investigating inappropriate payments to police officers and other public officials by the press. Pyatt had been accused of payments to police in the tragic case of Milly Dowler, whose phone had been hacked after her disappearance and murder, leading her hopeful family to believe she was still alive. As my tribunal concluded, the phone hacking inquiry concerning links between the police and Rupert Murdoch's newspapers began. Police officers had received payments of up to £130,000 over several years from the *News of the World* for information, including the royal family's contact details. The commissioner would still not tell me which person had received two sets of payments for my private data. Later, the BBC's home affairs correspondent, Tom Symonds, made contact to inform me that the corporation was investigating arrests, which he said 'possibly may be connected to [my] case'.[11] Anthony France, the *Sun* reporter, had been arrested along with two Met Police officers – one from my command (special ops) – under Operation Elveden.[12]

I was almost in disbelief when I read that France came out as gay during his trial, using it as a defence. A black gay reporter employed by *The Sun* had tried to out me, a black gay detective employed by the police, causing me great pain and upset.[13] France was found guilty of making payments to public officials under Operation Elveden, and sentenced to eighteen months' prison, suspended for two years, and ordered to carry out 200 hours of community service. However, his conviction was overturned on appeal. Police Constable Timothy Edwards and Detective Constable Sam Azouelos both pleaded guilty to misconduct in public office at the Old Bailey. Edwards, who worked at Heathrow and had received more than £22,000 for selling thirty-eight stories to France over three years, was sentenced to two years in prison. Azouelos was sentenced a month later to fourteen months in prison.[14]

At the same time, the retrial of the Stephen Lawrence murder case took place. After eighteen years of fighting for justice, Stephen's mother, Doreen, spoke outside the Old Bailey after the conviction of two of her son's killers: 'The fact is that racism and racist attacks are still happening in this country and the police should not use my son's name to say that we can move on.'[15] Stephen's killers Gary Dobson and David Norris were finally sentenced during the retrial. It had been thirteen years since the inquiry that had exposed the institutional racism at the heart of the British police. One of the original panel members, Dr Richard Stone (at the time President of the Jewish Council for Racial Equality), wrote an article in which he wondered what had changed:

> *In this country we waste an awful lot of talent. Bright children from second-, third- or even fourth-generation [black] families from the former colonies are too often denied the equal opportunities that are offered to their white schoolmates. When, on top of this, some of them are also submitted to arbitrary stop and searches by aggressive police officers, they understandably grow angry with society at large.*[16]

No sooner had the hearing finished and the tribunal retired to consider its decision than the police leaders again reminded me that if I did not return to work immediately I would be dismissed under UPP/A. Despite everything, I still didn't want to be dismissed from what had long been my dream job. What I didn't understand was why they were so desperate to have me back. To avoid being dismissed by the commissioner, I sent superintendent O'Connor a letter informing him I would return to work,[17] which he acknowledged.[18] O'Connor – despite being involved with me, as my senior – never gave evidence or appeared at the tribunal.

Following this, an appointment was made for me with occupational health to see Dr Cahill-Canning the day before New Year's Eve. She told me that it would require a 'tremendous effort' on my part to return, given everything that had happened. But I was genuinely willing. I knew that, after watching me sit through the hearing and knowing that they had given evidence against my two claims, my return would baffle my colleagues. But I couldn't free myself from the Force, because I felt guilty about neglecting my duty to my community. I'd sworn to serve them, so I couldn't just quit. Throughout my service I'd been called to plenty of domestics, and I'd never really understood why so many married victims of violence went back to their abusers (almost always women returning to men). Now I felt a spark of understanding. The police had mentally abused me, but I felt unable to leave. I was institutionalised. I was like a perp who committed crimes to return to the structure and order of prison.

After our appointment, Dr Cahill-Canning sent a memo to management saying that I was able to return, but should be put on a recuperative duties' work schedule.[19] She wasn't saying that I was well, and my reintegration would have to be managed. She also let my GP know.[20] I was then required to undergo re-vetting by the police on behalf of the government, as I'd been off sick; my security clearance had been maintained.

Eight days after I wrote to O'Connor, the Force held another gold group, chaired by Detective Chief Superintendent John Prunty. Superintendent O'Connor, Diana Hills from HR,

Lesleyanne Ellis and John Fisher from professional standards, and Dr Cahill-Canning, amongst others, sat at the gold table. They discussed how they were going to deal with me upon my return.[21]

In early January 2012, whilst the tribunal was deciding its judgment, Detective Chief Inspector Melanie Bailey of St Pancras International Special Branch emailed me, asking to meet with me before my official return.[22] She informed me I would be joining 'Team 1' at the station. My two future line managers worked under her, a Sergeant Kieran Witherington and Inspector Karen Yearley. I wasn't aware that Bailey and Yearley had supervised my Heathrow Terminal 3 sergeant after she was transferred.[23] Unlike Heathrow Airport, the several teams at the international station covered both the embarkation and disembarkation of the European mainland trains.

I would continue to gather intelligence concerning individuals in order to identify potential threats of national security, terrorism and espionage, utilising the provisions of Schedule 7 of the Terrorism Act 2000. Special Branch officers were routinely posted to other Eurostar terminals, including Gare du Midi in Brussels, Gare du Nord in Paris and Lille. Prior to meeting her, I sent Bailey an email – I wanted things to be clear and open, so that there were no misunderstandings on the part of either of us, as to what we were hoping to achieve with my return. I would no longer tolerate racist or homophobic behaviour from the police officers I served alongside, towards me or others. The chief inspector said she was keen not go over the employment tribunal, so that I could put it all behind me, but not before addressing two specific issues I had mentioned in my email. She began by addressing racial profiling and the terrorism legislation. Bailey said that the government had given the police and other agencies clear instructions as to who to stop with regards to terrorism and those who pose a threat to troops and British people in the UK. I told her that I didn't have an issue with terrorism legislation – or I wouldn't be in the role I was in – and that I wasn't naive.

'But do you understand that officers don't need a reason as to why they stop people?' she asked.

'Yes, I know this and I'm not challenging this. But you can't just stop people based on the colour of their skin,' I replied.

Bailey gave me a long look. 'Yes, well – we need the power to stop people. Usually the people we stop are from countries considered to pose a threat to the UK, and those people are generally not white,' she said, carefully.

In the minutes of this meeting, Bailey said, 'The threat assessment worked to by Ports staff came from national level and was based on the perceived threat to the UK and UK interests abroad . . . It was on this nationally assessed threat that Ports officers based their stops/examinations . . . The ethnic make-up of persons stopped under the legislation should therefore reflect this current threat.'[24] My colleagues had to 'perceive' who presented a threat; their perceptions were not always from a place of thoughtful consideration.

Bailey sent me an email with various policies attached:[25] use of the internet, media relations, business interests, secondary employment and political activities, and standards of professional behaviour. Bailey had read online that I had been invited to talk at the LGF's 'Being Me' event (for ethnic minorities within the LGBT community) prior to my return. I had also been asked to take part in a *Desert Island Discs*-type programme on Gaydio, a gay radio station, and had been invited to appear on Channel 4's 4thought.tv to discuss gay marriage in the UK. I wasn't back at work yet, and none of the activities had anything to do with the Force – I was going to do them in a personal capacity, and I wasn't being paid. However, Bailey wanted to remind me of breaches of professional standards and told me that I needed to seek her permission first. She wrote: 'If you have a copy of the

MPS logo anywhere on your BLOG this should be removed immediately.'

The judgment of the Reading tribunal was delivered to the lawyers, who sent it on to the commissioner and me.[26] I was hoping to be part of the small success rate at employment tribunals. Astonishingly, just 5% of those who fight are successful. I couldn't bring myself to read the judgment. I put it to one side until I was mentally ready to read it. Other people, however, did. And what they read was that I had won.

I had proven that I had been subject to discrimination, harassment and victimisation on the grounds of both my race and my sexual orientation.

I had also proven that the commissioner had indeed leaked my private data to *The Sun*.

The BBC was the first to report the verdict online, on 20 February;[27] it was a *BBC London News* headline on the same day, and reported in the national and international press. The headline of the BBC story read: 'Met officer Kevin Maxwell wins discrimination case.' *The Guardian* reported that Scotland Yard deliberately leaked a 'distorted account' of my claim to *The Sun*.[28] Even the *Daily Telegraph* weighed in over the data breach.[29]

The *Evening Standard* wrote about my mental collapse after being bullied and my colleagues attempting to publicly out me, accompanied by a picture of me biting my lip as I walked into court.[30] Unsurprisingly, many black and gay publications covered my plight. *The Voice*, Britain's black newspaper, wrote that I had got 'justice'[31], and the *Pink Paper* wrote about the environment at Heathrow being 'so toxic',[32] quoting my solicitor Simon Cuthbert as saying, 'Such alleged practices and behaviour have no place in a modern police service.' Simon reminded the crime editor of *The Times*, Sean O'Neill, that I had 'never taken a single day's sickness' prior to my diagnosis and that I had been an 'exemplary officer'. O'Neill wrote that

I had been 'shunned, ignored and insulted' by my colleagues.[33]

 On the front page of the *Islington Tribune*, Claudia Webbe, my local councillor and senior advisor to the Met, called on new commissioner Bernard Hogan-Howe to apologise, saying that I'd been treated 'horrendously'.[34] She wrote a letter to the commissioner and Mayor Boris Johnson, describing a 'direct failure of leadership'.[35] Claudia was supported by my MP, Emily Thornberry, who was the shadow Attorney General at the time. Emily told the press: 'It is appropriate for the commissioner to apologise. This is the police force in the twenty-first century. They should apologise. He was right, they were wrong.'[36] Hogan-Howe did not apologise. Instead, Scotland Yard told the BBC that 'it was disappointed at the tribunal's findings and would launch an internal investigation'[37] – an investigation that would be supervised by the IPCC.

 I wasn't surprised that Scotland Yard responded in this way. Although I'd succeeded at the tribunal, I wasn't a winner. I knew I was still in trouble. When I heard LBC radio talk about my case at 5.20 p.m. the day I received the judgment, I realised just how much trouble I was in. I had just publicly embarrassed the commissioner. I had seriously antagonised my police bosses by putting a crack in their armour. They weren't going to be happy about re-employing me; they were going to find a way to get rid of me.

 Arpita wrote to me from her new law firm, saying she was pleased overall with the result.[38] It was poignant for her, because it was the last police case of her career and effectively ended ten years at Russell Jones & Walker. She also told me that the *Guardian* reporter, Vikram Dodd, had called her to express interest in doing an interview with me for a feature article. This was the last thing I wanted to do. The seniors at counter terrorism had forty-two days to appeal the judgment and I knew they were going to go for it. I decided that the best thing to do would be to step back from everything and reflect and decide my next move. Vikram wasn't the only journalist who wanted to speak with me. Benedict Moore-Bridger of the *Evening Standard* had already written about me and contacted me on Facebook. I wrote him an email back: 'Whilst I am still a crown servant and dealing with other matters I don't want to give [them any] further reason to [treat me] differently. I don't want to sensationalise my experiences. I genuinely want to raise awareness of the "real" problems faced and the stigma that exists.'[39] I told Sean O'Neill, who had contacted me on Twitter, the same thing. I continued to tell all the journalists who contacted me that it was never my intention to exploit my experiences. I had fought for something much more serious than fifteen minutes of fame. I had fought for equality.

I received some intense abuse online. One officer asked, on an external police forum, 'if [I] couldn't hack it in the Force, why didn't [I] become a hairdresser or cabin crew?' I tried to channel my energy into reading the messages of support. One stood out to me in particular – someone named Matthew wrote me an email: 'As an out, black, gay disable [*sic*] man, I have constantly faced and challenged society . . . I have won a lot of battles and lost – or should I say I made sure I had the space to air my views, bluntly and candidly. Space and time are great healers, Mr Maxwell. Hopefully, it will not hurt [you] as much.'[40] It was testimonies like these that made me feel like it might have been worth it. I had gone into the police force to help other people; maybe, by fighting for justice and equality, I could help them in another way.

In the aftermath of the judgment, Bailey called me, asking if I was coming back to work, even though they'd just sent me on annual leave before the judgment was delivered. She told me that if I was returning I wouldn't be unable to 'go on' about the employment tribunal. 'You have to forget it,' she said. 'You have to understand that you are going to have to let the *Sun* thing go. Think hard about what you want. Your return won't be easy . . . you've made a lot of allegations.'

Kavanagh, who had made the strategic decision to dismiss me under UPP/A and had been promoted to a deputy assistant commissioner of the Met, replaced Sue Akers as head of Operation Elveden. He was later promoted to the chief constable of Essex Police.

Although I wasn't due back at the police for several months, professional standards told me the leaking of my data was now *not* part of Operation Elveden, though I had just received a letter from Detective Chief Inspector Larry Smith from the operation, confirming that it was.[41] I was astonished to be told that the criminal leaking of my data in exchange for money was only being investigated as 'misconduct', and not even gross misconduct.

The day before my birthday, I found out the commissioner Hogan-Howe was lodging an appeal against the judgment in its entirety with the employment appeal tribunal, on grounds of 'perversity' and 'error in law'.[42] Now he was the appellant (the 'injured' party) and I was the respondent. The commissioner was seeking to overturn the judgment on the spurious claim that my memory was 'unreliable'.

This was the start of their retribution.

I was distraught and angry. I knew I would have to fight on. Too much had happened for me to walk away quietly. Having taken the advice of my lawyers not to 'cross-appeal' – in which case the whole matter would go before a new tribunal – I instructed them to resist the more than forty counts of discrimination the tribunal had found in my favour.[43]

The appeal, however, was the last straw for my marriage. Exhausted by what we had been through, especially by the leak, my husband had urged me to remove myself from the situation. But I couldn't fold now. Unable to understand and unwilling to stand by me, my partner got involved with somebody else at work. The continued struggle with the police had destroyed what little chance of survival our marriage had left.

In April 2012, the month when the police lodged their

appeal, the *Evening Standard* published an editorial comment in its newspaper about racism in the Force and Hogan-Howe, in time for the London Olympics (whose slogan proudly and ironically proclaimed 'London is Open').[44] Under the headline 'The Met is getting to grips with racism', the paper said: 'Mr Hogan-Howe is right to take a strong line on racism, it is a problem that must be kept in perspective.' I laughed out loud when I saw another favourable front page headline the same day, in the same newspaper – it was an all-out public relations drive. It read: 'I pledge to drive out Met racists' – this was Hogan-Howe's 'vow',[45] whilst he was at the same time trying to drive the racism proven in my case underground. His double standards were highlighted when the Met was forced to reveal that there were 2,720 complaints of racism, with 572 'locally resolved' (i.e. a slap on the wrist and a 'don't do it again'). Forty-two officers had been found guilty, with two losing their jobs.[46] The BBC later submitted a Freedom of Information request to the Met, and found that internal complaints of racism amongst officers had trebled in the past five years.[47] These figures were the backdrop to yet another racism case, after a young black man, Mauro Demetrio, recorded PC Alex MacFarlane of the Met telling him, whilst under arrest: 'You will always be a nigger.'[48] MacFarlane was found not guilty of racially aggravated intentional harassment at the judge's orders.

After the controversial fatal shooting of Mark Duggan by the police in August 2011, Neville Lawrence, Stephen Lawrence's father, spoke out at a meeting at Camden Town Hall. Drawing parallels between the suffering endured by the two families, and pointing out the similarities of their complaints, he said: 'You would think, after nineteen years, people would have learnt some kind of lessons and dealt with the parents in the right and proper way . . . Any black man or woman wanting to join the Met today would still have to know what they were letting themselves in for.'[49]

★

My annual leave over, I had to return to work. I knew things were going to be awkward and uncomfortable for me. I had publicly challenged the police over discrimination and wrongdoing. Commander Richard Walton had also just addressed all staff prior to my return. When I entered the main room at St Pancras, a large number of officers were sitting at tables chatting, others were on computers. When they saw me, some of them got up and walked out. To my great surprise, there were quite a few Sikh officers in the room. In over a decade of policing, I had seen fewer than a handful. I was pleased to see such a diverse and inclusive room of officers, though I was a little puzzled by why the room was so heavily weighted towards one minority ethnicity. One Sikh officer was sitting at a table surrounded by white officers, designing a mug for Special Branch to drink tea or coffee from. I learnt that another Sikh officer was a sergeant, and was to manage my team along with Witherington.

On 22 April, still upset with the police's appeal of the entire case, and about having to go through a new hearing as well as the end of my marriage, I sent Sergeant Witherington an email from home telling him I was feeling very low and 'quite depressed'. Under immense stress, professionally and personally, I had found comfort in alcohol for some nights. The only problem was that I had never been a big drinker. I had never taken drugs or smoked either. I just didn't do blind oblivion. The alcohol made me feel worse.

In hindsight, I shouldn't have given the police that ammunition, but I wanted to be honest and let them see they were hurting a human being. But as soon as I'd sent the email, I knew I had made a mistake and that it would be used against me.

During a shift three days later, Witherington called me into an office to serve me a notice under the Met's risk assessment and substance misuse policy.[50] I told him I was feeling low, and his response was to serve me with a notice that formal action would be taken against me if I abused alcohol. In the risk assessment Witherington stated: 'Kevin has been treated as self-referring under the MPS Substance Misuse Policy.' Strangely, he added: 'No effects of substance misuse has been noted at work.' Though he wrote that I had self-referred, I hadn't, because I hadn't abused alcohol. In an occupational health referral form completed two days earlier, Witherington confirmed this, stating: 'I am therefore referring Kevin to OH [occupational health] under the Substance Misuse Policy.'[51]

Witherington's risk assessment was crucial in several other ways. At the time it was completed, the commissioner was aware that I was struggling with my return to work, and it noted the 'possibility of reoccurrence of depression, and emotional anxiety' and 'disability under Equality Act 2010', and that 'Kevin has stated he is taking medication to help with depression. Kevin has stated these anti-depressants can cause side-effects'. It was very strange that they had forced me back to work whilst acknowledging how unwell I was.

At the same time, Witherington also served me with a memoir prohibition notice.[52] The commissioner informed me that I was not allowed to write about what the Force or police had done to me during my years of service. Bailey then gave me notice regarding what I could and could not say about race and sexuality issues in public. It turned out that speaking about these was forbidden too. I had a pile of papers I needed to sign to promise the police I'd never say another bad word.

I met with Dr Cahill-Canning at occupational health. We spoke about my return and the comment about my 'drinking'. She wrote to management confirming what they already knew: that there was no evidence of alcohol abuse in my history at all.

During another shift, I took my seat near to where the Sikh sergeant was talking to another South Asian officer. He said to his Asian colleague: 'Is it because I'm an ethnic?'

I thought: Whatever test this is, I'm not going to react.

At the end of the shift, I spoke privately with Witherington in a side office, to let him know what had happened, and to explain how I'd be dealing with it. I wasn't interested in being 'tested' upon my return, when I had been instructed to focus on putting the tribunal behind me. My focus was the job and getting better.

I decided that I would speak with the Asian sergeant one-on-one the next day, after some reflection at home. Witherington assured me that I could deal with the matter myself, but he relayed the conversation to inspectors Yearly and Bailey. I received an email from Inspector Yearley, who informed me that she had spoken with the Asian sergeant before I had had chance to.[53] I shared my dismay with her, copying in the Asian sergeant and apologising to him for any distress caused.[54] The Asian sergeant said his comment about 'ethnics' was 'not meant to offend anyone'. Management began an investigation to see if the Sikh sergeant's comment fell under the wrongdoing policy (i.e. if he had committed a disciplinary breach). Furious, he then wrote a stinging document about the institutional racism he had experienced within the Metropolitan Police.[55]

The investigation into the Sikh sergeant represented the pursuit of the third Asian officer connected to my case. The first one (who had provided the *Monkey Times* newsletters) had been sacked, the second (who had called the police lawyer Jacqueline Morris a 'coconut') had been disciplined and investigated personally by the head of the Met's Specialist Crime Review Group, Detective Chief Inspector Chris Burgess;[56] and now a third (for his comments about 'ethnics') was being investigated to see if he had committed any wrongdoing. Not a single white officer had ever been brought to book for the actual racism that penetrated the ranks from top to bottom.

The Sikh sergeant's direct challenge to management left them red-faced and at a loss. So they began yet another investigation against me for raising the issue. After the misconduct form was completed, John Fisher at professional standards wrote to Mark Jones, the new Special Branch superintendent, and Bailey and

Yearley: '[Neither the Asian sergeant] nor Kevin are allowed sight of this document.' Though they were investigating me – without my knowledge – Fisher made clear in his report: 'There isn't any "wrongdoing" by KM in the first place.'[57]

The investigation eventually stagnated, because they realised it was very difficult to pursue an investigation against someone, i.e. me, for not accepting inappropriate behaviour. The police truly had no idea how to deal with race issues or racism. I challenged the whole fiasco, and the new Special Branch head Jones curtly responded: 'The matter is now closed.'[58]

I was angry at myself for thinking I could return to policing. On 9 May, I served the commissioner notice of my intention to resign, and leave the police once and for all. My resignation created a new problem for the Force. If they dismissed me, they would have the upper hand – because it would mean a black mark against my name. But if I resigned, I might be able to say that I had been forced out. Their reputation would be further damaged.

On 30 May, at 3 p.m. – the end of my 7 a.m. early shift – I received an email from Witherington, to inform me that he was holding an immediate performance review for me, which was to take place the next day with Sergeant Shaun Hilton.[59] Performance meetings were formal, minuted meetings, convened to discuss issues of poor performance by officers. I had already given my notice of resignation, but attended the meeting anyway. I was physically sick before I went in. Witherington informed me that the recuperative measures set by Dr Cahill-Canning were being revoked with immediate effect. They told me that because Dr Cahill-Canning had allowed me to return to work, this is how I would now be treated – i.e. with no concessions for my disability: there was 'an expectation that performance will fall in line with [that of my] colleagues', they said, though Witherington called the meeting a 'progress review', not a 'performance' review.[60]

The stress, the lack of support and the level of pressure from my seniors and the Police Federation caused a second emotional collapse. I was now unfit to serve out my notice period. I couldn't sleep, eat or rouse enough energy to shower. I was broken, frightened, exhausted.

Management sought further advice from Dr Cahill-Canning – according to my Fed rep at the time, her senior job had been jeopardised by the support she had shown me. SO15 wrote to HR that occupational health's input and Cahill-Canning's actions concerning me had been 'less than adequate'.[61] In an email to Dr Cahill Canning, Superintendent Jones again mentioned my consumption of alcohol.[62] Dr Cahill-Canning repeated to management that she had explored my consumption of alcohol again in further detail: it was 'actually very modest and he is not abusing alcohol'.[63]

Dr Cahill-Canning wrote to management to inform them that she was referring me to see a psychiatrist about my fitness for duty prior to my leaving the police – to Dr David Price, the fourth psychiatrist I would see, after Dr Oxlade, Dr Hindler and the Asian psychiatrist at the St Charles centre.

As I was leaving Dr Cahill-Canning's office after a meeting with her on 11 June, she told me to be careful what I said to my seniors, as they were using everything I said against me. She then asked me if would I like a copy of the second occupational health file held on me. I was shocked. I had not realised there was a second file. I told Dr Cahill-Canning that I would like to see a copy of this file.

A case conference was held without me. There were eight people present, including Bob Crawley – the head of Health and Wellbeing – Dr Cahill-Canning, Diana Hills from HR, Superintendent Jones, Chief Inspector Bailey and Sergeant Witherington. Bailey told the meeting, 'The MPS is working towards Stage 3' of UPP/A (i.e. towards ousting me under UPP/A – chief inspector D'Orsi and superintendent O'Connor had in their previous attempt got to Stage Two of this process). She again asked that my vetting be suspended, because I would likely to go to the press and write a book about my experiences. The meeting finished with them agreeing that I posed a '9.5 on a scale of 1 to 10' challenge to the police.[64]

The next day, I signed for a Special Delivery parcel from occupational health.[65] The first file was purely general medical documentation. This second file was filled with secret documents that management were producing about me, and which they (the police leaders) had been legally required to disclose (which they had not done). Occupational health, who attended the gold groups and other high-level meetings, had been placing copies of the documents they were sent or given by management in my second medical file; management weren't aware of this, because they couldn't see that file without my (the patient's) consent.

The file confirmed my suspicions: the police had wanted me to return to work so that they could get rid of me lawfully. Bailey had even written to Diana Hills at HR: 'If it is not sorted within 4 months my next stop is Cressida [Dick] and leaving my warrant card with her until it is sorted!!'[66]

Bailey had written a report to her senior colleagues in counter terrorism – which was passed through the Force to those at the top – asking for the suspension of my vetting,[67] and thus my security clearance, which would have meant that I would be out of counter terrorism and so out of my job. She had bullet-pointed all the different ways in which the commissioner could get rid of me now that I was back at work, including 'self-declared misuse of alcohol' (I had done no such thing), 'mental health issues declared' (the depression), and that 'his employment tribunal against him that is still unresolved to him' (they, not I, had appealed). Bailey reiterated: 'He has been using alcohol as a comfort blanket and has been drinking spirits up till the early morning hours.' Though I accept that I had been wrong to share my angst with the police, Bailey had read Witherington's risk assessment the month before, which stated that 'no effects of substance misuse has been noted at work', as well as Dr Cahill-Canning's medical note, which stated there was no evidence of alcohol abuse – but she did not share this information with the others. But though I was not abusing alcohol, what Bailey forgot, in her disdain for me, was that people do drink when suffering from depression.

Bailey finished her report by stating that my use of social media posed the 'greatest threat' to the police service, but her explanation for this was redacted. Whatever it was Bailey had written, the specialist crime directorate SCD26, who administered the police's vetting on behalf of the government, didn't agree and my security clearance – which I'd just gone through again – was maintained. Bailey wrote so many hateful reports – including one to Bob Crawley, the head of Health and Wellbeing, saying I had submitted 120 'claims' to the employment tribunal[68] (118 claims more than I had) – and was forwarding every single email I wrote to professional standards, that the professional standards chief at counter terrorism wrote to her:

> Melanie . . . can we discuss your specific request . . . I am not convinced that any meaningful misconduct assessment can be made of the contents of the just [sic] the email below. If you have any concerns about any misconduct you should say what they are . . . . Can we discuss what you need from PSU [the professional standards unit] and then what we can deliver. I don't want you to have expectations of something happening, if it is not.[69]

I discovered that management had even recorded how long I spent in the toilet. Yearley wrote to Witherington on one occasion, when she saw me go into the men's washroom but didn't see me come out! She asked a colleague to go see what I was doing; he reported that 'a cubicle in the room was locked but noises could be heard from within'.[70]

On 19 June 2012, Diana Hills, from the directorate of resources, wrote to my seniors, including John Fisher and Superintendent Jones: 'Dear All, can we meet on this one please. Basically we need to find him a post so that he can be instructed to return to work or go [*sic*] sick.'[71]

Dr Price answered management's question whether I could continue to do police work until I left, even though I was unwell; he made a full, detailed and fair report, accurately recording my description of my mental state (which was appalling) and my emotional response to the trials I had faced, stating that he did not believe I was 'oversensitive'. In concluding his report, Dr Price wrote: 'Mr Maxwell is suffering from clinical depression.'[72]

Based on Dr Price's report, Dr Cahill-Canning declared me 'unfit' for operational duties, but fit for other duties. Superintendent Jones emailed me to order me to work, in a CCTV room on the other side of London, in Sydenham.[73] Sydenham, the place infamous for being the site of the murder of Daniel Morgan, a private investigator – in 1987, an axe had stopped Daniel from exposing corruption in the Met.

I said no.

Commuting there daily on public transport would just be too much for me. I was suffering with serious depression and extreme irritability, and this meant that noises on trains, people on phones – texting or talking loudly – and any music sent me into despair. My anxiety would not allow me to be crammed into a tube train during rush hour like a sardine, without experiencing terrible claustrophobia. I didn't have much left, and my health and well-being was my priority. I had a moral responsibility to disobey an unjust order.

Superintendent Jones sent me another email: 'DC Maxwell, The content of this email constitutes a lawful order. I am aware that you did not attend work as required yesterday and to my knowledge you do not have any authorised leave nor have you reported sick. You are therefore absent without leave.'[74] It wasn't possible for me to take sick leave, as this would mean they would restart the UPP/A.

On 3 July, Jones emailed me about my resignation.[75] The next day, I replied saying that I would leave the police on 17 September – the date of the employment appeal tribunal pre-hearing – which thus constituted my second attempt at resigning, now with a date, after I had given my initial notice to resign on 9 May.[76] Dr Cahill-Canning wrote to me: 'I was saddened by your email earlier today that you are planning to resign in September. As you know, I hold you in high regard and if you leave, the Met will be a poorer place. I can understand the pressures placed upon you associated with this decision.'[77]

I sent Jones a letter from my GP about my 'ongoing' diagnosis of 'severe depression'.[78] My GP also responded to the fact that I'd been moved to the other side of London and would have to commute every day: 'This is adding to his anxiety and I would support that he is currently unable to do the journey due to his illness. When somebody is suffering from extreme anxiety it is often the case that it can be detrimental to their mental state if they have to face unfamiliar journeys, meet with new people and be in unfamiliar surroundings.' The Transport for London website stated the journey would take an hour each way. The next day, Superintendent Jones wrote: 'I have informed Commander Walton of the fact that you have formally tendered your resignation as of Monday 17th September 2012. He has consequently accepted your resignation' – but added that his earlier order, that I work in the CCTV room until I left the Force, still stood.[79]

A few days later, Dr Cahill-Canning wrote to management, and did something utterly unexpected: she disagreed with my GP, my primary care giver, and said that I could travel on public transport whilst unwell: 'I do not concur with the GP's opinion.'[80]

The seniors at Scotland Yard were delighted. They now had

their green light to dismiss me. The next day a notice was completed, which I received on 18 July, saying that I was being investigated for insubordination (disobeying a lawful order) – an internal 'gross misconduct' breach under the Police Codes of Conduct – for my failure to attend work (absent without leave).[81] Witherington completed the initial report on behalf of management. Jones sent me a further email, saying 'I am aware of the conflicting opinions', but his position remained unchanged.[82] I was to spend my final weeks in the CCTV room, or I would be dismissed. That was the end of it.

To this day, I do not bear Dr Cahill–Canning any ill feeling. But what she did sealed my fate. My final weeks in the police were miserable, difficult and fraught with more fighting.

In late July, Witherington sent me three resignation forms to complete,[83] but I had no lawyer (Simon Cuthbert had emailed me to say that he was away on holiday until August)[84] and no Police Federation rep to advise me, as I explained to Bailey after she had emailed me about the forms.[85] I did not know my rights. I did not know what to do.

I had stopped using the aid of the Police Federation; its support had been patchy at best and undermined me at worst, and I could no longer endure having even my supposed defenders against me. This now meant that my insurance, which had paid for Russell Jones & Walker solicitors, had ceased. Legally, I was on my own.

In mid–August, I received a second letter from the police,[86] which was a notice that I was being further investigated for failure to attend the misconduct interview about the first breach (I had been too ill to go). My resignation would now be delayed, as it was my intention to challenge the alleged breaches at the misconduct hearing.

I also received a letter notifying me that I was to receive a Diamond Jubilee Medal from the Queen, for my loyalty and dedication to policing. It was a horrible irony.

The unfair treatment I was given was highlighted in an email Bailey wrote to others, with the subject line 'Advice regarding Kevin Maxwell'. She had now been promoted to acting superintendent of Special Branch (Heathrow and St Pancras), because Superintendent Jones was sick: 'D/Supt Jones is now certified sick and does not have a return date.'[87] Jones was free to return once he felt better. I had been forced back, again and again, to the lasting detriment of my health.

Emails between Diana Hills and Lesleyanne Ellis highlighted the Force's thinking. Hills wrote, 'Options around suspending him and taking him off pay would appear to be a non starter at this stage if the suspension negates him being instructed to attend work and the pay issue perceived as victimisation with little or no precedent.'[88] Ellis replied, 'The views in [sic] suspension remain the same. If he doesn't resign a gross misconduct hearing will be the next step.'[89]

The press reported I was making a short film about my experiences in the police, with the sub-headline: 'Policeman's film shows Met racism against him'.[90] I used the film, *My Fight for Justice*,[91] to create a crowdfunding campaign on Indiegogo, to see if the public would either give me some financial support to hire a new lawyer, or point me in the direction of one who could help me fight the police's appeal against my two successful claims.

Since my career with the police would soon be over, and as the only other area of expertise I had was in media, I had enrolled on a BBC Academy course. I was being taught by Maddy Allen, head of production at Keo Films, and she introduced me to her colleague Toby Sculthorp, who had produced the BBC documentary *The Secret Policeman*. I'd actually signed an exclusivity deal with Keo to develop and pitch programme ideas and formats featuring me, an unusual move in the industry for an individual who didn't already have the support of a broadcaster – but they believed in me and my potential.[92]

On 17 September 2012, I attended the pre-hearing of the employment appeal tribunal in the City of London. I researched the case law myself and wrote my own skeleton argument.[93] The employment appeal tribunal judge, His Honour Judge McMullen QC, said I needed to find proper representation to fight the police at the full appeal hearing.[94] Toby Sculthorp explained that he thought he knew a lawyer who might be able to help. His name was Jason McCue and he ran the human rights law firm McCue & Partners.

Two days after the appeal pre-hearing, Bailey wrote to Nigel Foster (the project lead for Met Change), saying that she was 'wracking [her] brains' about how to get me out. The police chiefs and their lawyers were concerned that a finding of misconduct would be the wrong route, and that they should be using UPP/A, going straight to Stage Three. She asked him 'not to forward email [*sic*] to anyone else.'[95] Foster replied that he had met with the acting Chief Superintendent Nicola Dale and Chief Inspector Kirsty Andrew to discuss the case. He said it wouldn't be appropriate to suddenly 'switch' from misconduct to UPP/A given the 'inherent risks in adopting this approach in terms of raising the prospect of further discrimination claims for DC Maxwell.' Foster reasoned: 'A decision was taken to deal with this matter as a misconduct issue and this far down the road it must remain as that.'[96]

In September, I was informed that my resignation had been processed. In October, I received in the post my P45, the tax form ending my police employment with immediate effect. The Force had terminated me on 17 September, before disciplining me – which was a mistake. They had even published my resignation internally within the Force notices, for all to see.[97] My seniors were meant to dismiss me at the misconduct hearing they had planned and which I was going to challenge, but had ended my employment on the accepted resignation date. I could now claim that I was forced out of my job.

I shared my dismay with the commissioner,[98] pointing out that I had attempted to resign (the resignation notice I had given him, informing him that I was going), but that he had then begun a performance management action negating this (the performance meeting with Witherington and Hilton in May). I had then attempted to resign a second time (when I informed Jones of my leaving date, but been subjected to two gross misconduct breaches (in essence stopping this second attempt by me to resign). I had planned to challenge the misconduct breaches (withdrawing my resignation), but had instead received the P45 terminating my employment.

In response, the commissioner reinstated me, despite having issued the P45 and backdated my pay so that dismissal proceedings could continue regarding my insubordination (my refusal to travel to Sydenham whilst unwell) and failing to attend the misconduct interview, and even though I had signed no reinstatement or other re-employment form. Resignation or not, they were going to chase me out.

The Force had made such a mess of pursuing me, that the number two at Scotland Yard, Deputy Commissioner Craig Mackey, was forced to personally write to me: 'I have had an initial look at the chronology of events which led to your resignation being progressed despite the fact that you had not submitted any of the necessary paperwork. There does appear to have been a systems failure.'[99] It was a mistake that could not legally be undone. You cannot simply reverse a termination: once an employee has been issued with a P45, they have to be formally re-employed, by mutual agreement. Commander Richard Walton writing that I had been terminated in 'error' was not enough.[100]

Walton had begged Mackey not to write me the letter, because if he did, he, Walton, couldn't 'protect' him and the commissioner from further challenges from me: 'My humble advice would be that to protect both the commissioner and the deputy commissioner, this letter should go out from someone within SO, either ACSO [assistant commissioner, special ops] or myself on behalf of the commissioner. If the dep. commissioner is still keen to send the letter from himself then of course we'll craft the response for you.'[101]

In October, after a meeting with Jason McCue, his partner Matthew Jury and their associate solicitor Courtenay Barklem (who would look after me day-to-day), McCue agreed to help. McCue were quick to write to the police: 'We note that your letter dated 15 November confirms and accepts that MPS was wrong to terminate our client's employment on 17 September 2012, the date of the P45. Thus, our client has accepted MPS's repudiation and as a result his employment at MPS is now at an end, as from the date of the P45.'[102]

Despite the standoff, the Met had pushed ahead with dismissing me.

Lesleyanne Ellis and Ingrid Cruickshank of professional standards had buckled down to work out how they could possibly get me out for blogging. In November Ellis wrote yet another misconduct report about me and forward it to Cruickshank.[103] Cruickshank then forwarded it to Detective Chief Inspector Paul Monk of professional standards. She wrote:

> *Sir, this officer featured on the risk register [i.e. considered a risk to the police] when I was staff officer in relation to his various E/Ts [employment tribunals]. Maxwell has been blogging for some considerable time. I am happy to assess this as gross [misconduct] . . . and commence an investigation. I am mindful however of the following issues: the officer is highly likely to be dismissed in relation to being AWOL [the first breach they were trying to oust me with]. I would like to proceed, and get as far as possible with the investigation [for blogging] prior to his hearing [for being AWOL].*[104]

★

I spent much of these days in reflection. I wondered what advice my mum would have given me. I wasn't sure she would have forgiven the police for what they had done to her child, and she had been a very forgiving person. But I still wanted to ensure I kept doing the right thing by her and me – to always be a better person than them. She had always advocated rising above hate, and I didn't want this to consume me. But I now knew unequivocally why many people of colour hated the police and lashed out. I attended an Alternatives to Violence Project workshop, which looked at essential skills in handling conflict. I wanted to turn all the anger I had into something positive.

We were now only days away from the misconduct hearing on 17 December. By this time, I neither recognised the hearing nor the legitimacy of the police. My new legal team were in complete agreement. Courtenay wrote, 'We're disengaging with the misconduct process as we do not recognise its validity because they've already wrongly dismissed you.'[105]

Their behaviour was part of a series of related discrimination, harassment and victimisation, which represented a repudiatory breach by the Met of the working relationship that existed between me and the police.

The police would not give my lawyers advance notice of who the misconduct panel members were, and refused to hold the hearing in public to ensure transparency. Without notice, witnesses for the police were called.

I was, once again, very unwell on the day of their hearing, which took place without me or any legal representation.

One week after my eleventh year in service, the commissioner dismissed me without notice for a second time (if that is possible), for insubordination. My refusal to follow an order (to attend work whilst sick) amounted to gross misconduct, he claimed, 'discrediting the police service and undermining public confidence in it.'[106]

For them, I was now another statistic, another unemployed black man, ousted from the police because he had dared to stand up for himself. The police needed something on me to ruin any future work opportunities and they were going to get it, whatever it took. Assistant Commissioner Cressida Dick – my most senior line manger, who had taken over special operations from John Yates – did nothing to stop Scotland Yard's destruction of a black gay detective. On the day of my dismissal at 5.24 p.m., Dick received an email from Commander Richard Walton informing 'Cress' that I had been successfully forced out of the police service.[107]

Earlier in the year, on 14 August, police commissioner Bernard Hogan-Howe was speaking at an event called 'Policing in the World's Greatest City' held at the Stratford Picturehouse. It was a talk about the challenges facing policing in London, so I purchased a ticket and attended, to see what he had to say. At the end of what I found to be a very unsatisfactory discussion, the microphone was passed around for questions from the audience. I raised my hand and it was passed to me. With my fingers wrapped around the microphone, I took a deep breath and spoke.

'If you are so serious about ending racism in the police, why are you appealing cases like mine?' I asked.

The head of every senior police officer sitting in front of him swivelled towards mine.

'Kevin,' Hogan-Howe said. 'You probably don't want to talk about this now.'

The audience was silent.

'No, it's fine,' I replied, prepared to stand my ground.

The chair of the event, Dave Hill of *The Guardian*, stepped in and my question went unanswered. Nevertheless, I had asked. I had stood up, and I had made myself heard.

Following this event, the Force upgraded its 'risk of reputational damage' from medium to high, because I had directly challenged Britain's most senior police officer in such a public way.

The American author Terry McMillan once wrote about how it was going to be 'hard' for her son, going out into the world as a black man, and that she hoped that he had Malcolm X's 'courage, insight, wisdom'. She added: 'Men are made, not born,' and said, 'I hope he will be strong enough to say no to anything that will strip him of his power.'[108] I'd had enough. The police had burnt me, but a man had risen from the ashes.

I no longer considered myself subordinate to any person.

PART THREE

13

Down and Out

Less than twenty-four hours after the misconduct hearing, on 18 December, Bailey and Witherington called at my home and left a letter.[1] It would have been more appropriate to go through my lawyers – Jason McCue described the decision as 'outrageous' – but, then again, it would have been much less intimidating. On behalf of the commissioner, Witherington reminded me that failure to return the police items in my possession would lead to me facing a criminal offence. I had no desire whatsoever to hold on to the police equipment. The letter also instructed me to sign the Official Secrets Act, to stop me from speaking out about my experiences. They were not secret, but on the public record. The same day, Bailey sent an email to numerous people in the police, including their lawyers, vetting and professional standards, to make sure everyone knew I'd been forced out.[2]

I walked to Islington Police Station to return my equipment, which included my warrant card and two Special Branch security passes for Heathrow and St Pancras. The front desk officer refused to take them and called for his acting sergeant. The sergeant in turn contacted his inspector on the radio and they finally agreed to take the items, giving me the same sort of receipt that is handed to arrested persons for their belongings.[3]

The Force were now keen to prevent all the details that had

not been heard in tribunal from becoming public. This included the secret documents written by Bailey and others, and the very existence of the *Monkey Times*. They suggested that the CEDR (Centre for Effective Dispute Resolution) mediator, Fiona Colquhoun, could facilitate a meeting. I'd be given a fair reference; they'd get to bury the evidence.

There were, however, certain conditions attached to this mediation. I would have to drop all claims and sign a confidentiality agreement forbidding me from ever talking about my experiences again.

Employers contemplating dismissal of an employee they are, or have been, in dispute with, will hold meetings which they say are on a 'without prejudice' basis, so that they can entertain discussions about dismissal whilst offering to pay a sum of money to the employee *if* he or she signs a compromise agreement, without any admission of liability such as racism and/or homophobia.

I attended the meeting with my lawyer Courtenay at the Novotel London Waterloo. I sat in one room with Courtenay and the police leaders were in another (we didn't see each other); the mediator went back and forth between us. Fiona had never dealt with a case that had attracted so much attention from the senior ranks; she remarked that she couldn't believe how many police chiefs were sitting next door. She told us that it reminded her of the film *Fair Game*.

I was told that if I settled all claims and agreed that the police played no part in my ill health, I'd be granted a reference. As far as I was concerned, I hadn't done anything to cast a stigma on me, or reflected badly upon my probity or integrity in any way. There was a difference of opinion regarding how I left the service – with the issuing of the P45 having terminated my employment before *their* dismissal hearing – but either way, I had no shame in being forced out of a job after fighting discrimination and wrongdoing. I hadn't stolen, hurt somebody or lied. I was different in an institution that did not understand difference.

I refused to allow myself to be subjected to any further abuse from my employer.

Settling and accepting a reference would have been an admission of guilt on my part, and I knew I was not the guilty party. The police have destroyed too many black lives, and it didn't start or end with Stephen Lawrence. I wasn't the first and won't be the last to be wronged by the Force.

So mediation did not work.

I would have to keep fighting their appeal against the tribunal decision.

My marriage had fallen apart long before, and we'd handed our notice to our landlord. I asked my husband whether he'd be willing to cover the rent until I found a job, but he refused. I understood, of course, but it left me in a very hard position. In fact, I was jobless, applying for benefits, and homeless. I left everything we'd owned together with him and began to carve my own lonely path.

I moved into Clink 78, a 600-bed hostel, a former Clerkenwell courthouse that used former prison cells as bedrooms and was next to a working police station. The irony was not lost on me. The old courtroom, known as The Dock (as part of the hostel's aesthetic), had tables and internet terminals. I shared a room with thirteen other beds that were occupied by different people every night. There were no curtains and no privacy. I cried myself to sleep often, quietly.

Feeling like I'd left the old me behind with my belongings, I found it hard to get up in the mornings and lacked the motivation to do anything. Friends offered me a bed but I couldn't bring myself to impose. 'Come home to Liverpool,' said my sister. But I was no longer sure where home was, or what it meant.

I was walking from the hostel towards King's Cross station, when I heard somebody shout my name. I looked up and saw a man over the road, on a bicycle.

It was my old counsel, Kweku. After a brief chat, he agreed to help me fight the appeal, so that the work he had done at the original tribunal would not have been in vain. The only problem was, I didn't have the money to pay him.

McCue wrote to the Police Federation about funding my fight, which they were still legally obliged to do under their funding policy.[4] The Police Federation said they would pay for Kweku, but refused to pay any monies to McCue's firm (Kweku was my barrister, whilst McCue were my solicitors). They said the only option for me was to go with one of its other retained law firms, Pattinson & Brewer, instead of Russell Jones & Walker.[5] The Force would keep the same lawyers throughout. The union continued to put me at a disadvantage. In the meantime, the employment tribunal accepted my third claim, under the new Equality Act 2010, regarding the 'dismissal',[6] and gave me a new case number.

I prepared for the employment appeal tribunal hearing of claims one and two from the police, i.e. the claims of discrimination and leaking of personal data. But first I had to read the original judgment by the Reading tribunal, which I'd avoided doing whilst I recovered from the trauma of the tribunal proceedings. In the absence of an adequate explanation from the police as to why I was treated differently, the tribunal had to uphold my complaints unless the commissioner 'proved' that no discrimination was committed. It's called burden of proof. Proof initially lay with me, until a *prima facie* case was established (that is, enough to show that discrimination had occurred) – then burden shifted to the police chief.

In its reserved judgment,[7] the Reading tribunal started off by stating that I was 'black', because the police had challenged my mixed race. Though it said I was a 'personable, well-presented individual' who was 'respectful' and 'passionate' in my evidence, presenting as someone with 'a very real feeling of injustice', but then went on to criticise me. The employment tribunal judge, Richard Byrne, said it 'appeared' that at times I took offence over matters which, considered objectively, were not justified. The example he used for this was Dr Palmer, the police medical officer, against whom I had brought no complaint, though she had discussed my medical condition at the gold group without my consent. Byrne continued that I had presented as someone 'sensitive to a high degree of himself and those around him'. The tribunal, like the psychiatrists who worked for the police, put the onus of dealing with racism and homophobia on me and focused on my reaction to it, rather than on the actual racists or homophobes. The tribunal used the word 'perception' when discussing my experiences, because my white colleagues had, en masse, described my experiences differently to me. This also contradicted the legal definition of a racist incident following Stephen Lawrence's murder: 'Any incident which is perceived to be racist by the victim or any other person.' The establishment had long used the excuse of perception: in his 2009 book *Policing Controversy*, former commissioner Ian Blair writes, regarding the fallout from the Tarique Ghaffur case: 'Like many who had faced prejudice in their lives, however, Tarique seemed to see slights where none were meant.' Blair writes that he felt 'good about the way Tarique had been handled' and 'regarded the noise of the BPA as no more than that.'

The tribunal said my Terminal 3 sergeant acted 'businesslike', which I may have *perceived* as unfriendly and cold. It said she 'did not go out of her way to welcome' me, because she was 'relatively disinterested in [me] personally'. On her comments about not getting 'above [my] station', this was explained as happening because my sergeant was not supportive of my aspirations and unlike her relationship with my (white) colleagues, she had an 'arms' length relationship' with me because 'there was clearly not a close working relationship' between us (she was my supervisor), which gave me the *perception* that she had issues with me. Given this, the tribunal couldn't conclude discrimination.

My sergeant had confirmed that my black colleague had volunteered to mentor me but that she had decided to do it herself, and yet, the tribunal said, 'she took no steps to apply that mentoring'. The police claimed the mentoring scheme didn't exist. The tribunal said that my sergeant had given an adequate explanation as to why the mentoring wasn't done. Though it was brought up in tribunal, the tribunal made no comment regarding my sergeant backdating my tasks.

The tribunal accepted that I was criticised for using the wrong computer terminal to communicate about annual leave and that my sergeant's evidence was 'inconsistent': first she did not recall the incident, but then she said she'd given me an opportunity to do it again, using the right computer. The tribunal said that I had a 'clear recollection', and that it was an act of race discrimination (it took place), but 'out of time', i.e. not in step with modern policing. Regarding the correction/amendment of my intelligence reports, the setting of the office alarm and the unlocking of the safe, the tribunal said that I did not show 'primary facts' from which the tribunal could draw a conclusion about these 'general' allegations of humiliating and prejudiced treatment. Though this was also brought up in tribunal, the tribunal made no comment about my sergeant supporting white colleagues' job applications.

The younger officer on my team said that I told him I was gay during a lunch break; the tribunal stated that it was 'inevitable' he would tell the others. However, the two older officers didn't treat me any differently, as they were 'never close' to me anyway. The tribunal said there was not enough evidence to support the fact that my colleague had used the word 'poof', but that I may have taken offence to 'comments' made when a gay television programme was on(!). On my sergeant undermining my powers, the tribunal said that something did happen, but that she was entitled to do what she did. The tribunal said my sergeant's actions were 'entirely routine', and that the police had provided an 'acceptable explanation'.

About my colleagues stopping whoever they wanted to because they could, they denied this. My sergeant stated they were 'intelligence led'; another officer said, 'Whites were targeted as well.' An officer added, 'there is no face to terrorism,' though the police publicly state that Pakistan produces 75% of the threat to Britain. The tribunal said it wasn't satisfied that the primary facts had been established showing ethnic or racial targeting. Regarding the Islamic Awareness Day at the mosque – whether a colleague refused to eat the curry because 'they [the Asians] will have spat in it', another colleague refused to take her shoes off, and the general consensus was that imams were doing nothing to stop terrorist attacks: the curry-refusing officer denied being there with me, and the tribunal said it must have been another officer who spoke about the Asians spitting in the food. It was another female officer – not the one I'd identified – who had refused to take off her shoes. Judge Byrne said to me in open court, whilst I was in the witness box, that whether I agreed with it or not, the view that imams were part of the problem (of terrorism), was a 'reasonable view to hold'.

About my looking for accommodation south of the river, the tribunal said, 'While no doubt there were conversations about practical difficulties arising from living south of the river', my colleague's 'scum' comments weren't established on the evidence heard, and neither were the views expressed about Operation Trident.

Regarding the landing cards information, a colleague explained she did this to ensure she 'had not missed any intelligence', and another colleague, supporting her, said he looked at them afterwards to see if there was 'anyone on that flight relevant to intelligence'. The police said everything was intelligence-led and yet, as I said, they were retrospectively creating intelligence against those who posed no threat. The tribunal said it was happy with the basis on which passengers were stopped.

On the 'buffering' – officers pretending to stop white people to get to black and brown people – the Asian officer who stepped forward to support our white colleagues undermined their claim that it didn't happen by saying that it did, although he was fine with it. He may have been, but the law did not allow this. It was unlawful race discrimination and harassment, committed by the counter terrorism officers by 'creating an intimidating, hostile, degrading, humiliating or offensive environment'. I noted the tribunal had given the police a 'Get Out of Jail Free' card for this adverse finding – though the police didn't use this defence – by stating: 'The tribunal can understand that operationally it could well make sense for individuals of a particular ethnicity to be stopped by police officers of the same or similar ethnicity.'

My colleague's 'ranting on about homosexual sex' and 'taking it up the arse', and the 'as gay as a gay in a gay teashop' presentation at Paddington Police Station, were both ruled to be sexual-orientation harassment. They ruled that a reference made by my Terminal 5 sergeant to our Asian colleague (who defended the police's racist 'buffer' system) as 'one of those people' who wouldn't have got into Special Branch a few years ago was ruled racial harassment. The tribunal said that the sergeant who advised others to read about my plight with a 'large malt' in hand was 'disparaging', as his explanation that Quantrell liked malt 'does not ring true'. It was race discrimination and harassment, and sexual orientation discrimination and harassment. Regarding the 'lack of information' in the occupational health referral report and the Terminal 5 sergeant knowing nothing of the reason for my depression, the tribunal found him 'disingenuous' for saying that he didn't know the crux of the depression I was suffering from – because the wording of an email he had sent to the acting superintendent at Heathrow on 27 August could only be construed as indicating that he had knowledge of it. The tribunal said that he 'presented as a very controlled witness', and 'in [their] view there were many inconsistencies and inaccuracies in his evidence'.

Quantrell's 'that's life' comment to me, after I told him it wasn't easy being black and gay in the police, was race discrimination and harassment, and sexual-orientation discrimination and harassment. His curt email response to me was put down to the fact that he was 'frustrated'. Quantrell writing about staff being 'wary' of me, if they thought that I would get them into trouble over racism and homophobia because I wanted to progress my career, was both race and sexual-orientation discrimination, harassment and victimisation. Quantrell researching me to see if I was an 'okay' person and not a 'troublemaker' was considered by the tribunal to be both race and sexual orientation harassment and victimisation, because he doubted that I was a genuine case; the tribunal said: '[He] did not approach the claimant's allegations with an open mind.' Quantrell's careless use of 'queer' and 'faggot' to identify gay people at the case conference, his trivialisation of homosexuality, the tribunal considered to be discrimination and harassment on the grounds of sexual orientation.

Regarding the Regulation 28 sick pay letter, the tribunal stated:

> The claimant regarded his letter as confidential and said it was meant to go directly to the [B]CU [Basic Command Unit] commander from HR then to the assistant commissioner and that DI Quantrell should not have known about its contents . . . When DI Quantrell was cross-examined about the phone conversation of 9 November it was clear from his evidence to the tribunal that he was irritated at the contents of the Regulation 28 letter ('damaging our good name').

The tribunal accepted that Quantrell was aggressive in his tone to me, because he was angry and upset at what he saw as criticisms in the letter concerning himself. This was direct discrimination, harassment and victimisation on grounds of both my race and my sexual orientation.

The tribunal said that 'DCI D'Orsi on occasions gave lengthy self-serving answers to questions in cross-examination and there were a number of areas where he raised evidence that was not in his witness statement'. This caused the tribunal to generally approach his evidence with some caution. His clear focus was on getting me back to work, not on the discrimination I had experienced. Regarding my suitability for SO15, 'being black and gay', the tribunal accepted that, in the context of discussing options, DCI D'Orsi did say to me that if I moved to another policing role I would not face the issues I had at Special Branch: D'Orsi 'conceding that there were issues at SO15 arising from racism and homophobia' was discrimination, harassment and victimisation because of both my race and my sexuality. The tribunal found him 'disingenuous' concerning the question whether I wanted an investigation of the problems at work or not (he had told the tribunal that, during our meeting at the Place Hotel, I'd said that I didn't want them to investigate the racism and homophobia, but had not recorded this in his note about the meeting at the time). Quantrell had written a note about the meeting he had with me and D'Orsi: 'We discussed RTW [return to work] options and the thought that Ports was not as dynamic an environment as maybe other parts of the command.'

The tribunal said that, although Dr Oxlade expressed himself 'clumsily' at our consultation and his report's 'lighten up' comment was 'inappropriate', it accepted his 'professional view', including that about Asians and their lack of integration. It was ruled that his comments were not racist. It stated that I shouldn't have taken offence by proxy, because I'm 'not Asian'. Regarding stopping my pay and keeping it stopped, the tribunal agreed with assistant commissioners Rose Fitzpatrick and John Yates, when 'she [Fitzpatrick] drew a distinction between performing the duties of a constable and being on duty' and he [Yates] argued that 'one can suffer racism or homophobia in any workplace'.

Though it originally said that my curry-refusing officer had not been at the mosque with me (the tribunal said it must have been another officer), when it made its ruling about race harassment, however, regarding my data being leaked to *The Sun* — unlawful acts of victimisation on the grounds of my race and sexuality — it said that he *was* there: the *Sun* journalist had mentioned 'an officer with knowledge of the visit to the mosque' whose 'low-cholesterol diet . . . [had] led [him] to decline food at the mosque'. I didn't know about his low-cholesterol diet until cross-examination at the tribunal, and yet the tabloid had known about it two years before. It was incredible. The tribunal had completely contradicted its own judgment.

The two positive things I took from the judgment were that the Metropolitan Police's attendance management policy used against me (all those calls) after I had raised issues of 'great concern' to the Force was 'excessive' of the contact requirements, which was discriminatory, harassing and victimising because I was a black gay detective. And its conclusion that the commissioner and, in particular, 'senior police officers', had failed to comply with their own 'reporting of wrongdoing' policy. The police did not know how to deal with wrongdoing within its ranks.

On 19 March 2013, I attended the employment appeal tribunal at Fleetbank House in the City of London for the three-day appeal hearing for claims one and two, to uphold the proven discrimination and data leak to *The Sun*. Each day, a different friend came with me. Lesleyanne Ellis from professional standards was sitting with a man at the back of the court, directly behind us. The appeal was heard in front of the high court judge Mr Justice Supperstone. Kweku spoke for me and Mead spoke on behalf of the Met.

Mead, after giving his opening statement, shocked all of

us when he said the case had to be thrown out by the appeal tribunal because I was a threat to 'national security'. I'd gone from being a race opportunist – Mead was the one who had demanded that I decide whether I was black or mixed-race – to being a racist myself with a chip on my shoulder, to a national security threat.

During my time on the Force, I'd seen the 'national security' label used on staff like Ali Dizaei and members of the public to silence a threat to the Force. The police smeared what they feared. No one, including the general public, press and politicians, questioned the police when they said that something was a matter of 'national security', especially with attacks and attempted attacks against the nation on the rise since 7 July 2005. For a gay mixed-race former counter terrorism officer from Liverpool, it was a particularly painful and strange statement.

In early May, I received a call from Kweku, who was visiting his family in Ghana. He had been notified of the appeal tribunal's ruling and the judgment that was to be handed down. He then forwarded me an email: 'The judgment is still under embargo and cannot be revealed to anyone other than the parties and their legal representatives. Breach of this may amount to contempt of court.'[8] As I was finishing my breakfast at the hostel, the employment appeal tribunal delivered its judgment, publicly, through the Judicial Office. (Court judgments are available for the most senior courts, typically the Court of Appeal. From time to time, the Judiciary of England and Wales (judges and magistrates) and the Tribunals Judiciary publish a link to high-profile judgments or those it says 'set particularly important precedents'.)[9]

As *The Times* reported: 'Scotland Yard was found guilty today of discrimination, harassment and victimisation against a black, gay officer who was dismissed for "discrediting the police service".'[10]

Once again, I had proven in a court (a senior one) that I'd had my dignity 'violated' as a result of 'an intimidating, hostile, degrading, humiliating or offensive environment' whilst at the Metropolitan Police.[11] Scotland Yard had committed more than forty counts of unlawful discrimination against me because I was black and gay, and did leak my details to *The Sun*.[12]

The appeal tribunal rejected the police's claims that I could not be relied on to accurately recall events. The police, after all, had trained me to be meticulous, thorough and reliable when recalling evidence and events. The homophobic comments about 'taking it up the arse' and 'as gay as a gay in a gay teashop', were found 'out of time' on appeal, as I should have made the complaint when I fell ill, and within the normal three-month deadline. Quantrell's 'aggression' regarding the Regulation 28 letter, though harassing and victimising based on my race and sexuality, wasn't discrimination.

Though the police would still not acknowledge any wrong-doing towards me or others, describing itself as 'disappointed' (again), black and brown people did. Many wrote to me to thank me for what I had done. One prominent black figure wrote: 'I salute you for the enormous courage you have displayed in seeing this through. I hope that today's ruling will signal a new chapter of hope and renewal for you most importantly, and for others. Your case sends out such an important signal that such discrimination is not acceptable.'[13]

The Gay Police Association would not condemn Scotland Yard for its homophobic discrimination, but one gay police leader wrote to me privately, to acknowledge my fight for LGBT rights in the Force, saying: 'Your sheer doggedness has won much support and admiration.' Apparently he had 'moni-tored' things, and told me that he was supporting another officer who was perceived to be gay by his colleagues:

> *He is in a very very bad way mentally as a result of years of abuse and disappointment in the Met. I agree that we can trumpet as much as we like about improvements and advances*

> *but colleagues who harbour racist/homophobic views can by*
> *using guile and the unwillingness of others to stand up, still*
> *wreck havoc in an individual's life.*[14]

In stark contrast, the BPA was hot on the commissioner's heels.[15] Its president at the time, Charles Crichlow, later invited me to speak at the 13th National Black Police Association Conference[16] being held at the College of Policing (which took over from the National Policing Improvement Agency) in the West Midlands. Ruwan Uduwerage-Perera, chair of the Ethnic Minority Liberal Democrats, came to the talk in Coventry and wrote to me, 'You left a lasting and very positive impression on the audience today . . . People need to hear of your experiences so that they realise the need for police reform.'[17] I was glad that people understood why I had chosen to walk this difficult, lonely road.

Scotland Yard was not responding to the ruling, aside from describing itself as disappointed once more in the senior court's judgment. I decided that, since people needed to hear about my experiences, I should take my story to them. I agreed to be interviewed by national newspapers, radio stations and television channels. I would ask for no payment, for expenses or otherwise. The first interview I did was with *The Guardian*. My lawyer Courtenay and I travelled to the newspaper's headquarters in King's Cross. In the restaurant, we met Vikram Dodd, the crime correspondent. Vikram asked if we would like something to eat or drink. I said no. I was so worried about how it might look, taking free food from a newspaper during such an important interview, that I sat there for several hours, hungry, watching them eat. I dared not risk anything.

I told Vikram that I had been made to feel like an 'enemy of the state' by an establishment I had served dutifully for over two decades, if I included the cadet forces.[18] I had always felt that because I finally challenged the discrimination and wrongdoing in the police, they had set out to break, damage and destroy my credibility and me. Vikram noted that Scotland Yard had lost the appeal on 'at least 40 points'. 'Then they sacked you?' he asked. I said yes.

Vikram paused the interview and went outside for a smoke. After he came back, he sat down and said that he couldn't grasp how they had fired me after forty unlawful acts of degrading and humiliating treatment.

Though I've never considered myself a 'whistle-blower' (because I went to the police first), Vikram's *Guardian* article about the case questioned the police's treatment of whistle-blowers and said that their behaviour undermined claims from top officers that they could sort out wrongdoing themselves. The paper reported that I'd gone to the leadership 'privately' about my concerns, but it was the police chiefs who turned the whole thing into a very public bitter fight to stop me.

On a broader and more important issue, the paper commented on my belief that stopping and searching black and Asian members of the public under the guise of terrorism legislation fuelled resentment and was deeply worrying. I told them that I thought we should be catching terrorists, not creating them.

The *Times* crime editor, Sean O'Neill, who had covered my case closely, came to interview me at the McCue law offices in Knightsbridge for a feature for the paper's 'Times2' supplement. He brought along a photographer who had recently taken a portrait of the former American president George W. Bush. I didn't want to have my picture taken, because I had let myself go during this entire ordeal. I had been comfort-eating, but lacked any motivation to exercise. But both newspapers wanted a photograph to accompany their articles, so I did my best. Sean wrote that my fight against the country's biggest police force had taken its toll on me and that I was 'heavier than when I last saw him, fatter around the face and more dishevelled in a loose blue shirt'. One friend, astonished, asked, 'How could he write such a thing?' I replied, 'Because it's the truth.'

Sean's article brought a tear to my eye. It was quite something to see myself described as the person I was, and had always been, and not the dangerous element the police had made me out to be: 'He was every inch the model of a twenty-first century policeman: black, gay, intelligent, articulate, a university graduate from a working-class background in inner-city Liverpool. There was barely a box in the diversity dictionary he couldn't tick.'[19] Sean's succinct summary of the years of hell I had been through were spot-on too. He wrote:

> [This] was not just personal, but institutional . . . When Maxwell complained and sought to challenge the Metropolitan Police, the full corporate weight of the organisation was thrown into battle against him. More than 30 officers and staff – including his overall boss, the head of counter terrorism – lined up to testify against him at an employment tribunal. Even after he resigned and had been sent a P45, the Met decided to reinstate him so that it could hold a gross misconduct tribunal – behind closed doors.

I explained that I didn't celebrate after the high court judge's ruling, because the magnitude of the losses made it feel as though there was nothing to celebrate. 'There are no winners,' I told him. I just survived. Sean finished his two-page feature on me with the words: 'Mentioning Maxwell's name in policing circles was often met with raised eyebrows and a nudge-nudge suggestion that: "Well, he's got an agenda, he's making it all up isn't he?" For a man who the Met seemed to regard as an enemy of the state, he is passionate about Queen, country and public service.'

BBC television came to interview me for the news, at the McCue offices. I hated the way I looked and sounded. I was so exhausted by the ordeal, but was committed to making my story heard. The interview was broadcast at lunchtime on BBC One,[20] on 22 May 2013, and was scheduled to be shown throughout the day; but tragically, the soldier Lee Rigby was murdered that day, near the Royal Artillery barracks in Woolwich. Lee's murder by two black men was a terrible and senseless death that reminded me of the ways news reporting could be swayed by the tide of impassioned public opinion. A BBC producer told me that the corporation struggled to air programmes about police wrongdoing after the death or serious injury of an officer, because the public had no appetite for it. In fact, I remember this from my years in the Force. I had policed the funeral of Detective Constable Stephen Oake at Manchester Cathedral, guarding Prime Minister Tony Blair's car. Stephen had been stabbed to death in 2003 by would-be bioterrorist Kamel Bourgass during an anti-terror raid at a flat in Crumpsall. He had been killed in the line of duty. In September 2012, Dale Cregan, a white Englishman, killed two police officers from my former Force, along with two members of the public. Constables Nicola Hughes and Fiona Bone were ambushed by Cregan after he made a hoax call to the police. He shot them numerous times, firing 32 shots in 31 seconds, and threw an M75 hand grenade at them.

Knowing that so many officers had sacrificed themselves to protect the people they served sometimes made me feel immensely guilty for coming forward and saying that I had issues with the police. I never set out to challenge the police. There was a reason that policing had always been my dream. But it had become a nightmare, and I had a duty towards the minority officers of the future. I had to expose the injustices in all their ugliness. After an interview on BBC Radio Merseyside's *Upfront* programme (for Liverpool's black community) with the presenter Ngunan Adamu,[21] Courtenay and I travelled to the BBC's new headquarters in central London to be interviewed by Victoria Derbyshire live on air, nationwide, on BBC Radio 5 Live.[22] Some of my friends didn't want me to go on because they didn't like Victoria's style of interviewing. Courtenay wasn't sure himself, saying, 'We don't know whether these guys are going to be nice to you or not.'[23] In the interview, Victoria brought up the dismissal and spoke about the 'thousands' of allegations I had made, and then corrected the number to 'hundreds'. I corrected her, reminding her that more than forty acts of un-lawful discrimination had been committed against me prior to my so-called sacking, but there were only three claims: the discrimination, leak and dismissal. The court's own document, 'Summary of the Findings', listed the forty-one incidents (paragraphed) concerning Heathrow (forty-two, including the leak to *The Sun*) over a two-year period, covering my experiences at Terminal 3 and Terminal 5 before I fell ill, and contact after.[24] To report 'hundreds' of incidents or claims was simply a way to make me look vexatious.

I found that many people misunderstood how discrimination law worked. In my claim, I wrote down what took place during my time in the Met until I fell ill. There was no itemised list or rota of names. I simply put down on paper what had happened, as faithfully as I could recall. My lawyers at Russell Jones & Walker used this document to work out where the commissioner may have broken the law and discriminated against me. One incident could bring about numerous breaches of equality. One interaction could have been both racist and homophobic – resulting in six counts from one interaction: race discrimination, harassment and victimisation with sexual orientation discrimination, harassment and victimisation. I hadn't picked these acts out and slotted them in; the law viewed my treatment according to understood parameters.

At the beginning of July, Courtenay and I travelled to the ITV television studios on London's Southbank, to appear alongside the chairman of the UK Parliament's Home Affairs Committee, Keith Vaz, on *Daybreak*, ITV's live national breakfast show at the time. As with BBC Radio 5 Live, I didn't want to do it for several reasons, one being that the one of the two hosts, John Stapleton, had been a long supporter of the police and I didn't want to get into a tit-for-tat spat with him – but my lawyers wanted to keep the conversation going. The interview went as expected. After I talked with Stapleton about discrimination and wrongdoing, he reminded the viewers that I had been 'dismissed'. At 6.55 a.m., he read out the Met's statement: 'Since that time, there have been changes across a number of areas, including how to report wrongdoing and managing employees on sick leave.'[25]

In contrast to this statement, in yet another report about racism in the Force, the IPCC said that Met investigators were often wrongly rejecting allegations of racism simply on the basis of an officer's denial: 'The force tends to respond only to "overt" racism such as the use of the word "nigger" and when other evidence such as mobile phone footage or whistle-blower testimony is provided.'[26]

I wasn't surprised to learn that two thirds of appeals concerning racism complaints rejected by Scotland Yard were later upheld by the IPCC. Unveiling the report, Deborah Glass, the IPCC's commissioner for London, said that racism remained a 'toxic' issue for the Met and that big changes were urgently needed. Channel 4's *Dispatches* followed up with national statistics highlighting the failings within the police. The figures were staggering, and it wasn't only the Met – Britain's largest force, which polices the country's most diverse city. Though it upheld just 20 out of 4,730 allegations of racism, or 0.4%, three other Forces – Greater Manchester, North Yorkshire and Lancashire – upheld none of the allegations reported to them, which at Manchester (my former Force) numbered more than 500.[27] Though you cannot legislate against them, prejudice, bigotry and suspicion of the 'other' – the young black man, the veiled Muslim woman, the gay person – is prevalent throughout our society, and as long as our institutions, like the police, uphold those suspicions, we will never break out of the shackles of racism, Islamophobia or homophobia.

An article in *The Guardian* from July 2013 by Hugh Muir, entitled 'Racism and the police: an insider's view', cites Leroy Logan, the black former superintendent who had just left the job after thirty years:

> *'The problem is cultural,' he says. 'If officers felt they were going to be held to account, things would be different.' . . . 'Too many sergeants are constables with stripes,' he says. 'They don't want to be unpopular. In terms of race, they acquiesce. They see things, hear things and do nothing. If someone is a whistleblower, they talk them out of it. They don't want to be seen as agents of change.' And so, he says, the culture persists and swallows people. . . . 'During training, you would see raw recruits radicalised – there is no other word for it. They'd meet a certain kind of officer and within weeks it would change them.'*[28]

In the meantime, my fight went on.

With the appeal judgment delivered, the Reading employment tribunal gave notice of the remedy hearing for claims one and two (the discrimination and leak to the *Sun* newspaper),[29] about the impact of the unlawful acts committed against me.

Though the police commissioner had been found liable for racism and homophobia towards me, there was no causation report as to what made me ill with depression. In this claim of psychiatric (personal) injury, as opposed to injury to feelings, both the police and I were allowed to submit our own reports. The police wanted to avoid this. On top of the commissioner being found guilty of discrimination, it would be bad for the Force to have been the official cause of my depression. At the same time, Parliament published my evidence to the Home Affairs Committee on leadership and standards in the police,[30] which the *Independent* newspaper ran with a photograph of me outside the Houses of Parliament.[31] In that evidence, it was noted that the high court judge, Mr Justice Supperstone, concluded that the police commissioner had made an appeal that was 'without merit'. The commissioner had pushed for the appeal to his detriment and at considerable cost to the public purse. D'Orsi and Quantrell had been promoted to police superintendents.

Including the number of hours worked by officers and staff, together with emails, documents, statements and meetings in luxury hotels throughout the country, witnesses at tribunal, a six-week hearing and an appeal, my case was estimated to have cost the taxpayer two million pounds. Much of this went on the police's legal fees, in particular to its barrister, Philip Mead. The Force would not disclose his fees and public money received, despite a Freedom of Information Act request.

In June, I received a letter that said that the employment tribunal was to have a case management discussion to hear the third claim, the 'dismissal', at the aptly named Victory House court in central London.[32] My lawyers were concerned. Counsel wanted us to have the same judge, Byrne, from the initial hearing, to give me *any* chance of success again – because, they said, 'All the others are pro-police.'[33]

The hearing was postponed whilst the judge for claim three was decided.[34] The employment judge, Judge Potter, later said that 'the claim will remain at London Central', despite Kweku arguing for it to go back to Reading.[35] Judge Lewzey said the third claim would be heard in January 2014 over three weeks at the Central London tribunal, and following this the remedy for all three claims (if the third was successful) was to be heard in March 2014 by the Reading tribunal.[36]

I wasn't interested in overturning the dismissal – or I would have appealed to the police reinstatement panel at the Home Office (the Police Appeals Tribunal), who could have reinstated me due to the flaws in the process – because I didn't want to return to the police. It was over for me. I didn't want to go back like Gurpal Virdi had, after his racism case. When he finally left the police in 2012, Virdi was only the twelfth officer of colour to have completed all thirty years of service in London. Years later, the Sikh former officer was arrested for a second time by Scotland Yard whilst running to be a local councillor in London. He was accused of sexually assaulting an underage prisoner some thirty years earlier whilst on duty. Virdi's case went to trial with a jury taking less than fifty minutes to clear him of all charges.[37] The judge noted the likelihood of a conspiracy behind the case by the police.

I wanted a tribunal to rule that what had been done to me was discriminatory, that they had forced me out, so that it couldn't happen to others when they challenged wrongdoing in the police. There were many obstacles. The Police Federation wouldn't fund the lawyers at McCue. The police's misconduct panel was also protected by judicial immunity (similar to a military court martial).

Like Russell Jones & Walker, McCue wanted me to settle the claims. 'I believe it has gone beyond settling,' I said curtly. Courtenay reminded me that 'the employment tribunal can award costs against someone acting unreasonably'.[38] Claimants were often threatened with the cost of losing; if the police lost, the public would pay.

The Met arranged for me to see its appointed consultant psychiatrist, Dr David Gill in Harley Street, for *their* medical report on me.[39] Dr Gill was now the fifth psychiatrist I was to see. I had to consent to his seeing my medical records from birth.[40] Dr Gill asked that I be accompanied, so Alice, a friend I had made in the hostel, came with me. I researched this doctor before I saw him, having learnt the hard way from my experience with Dr Hindler. Dr Gill had just written a public report, 'Proving and Disproving Psychiatric Injury'.[41] I could guess why the Met had chosen him. Alice and I arrived just before 10 a.m. Dr Gill outlined what his role was and that he had been given two tasks by the police: to assess (1) the impact the found discrimination had on me and (2) whether I was disabled under the Equality Act (if not, the police's treatment after I returned could be justified despite Witherington acknowledging 'disability under Equality Act 2010' in his risk assessment). Dr Gill asked me questions about my childhood, and my service in the cadet forces and the police. He said he was sorry about the breakdown of my marriage, of which he hadn't been aware, as the police had not told him, and also sorry to hear that I was on benefits and living in a hostel. Afterwards, Alice, who had sat behind me listening, said she found the consultation 'strange'.

In her notes of the meeting, she wrote: '[Dr Gill] stated that he thought it was evident that Maxwell was wronged and that the experiences with the Metropolitan Police had clearly affected him mentally.'[42] Dr Gill pointed out that his allegiance (my word, not his) didn't lie with the police (I assumed he meant that it lay with the tribunal). To my surprise, I found Dr Gill to be a thoroughly nice man. I felt at ease with him and trusted him. He was everything I had hoped the doctors Oxlade and Hindler would be – empathetic. After an hour and a half of talking and answering questions, he informed Alice and me that he would be unable to complete his report because he needed more time, given the complexity of the case and impact on me. Between us, we arranged for me to see him again the next month. Alice and I thanked Dr Gill and left to head back to the hostel.

Following my previous interview with the newspaper's crime correspondent, *The Independent* asked for my view on arbitrary terror arrests for which the police were under fire.[43] The IPCC were investigating twenty-five complaints about Schedule 7 detentions, the law that allowed officers to detain people for up to nine hours without reasonable suspicion that they were involved in terrorism. Failure to cooperate could mean facing up to three months in prison. This was more than enough to intimidate anyone. Scotland Yard was facing legal action after being given an ultimatum to hand over evidence alleging misuse of the powers by officers. Those same powers I had told the tribunal were being misused. The police watchdog gave the Force seven days to hand over its findings, after the Met's 'consistent refusal' to investigate the wrongdoing.

Britain's biggest Force refused to disclose why some passengers were stopped, many of them being ethnic minorities. My former colleagues at Heathrow had just used the controversial law to stop David Miranda as he went through the airport on his way to Brazil where he lived with his partner, the *Guardian* journalist Glenn Greenwald (who was involved in the Edward Snowden case).[44]

As reported by the *Evening Standard* in November 2013, the UK's Supreme Court used a judgment 'on the use of terrorism law to convict the London student, Mohammed Gul, for posting al-Qaeda and Taliban material on YouTube' to '[warn] that Schedule 7 powers used to detain the boyfriend of journalist Glenn Greenwald at Heathrow could lead to "serious invasions of personal liberty" and called on ministers to respond by narrowing the "wide" definition of terrorism'[45] – that carte blanche my former colleagues enjoyed. My views on Schedule 7 and all terror legislation remained the same. I had said before that if it is not done properly it can undermine the integrity of the police's anti-terrorism efforts.

Not long after the appointment with Dr Gill, I received a letter from the employment tribunal asking me why I had walked out of the consultation with the doctor and to give the tribunal an immediate explanation.[46] I was stunned, as no such thing had happened; I never even had a toilet break. Alongside their letter to me, the tribunal attached a letter from the police's lawyer, Jacqueline Morris. In this letter, Morris told the tribunal: 'Dr Gill has advised the respondent that he was unable to complete his examination of the claimant because the claimant left the examination midway through the appointment.'[47] Alice was furious. She wrote to Dr Gill, 'I am baffled at your dishonesty. If this is an attempt to discredit Mr Maxwell, I cannot help but think that you have only discredited yourself by uttering such a bald-faced lie.'[48]

The material from the tribunal to me also included a two-page draft order Morris had written to the tribunal, stating that as I had walked out midway through the consultation, unless I agreed to a further examination with Dr Gill the psychiatric injury part of the case should be struck out. I believe that they had found out that Dr Gill had felt empathy for my plight, and this the police could not allow. I wrote to Dr Gill about the strange letter from Jacqueline Morris to the tribunal.[49] He responded:

> *Those who provided me with instructions appear to have said that I was unable to complete my assessment because you left the appointment midway through. My understanding of events is different, in that after about one and a half hours or so, you were starting to get upset, and it had become clear that we were not going to be able to finish what was inevitably going to be a long interview in the allocated two hours. Accordingly, I advised that we end there for the time being, and reconvene for a second appointment, and you kindly agreed.*[50]

Dr Gill said that the position the police had put him in had affected the trust between us that was necessary to carry out his medico-legal interview, 'especially in such a highly sensitive matter as the present case'. He finished with the words: 'I feel that I have been put in a difficult position.' He then stated that he had recused himself from the police and from acting for them, and returned their papers to them.

I wrote to the central London employment tribunal about Morris's untrue letter concerning Dr Gill, copying Morris into the communication.[51] I even attached a copy of Dr Gill's letter to me. A couple of days later, McCue wrote to the employment tribunal about the matter, attaching a copy of Dr Gill's letter to me and Morris's letter to the tribunal. Referring to the fact that the police now had no opinion on me by a medical expert, McCue wrote:

> *This situation was caused by the respondent making disin-genuous statements regarding the claimant in its application for strike out sent to the tribunal dated 1 October 2013. Dr Gill, who was to be the respondent's own medical expert, agrees that the respondent is wrong to claim before the tribunal that the claimant had walked out of the consultation midway through. He clarified that this is not what happened at all, as in fact it was the doctor who asked to end the interview early.*[52]

Through their own continued spitefulness towards me, the police now had no medical report to put an end to our dispute, and I would have to see another psychiatrist on the public purse to conclude this chapter of my life.

14

Darkest Before Dawn

At the beginning of November, I received a letter from the IPCC. In it, the deputy chair Deborah Glass acknowledged the 'impact of the leak' to *The Sun* and said that the decision of the IPCC was to uphold the complaint to them that the leak did come from the Met.[1] She noted the 'strong recommendation that the MPS should acknowledge the overall distress caused and apologise'. Of course, I did not receive any apology from the police, although the Met went on to apologise to my estranged husband for leaking my data and endangering him.[2]

With the Police Federation refusing to fund McCue to fight the remedy concerning claims one and two, never mind claim three, my relationship with them ended. If I still wanted to hold the police liable for my illness, I had to go with the employment solicitors Pattinson & Brewer, the only firm the police union would pay any monies from my insurance to.

Along with the personal (psychiatric) injury pursuit for claims one and two I decided that I had to also get claim three – the dismissal – out into the open, and so force the commissioner to disclose further documents that would point to his wrongdoing into open public debate. I had told McCue I was going through with this claim 'on a matter of principle if nothing else'.[3]

In November, Alice and I attended the preliminary hearing

(case management discussion) for claim three at the Central London employment tribunal. With no legal representation, I sat alone at the claimant's table whilst Mead and Morris sat at the respondent's. Out of the corner of my eye, I could see Alice shifting with frustration at the hostile atmosphere in the tribunal. Nevertheless, four years after I was first diagnosed with the depression the police had so strenuously denied, their barrister Mead told the tribunal that he now had 'formal instructions to concede the fact of disability'.[4] The tribunal concluded that 'the claimant is disabled for the purposes of [the] Equality Act. He suffered from depression at the material time'.[5]

But that wasn't all. As the hearing was wrapping up, Mead spoke again. He disclosed that one of the members of the white three-man panel that had 'dismissed' me from the police was a lay member of the central London employment tribunal, literally the tribunal we were sitting in. When a police officer faces a disciplinary misconduct panel, he or she usually presents themselves before three senior police officers, just like a military court martial. In my case, one of the officers was substituted for a member of the London court, Roger Lucking,[6] sitting with Commander Dave Martin and Chief Superintendent Simon Ovens, and nobody decided to tell my former lawyers or me. Lucking's identity was only revealed just under a year later. I raised this conflict of interest with the tribunal,[7] but was told it would be 'placed on the file'[8] and that a judge from outside London would now look into claim three's resolution.

I decided to go ahead with the third claim and agreed to a new judge being brought in from the counties, not because I believed the proceedings would swing in my favour – impossible in the circumstances – but so that all the documents would have to be disclosed in the new proceedings. Without these documents, this book would not be complete. The public – the people I'd served faithfully, the people whose opinion mattered to me – would be able to judge the truth for themselves. My Manchester police records – such as the grievance, Dr Hindler's report and the undisclosed Met documents, like the *Monkey Times* for example – would all become public (disclosed and bundled into the open court files) as part of the proceedings for claim three. More importantly, this included what took place at the secret misconduct hearing, with Lucking's involvement.

Writing in *The Independent* and citing my case, Paul Peachey, the crime correspondent, said that the last, and only, time the police had held a public misconduct hearing was for Simon Harwood, 'the thuggish police officer who struck a London *Evening Standard* newspaper-seller during the G20 riots'.[9] Harwood had struck Ian Tomlinson and pushed him to the ground. His face was covered by a balaclava and he had hidden his shoulder numbers (something riot officers often did). Tomlinson got up, walked about sixty metres, then collapsed, his face grey. An ITV reporter and a medical student who attempted to give medical aid were forced away by the police and police medics. On arrival at hospital, Tomlinson was pronounced dead. Later, Harwood would be acquitted of the manslaughter of Tomlinson at a criminal trial. Tomlinson's family described the police misconduct hearing as a 'whitewash'. Both the inquest and court hearings exposed systemic police failings, and raised the question of why Harwood was allowed to remain an officer when there was a stack of previous allegations against his name.

Binder Bansel, the partner at Pattinson & Brewer (my third law firm) held a meeting with me along with the assistant solicitor, Joanne Cameron. Binder was only authorised by the Police Federation to fight the remedy concerning claims one and two (whether the police had caused me mental abuse, and whether any compensation was due), but he was so concerned about my treatment following my return to work that he advised I write to the Police Federation to seek its approval for him to act for me regarding the third claim.[10]

However, Binder also had a few concerns. He didn't think

I was well enough to go through another tribunal process at that time; there also wasn't a lot of time for him to read the papers in the case before the hearing; Kweku, my former barrister (who had in the end agreed to help with claim three), was no longer available, due to having to work on another case.

Binder asked me if he could write to the tribunal for a postponement until he felt I was fit to give evidence.[11] I agreed and visited my GP for his expert opinion. In his medical report, my GP wrote: 'In my opinion he remains vulnerable [as] regards his mental health . . . As his medical practitioner, I think the date set is too soon in view of him having to meet with and work with a completely new legal team. It would affect his mental health at this stage. He will require more time.'[12] The police's lawyer, Jacqueline Morris, objected on behalf of the commissioner.[13] The central London tribunal supported the police and refused to postpone the hearing. Not only was I unwell, but Binder had to find alternative counsel. He eventually found the barrister John Horan, of Cloisters chambers. The tribunal would be overseen by Judge Alastair Smail, brought in from Watford.

As the day of the hearing for claim three came closer, a new bundle of documents and witness statements was exchanged. The bundle again excluded unredacted documents; the Force told Binder that any further documents were considered 'not relevant' (by the police).[14]

It was my right in law to see everything, especially the minutes of undisclosed gold groups, and other undisclosed documents which dealt with my management. I also, crucially, required the metadata showing the changes to the previous documents disclosed, like the gold group minutes (and any other documents that had been changed).

At first, and unsurprisingly, the commissioner resisted disclosing these further documents, and Judge Smail supported him. It wasn't until my new counsel threatened to proceed with a tribunal order, that the police decided to disclose rather than be forced to hand over documents – if their resistance became publicly known, it would look very bad for them. The disclosed new documents revealed that further gold groups had been held without my knowledge.

One particular gold group meeting stood out. In it, the MPS said they accepted my resignation, but were determined to pursue dismissal if I didn't return to work. The group also discussed occupational health disclosing the secret documents written by Bailey and others about me. Bailey told the meeting: 'Maxwell's OH [occupational health] file, in its entirety, has been given to him by OH.' Commander Richard Walton said it was an 'error of judgment to disclose [the] file', though I had lawful access to this medical file, as it was about me.[15]

Other documents from my seniors that I read saddened me, but Bailey's report requesting my suspension, now unredacted, shook me to my core.[16] It was written by her the same day I instructed my lawyers to resist the appeal by the commissioner against my successful claims concerning discrimination and the leak, and the same day that the Sikh sergeant at St Pancras wrote his stinging report about racism in the Metropolitan Police, and particularly counter terrorism.

Unbeknownst to me, my seniors had been going through my social media to see if they could find anything to discredit me whilst I was fighting the appeal of claims one and two.

Over the years, ethnic minority members of the public and staff had written to me privately about racism in the police. Some messages I saw and was able to read and respond to, others not. Under the heading of 'Dissatisfaction with employer & use of social media', Bailey wrote that documents attached to her report at '1F' (which have never been disclosed to me) 'suggest that KM is in receipt of a message from a Twitter account that has also been sending messages to what appear to be AQ [al-Qaeda] sympathisers.' She went on: 'The document at 1G contains an extract from an Islamic Human Rights Commission report where evidence presented by DC Maxwell at his employment tribunal is referenced' and 'clearly this puts him again in the public arena where he may be judged by some as an approachable target.'

I felt that, for some people, Bailey's report would have had a clearly negative interpretation. I was informed that Bailey did not, or mean to, connect me to those who sympathised with al-Qaeda. But given the other things she had written about me, it was hard not to feel that this was intended to harm my reputation. Bailey had after all written it in order to have my vetting suspended, which would have meant that I would be thrown out of the police.

To this day, I am unaware of any such message being sent to my Twitter account (it's never been produced). It is on the public record (this book documents it) that, although I am neither Asian nor Muslim, I have spoken up for Asian people who I believe have been victims of racism (as per evidence presented by me at tribunal). I detest all forms of hatred, including towards white people, like my mother. The Islamic Human Rights Commission report Bailey cited was a news article by the UK Muslim organisation – which, though legitimate, I have had no dealings with – which reported on the comments I made at the open employment tribunal whilst in the witness box.[17]

What made Bailey's report all the more nonsensical was that she had written it forty-one days before her boss, Superintendent Jones, gave me that 'lawful order' to return to work in 'counter terrorism' whilst unwell until I left the police, or else I would be fired. I'd also just been re-vetted by the specialist crime directorate SCD26 and my security clearance had been maintained.

Even if I accept that it was never Bailey's intention to be hurtful towards me, reports like this can and do have serious consequences for law-abiding people of colour. Imagine if I wasn't who I am – a gay man raised a Catholic – but Asian, and Muslim? 'No smoke without fire', the rumour mill would say.

Abdul Rahman, an Asian former Met officer, had been

accused of attending a 'terror training camp' before joining the Force. He resigned from Scotland Yard after senior officers revoked his security clearance. Rahman sued the commissioner over discrimination, denying attending any training camps. After a five-year legal battle, an employment appeal tribunal ruled that his case could be held, but in secret. Mr Justice Mitting, a high court judge, ruled that Rahman and his legal team be banned from parts of the hearing that concerned issues of 'national security'. Scotland Yard had applied to have Rahman's case heard in secret as it wanted to protect its intelligence, which was the basis for the judge's decision. Rahman's lawyer, Jasmine van Loggerenberg of Russell Jones & Walker, the police union's main firm, highlighted that he'd never been arrested, questioned or charged under terrorism legislation. The final outcome of his case is not known.

My MP, Emily Thornberry, wrote to James Brokenshire, the Conservative minister of state for security and immigration at the time, about the police going through my communications, which was protected by a warrant under the Regulation of Investigatory Powers Act 2000 (RIPA). The minister said it was 'unlawful' for him to confirm its existence under section 19(1) of RIPA.[18] RIPA is an Act that regulates the powers of public bodies to carry out surveillance and investigation, covering the interception of communications. The Home Secretary has to sign any such warrant for the police commissioner. RIPA was intended for the purpose of preventing or detecting serious crime and for safeguarding the economic well-being of the UK – and I, by seeking justice for the discrimination I faced (the racism and homophobia), was apparently enough of a threat. As long as I had been in the service, flimsy RIPA warrants had been signed off to spy on those whom the police leaders deemed a threat. My taking on the police force had turned me into one.

★

On the second morning of the new employment hearing, as I was getting ready in the hostel, exhausted and tired by everything, I slipped in the communal shower and fell unconscious. After waking, I was very worried because Judge Smail disliked me already and would think I was making excuses in order not to begin giving my evidence for claim three, that I – rather than go to hospital – travelled to the tribunal in my suit in a state of confused concussion, bloodied and bruised. My lawyers asked that the hearing be postponed, but the judge refused until my counsel, John, demanded it. My lawyer Joanne travelled with me to St Thomas's hospital. I was seen at accident and emergency, and then, given my depression, I was also seen by a mental health nurse.[19] He expressed his confusion as to why a hearing was taking place given the mental state I was in, and wrote as much to the tribunal.[20]

After I returned to the tribunal, still reeling, Judge Smail said the only way the hearing was going to be postponed was if my GP wrote to him. I travelled from the tribunal to my GP's surgery for an emergency appointment. The supervising doctor – my GP was not on duty – wrote to the judge:

> *He has been suffering with marked reactive depression . . . for which he takes daily anti-depressant medication. He came to see his own General Practitioner . . . as his mood had deteriorated . . . [My usual doctor] wrote a letter stating that his court date should be postponed . . . as he wasn't fit to attend due to his current mental health. Unfortunately, this letter wasn't taken into full consideration and the hearing went ahead as planned this week. Mr Maxwell's health wasn't conducive to attending court in any case, but having done so, this resulted in a significant worsening of his condition.[21]*

The senior doctor finished by stating the fact that I was not fit to be cross-examined or give instructions to my lawyers, now or in the immediate future.

Binder wrote to me[22] about correspondence he had received[23] from Judge Smail: 'The tribunal remains hostile to the notion of the hearing being postponed.' The judge also threatened costs against me, which Binder said was 'unduly harsh and unsympathetic to your plight.' My lawyers were so concerned about Smail's hostility that they told me, further to their meeting with counsel, that I should look at the *Equal Treatment Bench Book* and consider whether any aspects under 'vulnerable adults' applied to me.[24] Section 20 of the Equality Act 2010 expects courts to make reasonable adjustments in order to remove barriers for people with disabilities, like depression.

I had to go and see two further psychiatrists, numbers six and seven, one for police's lawyers again (because Dr Gill had refused to work for the Force) and one for mine, to assess my mental capacity to give further evidence and the cause of my depression (which the police now admitted). They were odd and unpleasant meetings, though both doctors acknowledged I had suffered from severe depression. Dr Christopher Howard at Harley Street asked if I had been bullied at school – I hadn't: my primary-school and secondary-school days were some of the happiest of my life. In light of the fact that I was gay, Dr Paul McLaren (who now worked at the Priory with Dr Hindler) asked whether I had been 'sexually abused' as a child (nothing could be further from the truth). My friend, Stephe, who came with me, wrote 'how odd' and 'unnecessary' the comment had been.[25] My life was examined for faults, and they considered the question whether I had overstated the level of prejudice in the police.

In June 2014, a new hearing began. The Met's witnesses denied treating me differently because of my race and sexuality. Chief Inspector Bailey and Lesleyanne Ellis did not provide a statement or appear. Judge Smail said the incident with the Sikh sergeant, and Sergeant Witherington going behind my back and betraying my confidence, was 'unfortunate'. Witherington stood by his actions. After congratulating him on passing his inspector's exam, the judge asked Witherington to comment on my progress and documents at Manchester, though he had never served alongside me at this Force.

Superintendent Jones commented in tribunal that, because of my success in proving that the 'Schedule 7 stops' (the 'buffering') had been based on racial discrimination, the police had had to change how they implemented terror legislation.

During the hearing, the Met sent more documents that they should have disclosed years ago. There were documents from Commander Richard Walton's 'personal (email) folder' on me going back to spring 2012, including an email to Assistant Commissioner Cressida Dick expressing concern that I'd succeeded with the discrimination case concerning Schedule 7 stops made under terrorism law.[26] Under the Data Protection Act, Dick had an obligation to disclose all documentation she held about me. She is now the commissioner of the Met Police (the first woman to hold that post). She has spoken about more stop and search around the issue of knife crime, with an emphasis on tougher sentences for 'teenage thugs'.[27] If I've learnt anything from the police, more stops are not the answer and neither is heavy-handed policing or longer prison sentences.

There is little research on whether stop and search actually prevents and deters crime.[28] Section 60 of the Criminal Justice and Public Order Act 1994 (a blanket stop and search granting the police wide powers) requires no reasonable suspicion on the officers' part, and yet the Home Office's recent report found that this power, which is often used to reduce knife and violent crime, has no effect.[29] Under Section 60, black people are forty times more likely to be stopped and searched, 'doing untold damage' to minority communities.[30] Expanding the use of this tactic, as is often suggested, seriously fails to address the harm it does and has not come close to resolving serious youth violence. BAME communities have been unfairly impacted by stop and search actions. Young people without knives get stopped, are alienated, and some later get involved with them because they have already been labelled a 'thug'.

As the hearing progressed it was becoming apparent that the Force were still withholding documents, particularly from a gold meeting held after they had 'dismissed' me. My barrister John had had enough and demanded that the police hand over everything. The tribunal waited as the police's lawyer Jacqueline Morris telephoned Scotland Yard in open court to explain that she had to disclose the gold group they had failed to disclose earlier. Mead handed over a copy to Judge Smail, who postponed the hearing and went to read it alone in the back office. He returned, and told me that I wouldn't be getting a copy of the unredacted version of the meeting – though I had a right to this under data protection law – but did announce that he was disclosing one aspect of the gold meeting.

After 'dismissing' me a week before Christmas, ten days into the new year, a gold group was held at the top of Scotland Yard.[31] Under Commissioner Bernard Hogan-Howe's 'Total Policing' banner, this one was entitled 'Maxwell'. The meeting was held because, although I was now out of the Force, the leaders saw me as an even greater threat to policing than when I was in it, because I was still publicly challenging the police.

The gold group suggested that the only way to stop my pursuit of justice and equality was to arrest me. If they could arrest and successfully prosecute me, public opinion would finally turn against me and they would have negated the 'harm' I could cause them. The basis on which they wanted to criminalise me was fraud, for the video I had created for YouTube, the 'fight for justice' crowdfunder film. Hearing this was surreal. I wept in open court.

Everybody, especially a detective, knows that fraud is about deceiving people. I could not see how a public video asking for public help to fight a public appeal could be fraudulent.

Nevertheless, even Ellis told the meeting: 'There is a discrepancy with regards the quality of the evidence against Maxwell and whether there is enough evidence for a successful prosecution.' After reading this, my counsel demanded that Ellis attend the tribunal to give evidence, or a formal tribunal order summonsing her would be actioned. She eventually appeared and looked embarrassed about having been forced to come. She did not look at me.

I was not the only person seeking justice for discrimination whom the Met had considered arresting. Carol Howard, a black police officer who had been in touch with me privately through Facebook, eventually won her case for race and sex discrimination against the Met;[32] in February 2015, the *Evening Standard* reported that 'in a statement confirming the settlement – understood to be for claims for wrongful arrest and harassment – Scotland Yard said, "PC Carol Howard and the Metropolitan Police have agreed a final settlement of all her (existing) legal claims against the Metropolitan Police and accepted her resignation from the service."'[33]

After Carol won her claim, it emerged that she had been arrested by the police no less than three times. Carol said the arrests were motivated by revenge, because she had made a stand against bullying. The tribunal found the Met had tried to 'deflect' negative publicity by releasing details of her arrests. The arrests led nowhere and the allegations were dropped.

After a tough three-week hearing, Judge Smail handed down his judgment about what took place after I returned to work at St Pancras and leading up to my 'dismissal' (that is, the third claim).[34] According to Smail, I had not been on the receiving end of any further discrimination. His decision included a defence of the horrid documents written by Chief Inspector Bailey, who did not turn up in court.

On the subject of whether I had resigned or not, the judge said my challenge to the police having terminated me in 'error' and without my signing any resignation forms was significant, because it recorded my position as withdrawing the resignation: I 'deliberately' didn't fill in the resignation forms. But at no point did I withdraw my resignation. My email to Bailey from 3 August 2012 had stated that 'my resigning from the MPS stands', and in the final sentence of that email I'd said I was going to challenge what happened to me 'as a civilian', i.e. no longer a police officer. Although my email did mention delaying my final date, there was no response from the police until the issuing of the P45 ending our relationship on 17 September. Regardless of what I said, it is not possible to reverse a termination without officially re-employing the employee; and as far as my 'deliberately' not signing the forms is concerned – when I received the resignation forms, as documented, I had no legal or police union advice.

Judge Smail called the fact of the police changing public documents, like the gold groups minutes, to show the commissioner in a more favourable light, 'unsatisfactory features', and said that the police 'needs to take care' – though it was clearly, in my view, a case of evidence being added or altered after the fact.

Concluding, Smail said that I should have obeyed Superintendent Jones's order and travelled to Sydenham on public transport, though I was very unwell. The judge said that when Jones gave me the order in June, I had not established that my mental impairment was such that I could not travel. This statement was all the more extraordinary, because in his judgment regarding my mental state days before Jones's order, Smail had written: 'The claimant certainly comes across as mentally unwell in this email' – referring to an email I had sent on 1 June.[35] The Reading and London Central tribunals then ruled that it would be Judge Smail, the judge who was hostile towards me, who would hear the remedy regarding the successful claims one and two the week before Christmas – rather than Judge Byrne, who had originally ruled on them.[36] I had new counsel too, the barrister Giles Powell of Old Square Chambers, who was assisted by Jennifer Danvers of Cloisters chambers. Smail (fortunately) could not overturn the judgment of the two previous claims and over forty counts of unlawful discrimination and leaking to *The Sun*, so he attacked me in another way. He criticised me for writing an eighteen-page grievance at GMP, taking 'issue' with discrimination and wrongdoing there – 'single-spaced', as he pointed out. I was not aware of a page limit on what I could say about racism and homophobia. He called me, a black gay man fighting for his rights, 'self-centred and sensitive' for writing about my time at GMP.[37]

Though I was to be compensated, I had proved that I had been caused a personal injury (the tribunal found that the proven discrimination materially contributed to the 'causation, exacerbation and continuation' of my depression) as well as injury to feelings (being discriminated against), and though my bad health had been aggravated (by the leaking of my data to *The Sun*) – all by the Met – Smail said there was not a 'deliberate sustained campaign of harassment' against me. Even more odd was the fact that the judge wrote that when I was 'dismissed' (in December) for refusing to travel to Sydenham, I still had not 'recovered' from my depression; but also wrote that, months earlier (in June), when I was given the order to do so, I had not established that my 'mental impairment' was such that I could not travel, despite my GP saying otherwise.

Smail's judgment floored me, but it didn't shake my resolve. He had done as I had been warned by my lawyers, and as I had expected. Courts *were not* the place to battle race discrimination.

Ethnic minorities are hugely under-represented in positions of power, such as police chiefs, psychiatrists and judges. British courts have unjustly treated black people harshly for a long time. Their racial bias towards black and brown people is not new. Trials and judgments have ruined people of colour. In 2017, the Lammy Review – the independent review by the Labour MP David Lammy, sanctioned by the Conservative government

– investigated discrimination in the British justice system.[38] An *Observer* article from October 2018 describes how, at the time the article was written, for every 100 white men convicted of public order offences there were 494 offences for people of colour, many failing the 'attitude test' after a stop and search. There was a greater disproportionality of black people in English and Welsh prisons than in the US: black people represented 3% of Britain's population and 13% of the prison population, compared with 13% and 35% in America. And black people were nine times more likely to be stopped and searched for any reason under Section 1 of PACE (general searches) – a figure that had more than doubled since the report into Stephen Lawrence's murder (and was at its highest rate in over twenty years)[39] – three times more likely to be arrested,[40] three times more likely to be tasered (by stun guns)[41] and four times more likely to be detained under the Mental Health Act.[42]

Since 1990, there have been over 1,700 deaths in police custody or following contact with the police in England and Wales, as recorded by casework and monitoring done by INQUEST (the charity concerned with state-related deaths), resulting in no convictions. A disproportionate number of BAME people die 'as a result of use of force or restraint by the police'.[43] Scotland is not immune. Sheku Bayoh, a black man, died after being restrained by officers in Kirkcaldy in 2015. No police officer was charged over his death.[44] Stephen House, chief constable of Police Scotland at the time, is now deputy commissioner of London's Met. A UN human rights panel said, 'Structural racism [is] at [the] heart of British society.'[45]

For far too long, the police have mobilised an aura of untouchability against the families of those who have died in custody. The Crown Prosecution Service, which was criticised along with the police in the Stephen Lawrence Inquiry, works with the police on so many cases, yet is expected to be 'impartial', like the judiciary, when working against them in cases of death in custody, and such. The police and the state cannot objectively and fairly investigate themselves, especially when the blue wall of silence, that unspoken internal code of conduct, ensures that officers don't rat one another out. In criminal trials in which the police stand accused, jurors are often unwilling to convict officers.

As a result of the war on terror, so many people – in the press, in politics and amongst the public – have a mindset that defaults to excusing dangerous actions: 'It's a hard job, I couldn't do it.' They have to do what they have to do, in order to keep the peace. Often, public opinion has to play catch-up years later. Since the attacks of 9/11 and 7/7, the public have been encouraged to look to the police force as a tough but fair arm of the fight against crime and terror, doing a difficult job in frightening circumstances. Even more so now that counter terrorism is a routine part of policing. They are no longer servants of communities but soldiers in a war, and as with all war zones, there will be casualties. If we want safety, we have to accept those. But I disagree. If we look at it like that, the terrorists have won. People in positions of power and influence must speak out against bad policing, followed by robust action.

I thought Theresa May putting her name in the hat to become the next British prime minister after the resignation of David Cameron was a good thing, but it turned out I was wrong. I was no fan of her politics (what with the 'Go Home' vans suggesting that illegal immigrants should 'go home or face arrest', and the deportation of Commonwealth migrants on her watch), but when it came to the police, she was on point. She had spoken at the National Black Police Association Conference in 2015 about the lack of diversity within the service and the failings of stop and search. Not long before, she had confronted the Police Federation about their scandals and demanded reform. In April 2014, she had said this, regarding the reform of stop and search: 'Nobody wins when stop and search is misapplied.

It is a waste of police time. It's unfair, especially to young black men. It is bad for public confidence in the police.'[46] Never before had a Conservative Home Secretary taken on the police with such vigour. On becoming prime minister in July 2016, standing outside 10 Downing Street in front of the cameras, she said: 'If you're black, you're treated more harshly by the criminal justice system than if you're white.'[47] Her words were not enough. In June 2016, the month before May took over from David Cameron, 42% of under-18s in custody were from a BAME background. By March 2019, this had risen to 49%. As of October 2019, more than half of young people in British jails are BAME.[48] Since she resigned and Boris Johnson took over as Britain's prime minister, those 'burning injustices' May described continue to get worse. Many of these young people frame their understanding of, and interactions with, the state through the police – civilian 'enforcers'. Rather than the answer, policing is the cause of many crimes committed by people of colour. More white people use drugs but more black people are in prison for drug-related offences.

The Met commissioner Cressida Dick says the police is no longer 'institutionally racist'. Britain's most senior cop says the term suggests 'the Met of today is just like the one of 20 years ago.'[49] She's right, it's not. When it comes to racism, it's worse than it was two decades ago. The police cannot change from within, however much they think they can. The leadership's strategy to improve policing will always be safe and never implemented with urgency or compulsion. To truly engage with the changing times, the Force needs to embrace diversity and difference. The police need to examine hard truths. They need to actively listen and accept criticism, even when this means losing face and admitting they are in the wrong.

Writing this book has been the hardest thing I have done, traumatic at times, forcing me to relive the events. Yet it has also been therapeutic, ridding me of demons and hurt, so that I can move forward. Only I get to say how my story ends. They say it takes five years to deinstitutionalise yourself from the Force after leaving. With the end of my tribunal cases, my time is up. I will never trust the police again, and wouldn't call them if their help was needed. My heroes are those who stand up for equality and justice.

Though I will never look at them in the same way, I wish officers no ill. I acknowledge good police work, like with missing persons, and the bravery of officers fighting crime and terrorism, such as Constable Keith Palmer, who died protecting others during the 2017 Westminster terrorist attack outside the Houses of Parliament.

I don't think for a moment that there aren't good cops out there. In my time on the Force, I met a few. And I know more than most the threats faced by the UK and her allies. In 2017, there were 412 'terror' arrests in Great Britain, the highest since records began. Between 2010 and 2017, there were 2,029.[50] But the idea that racism is down to a few bad apples is long gone.

The police mentality that 'not all cops are bad' when it comes to discrimination and wrongdoing demonstrates that, as an institution and individuals, they are avoiding their collective responsibility and accountability to the public, as if to say 'They're not talking about us.' I am. The British police are the last bastion of vested interest. This needs to change, for the common good.

Do I forgive the police? It's not my job to forgive. They have to forgive themselves for what they did, and this involves accepting what they did. I never did receive an apology for the horrific abuse I endured, but I am beyond this. The person who criminally leaked my data, outing me, was never held accountable, and straight white officers who discriminated against me were promoted.

I was the one punished, the black gay detective who stood up against hate and wrongdoing.

Do I regret joining the police? Yes and no. I'm fortunate enough to say I was a boy with a dream who achieved it. I went from Liverpool 8 to SO15 (from riot-ridden Toxteth of the 1980s to the UK's counter terrorism command), against all odds. I gave up on my job, not myself. The police turned out to be nothing like I thought it would be, but everything my white liberal friends told me it would be, and more. If the police had been kind, I could have achieved my true potential. But I also accept that it takes a certain sort of person to be a police officer, and I wasn't it.

During my darkest days, my brother sent me a message from Liverpool:

> *You are unbowed and unbroken, resilient to the core, just like our mum, and how my own three children need to become in order to play a meaningful role in the life of the UK as a person of difference, in order to move the society forward that we live in. I'm proud of you as a man, as my brother, but most of all I am proud of you for giving others hope who may be going through similar experiences.*

Like my mum, I'm a firm believer that 'no hope breeds no hope'. Hope is all I had.

At her funeral, the final hymn was 'Here I am, Lord'. A line reads: 'I will make their darkness bright. Sometimes the brightest light comes from the darkest place.' I no longer allow myself to be downtrodden. I am not responsible for racism, but I have a role to play in ending it. Injustice *can* only be rooted out by continued action, like this book.

I was not and am not any of the awful things the police said. That's the truth.

I'm a believer in the fact that the public can force change in the police after reading stories like mine, that their awareness will be raised if people like me speak out. Through my efforts I sought to improve the climate in which black and other minority officers serve, and make things better for the public. I fought for racial, sexual orientation and mental health justice, through litigation, advocacy and education. I've tried to do my bit. Now it's up to others to drag this nineteenth-century institution into the twenty-first century.

Martin Luther King Jr was right, 'Freedom is never voluntarily given by the oppressor; it must be demanded by the oppressed.' Now I demand it each and every single day. [51]

For those who have suffered an injustice, and 'all the strong black birds of promise who defy the odds and gods and sing their songs', [52] I hear you. I know there is nothing more lonely or terrifying than not being heard. Your lives do matter. Your voices will be heard.

I understand the burden of being black. Our world *is* different.

So many of our stories don't end with the police saving the day. The police did all this to me, and I was *one of them* – I can only imagine *your* stories. But never forget, the best retaliation for prejudice and hate is success.

As I begin rebuilding my life after being forced out and the devastation that followed, and find a place where I can be at peace with this world, with who and what I am, and write the next chapter of my story, I say to all those fighting for a better world: never waver in your absolute belief that you can and will triumph.

I'm still asking you to believe – not in my ability to bring about change, but in yours. I believe in change because I believe in you.

Barack Obama

Acknowledgements

Thank you to my friend and cheerleader Jonathan Cooper, international human rights barrister, for introducing me to Laura Barber, deputy publishing director at Granta Books. I am indebted to Laura for believing in me and my story, for being so kind to and supportive of me, and for introducing me to my wonderful literary agent and advocate-in-chief, Emma Paterson.

I read that an editor doesn't change the author into someone else, but helps them to become who they really are. To my dear friend Alice Kim, who checked over my manuscript in fine detail and brought it to life, thank you so much. To my truly exceptional editor at Granta who gently edited me, Ka Bradley (you're one of a kind and amazing), thank you very much.

Thank you, Gesche Ipsen – your copy-edit was simply outstanding and got me to think about the manuscript differently. You have made the book so much better. To the rest of the Granta team, including my publicist, Pru Rowlandson, and Christine Lo, managing editor, I'm thankful for the contribution you all have made. To Dan Mogford: thanks for the cover design, and your patient fine-tuning. *Forced Out* has truly been a team effort.

To friends who stuck around and those who encouraged me to keep on writing the book when I wanted to give up, often, especially Stephe, thank you also. Thanks to Chris, for reading over the initial manuscript. Yaz, thank you very much for your support and encouragement during the final stages.

Thanks to my MP, Emily Thornberry, and Councillor Claudia Webbe, for never wavering in your support of me and for furthering black, gay and mental health rights.

Special thanks to Lucy, nurse practitioner at the NHS: you saw the depression, thus enabling me to fight it. Thanks to my GPs for being empathetic healthcare professionals. Thank you so much to my psychologists, Izzy and Kirsty, for listening to and helping me.

To my counsellors, Sonia and David, thank you both for your help and support, and counsellor Ruth, because of you and your kindness, support and overwhelming empathy for me and my mental health and belief in me as a person, I'm here today with this story of hope.

X

Notes

1. Against All Odds

1. For more on this, see 'Riots erupt in Toxteth and Peckham', *BBC News*, 1 October 1985 (http://news.bbc.co.uk/onthisday/hi/dates/stories/october/1/newsid_2486000/2486315.stm).
2. 'Toxteth riots: Howe proposed "managed decline" for city', *BBC News*, 30 December 2011 (https://www.bbc.co.uk/news/uk-england-merseyside-16355281).
3. Hansard, HC vol 18, col 744 (23 February 1982).
4. 'The Report of the Hillsborough Independent Panel', 12 September 2012.
5. 'Video nasty', Andy Byrne, *Liverpool Echo*, 24 September 1987.
6. Letter from John Walsh, St John Ambulance, 6 May 1996.
7. Letter from James Egan, St John Ambulance, 3 January 1996.
8. 'Windsor Scoop!', Jayne Atherton, *Liverpool Echo*, 2 June 1998.
9. See 'Stephen Lawrence: Gary Dobson and David Norris get life', *BBC News*, 4 January 2012 (https://www.bbc.co.uk/news/uk-16403655).
10. 'Report of an inquiry by Sir William McPherson of Cluny', The Stephen Lawrence Inquiry, 24 February 1999.
11. 'Linda Bethel's evidence to the Lawrence inquiry', *The Guardian*, 30 January 1999.
12. 'Sky's the limit for star talent', Barry Turnbull, *Liverpool Echo*, 22 February 1996.
13. 'Black officers tell of police racism', *BBC News*, 25 September 1998.
14. 'Police chief admits to racism in ranks', Kathy Marks, *The Independent*, 14 October 1998.

15. 'Application Form for Appointment as a Constable in the Police Service of England and Wales', KM, 20 April 2001.
16. Letter from GMP, 16 November 2001.

2. One of Them

1. 'Compensation but no police apology', Kevin Core, *Mersey Mart*, 13 November 2003.

3. Ways and Means

1. 'Shocking', Don Frame, *Manchester Evening News*, 18 August 2003.
2. 'Police union hits back', Neal Snowdon, *Manchester Evening News*, 19 August 2003.
3. 'Good Work Minute', divisional commander, GMP, 2002.
4. Letter to author (KM), 1 December 2002.
5. 'Scandal of the bogus crime figures', Sarah Lester and Lisa Roland, *Manchester Evening News*, 3 December 2002.
6. 'Operational move – Wigan DHQ to Bootle Street DHQ', 27 September 2002.
7. Letter from divisional chief superintendent, GMP, 3 October 2002.
8. Crime record, KM, GMP, 30 July 2002.

4. Pride and Prejudice

1. 'Sikh officer sent hate mail', *BBC News*, 3 March 2000 (http://news.bbc.co.uk/1/hi/uk/665598.stm); and see 'Gurpal Virdi: "I'm more of a fighter now"', Simon Hattenstone, *The Guardian*, 14 January 2002.
2. 'Sikh officer fired for race hate mail', Nick Hopkins, *The Guardian*, 4 March 2000.
3. 'Gurpal Virdi', Hattenstone, *The Guardian*.
4. 'Asian police officer: the Met set out to destroy me', Ben Leapman, *Evening Standard*, 3 June 2004.
5. 'A new force: part one', Simon Hattenstone, *The Guardian*, 20 March 2004.
6. 'Met Police still "racist"', *BBC News*, 22 April 2003 (http://news.bbc.co.uk/1/hi/england/london/2965475.stm).
7. 'First black chief constable welcomed', *BBC News*, 27 September

2003 (http://news.bbc.co.uk/1/hi/england/kent/3145826.stm).

8. 'Darcus Howe won't celebrate a black chief constable', Darcus Howe, *New Statesman*, 6 October 2003.

9. 'UK's first black chief constable appointed', Syreeta Lund, *Police Review*, 3 October 2003.

10. *Kill the Black One First*, Michael Fuller (London, 535 Books, 2019), p.257.

11. 'Black detective backs GMP', *Manchester Evening News*, 22 October 2003.

12. 'Scandal of Nazi police', John Chapman, *Daily Express*, 3 November 2003.

13. 'Call to sack Anderton after flogging remark', *Glasgow Herald*, 14 December 1987.

14. 'Black and minority ethnic youth unemployment "rose by 50% under the coalition"', Anna Leszkiewicz, *New Statesman*, 11 March 2015.

15. 'Police assault inquiry begins', *BBC News*, 21 February 2004 (http://news.bbc.co.uk/1/hi/england/manchester/3508037.stm).

16. 'Policeman puts the boot in', Stan Miller and Blaise Tapp, *Manchester Evening News*, 20 February 2004.

17. 'Policeman's kicks caught on video', *Manchester Evening News*, 13 August 2004.

18. 'Outrage', Nicola Dowling, *Manchester Evening News*, 21 February 2004.

19. 'Policeman puts the boot in', *Manchester Evening News*.

20. 'PCA to investigate police "attack"', *Daily Telegraph*, 20 February 2004.

21. 'No charges for policeman who kicked suspect', Nigel Bunyan, *Daily Telegraph*, 9 August 2005.

22. *LA 92*, dir. Daniel Lindsay and T. J. Martin, National Geographic Channel, 2017.

23. 'Policemen who attacked teen suspect are jailed', Fred Attewill, *Metro*, 9 April 2010.

24. 'Jail for PC who assaulted teen', Chris Osuh, *Manchester Evening News*, 28 April 2010.

25. 'Skull threat Greater Manchester PC faces hearing', *BBC News*, 12 March 2010 (http://news.bbc.co.uk/1/hi/england/manchester/8564131.stm).

26. Letter from divisional commander, GMP, 21 May 2003.

27. Report from inspector, GMP, 9 April 2003.
28. Memo from sub-divisional chief inspector, GMP, 17 April 2003.
29. Note from chief superintendent, GMP, 22 April 2003.

5. The Secret Policeman

1. *The Secret Policeman*, dir. Toby Sculthorp, BBC, 2003.
2. 'My life as a secret policeman', Mark Daly, *BBC News*, 21 October 2003 http://news.bbc.co.uk/1/hi/magazine/3210614. stm).
3. 'Senior officers agree plan to tackle racism', Helen Carter, *The Guardian*, 24 October 2003.
4. 'Pictures that shame police', Paul Gallagher, *Manchester Evening News*, 18 October 2003.
5. 'Police race shame is exposed by secret BBC film', Andrew Nott, *Manchester Evening News*, 22 October 2003. All quotes from the documentary can be found in the 'Transcript from BBC's "Secret Policeman" documentary', available at http://www.ligali.org/ pdf/bbc_transcript_secret_policeman.pdf.
6. Memo from Michael Todd, GMP, 18 August 2003.
7. Letter from GMP, 22 January 2004.
8. 'Four quit in police race shame', *Manchester Evening News*, 12 August 2004.
9. 'Anger of top cop', *Manchester Evening News*, 12 August 2004.
10. 'The Report of the Morris Inquiry', Metropolitan Police Authority, 2004.
11. 'Anger of top cop', *Manchester Evening News*.
12. 'I earned respect by rising above racism for 20 years', Tony Chana, *Police Review*, 31 October 2003.
13. Letter from divisional training sergeant, GMP, 12 November 2003.
14. Letter from Justine Curran, GMP, 24 June 2004.
15. 'Good Work Minute', divisional commander, GMP, 2004.
16. Bonus award notification, GMP, 12 October 2004.
17. 'Performance Appraisal (Annual)', GMP, 31 March 2004.
18. Email from inspector, GMP, 20 December 2004.
19. Report, 'Psychological Assessment for Undercover Training', Felicity Gibling (Adept Psychology), 18 January 2005.
20. Letter from National Undercover Training Selection Board, MPS, 9 May 2005.

21. 'Black cop wins case – but his tormentors are promoted', Lester Holloway, Black Information Link, 11 April 2005.
22. Reserved Judgment in case of *Charles Crichlow v Chief Constable of GMP*, 2005, Employment Tribunals.
23. 'Black cop wins case', Black Information Link.
24. Ibid.
25. Ibid.
26. Ibid.
27. Memo re: recognition of good performance, GMP, 26 April 2005.
28. 'Crime in England and Wales 2004/2005', Home Office Statistical Bulletin, July 2005.
29. Email from GMP, 13 May 2005.
30. 'Performance Appraisal (Interim)', GMP, 3 March 2005.

6. Shock and Awe

1.   'Surge in stop and search of Asian people after July 7', Vikram Dodd, *The Guardian*, 24 December 2005.
2.   'The fall and fall of Sir Ian Blair', Sandra Laville, *The Guardian*, 2 October 2008.
3.   'De Menezes family: Met claims were "sickening"', Richard Edwards, *Daily Telegraph*, 1 November 2007.
4.   See 'Stockwell One: Investigation Into the Shooting of Jean Charles de Menezes at Stockwell Underground Station on 22 July 2005', IPCC (available at http://news.bbc.co.uk/1/shared/bsp/hi/pdfs/08_11_07_stockwell1.pdf).
5.   'De Menezes: Met guilty of serious failings', Richard Holt, *Daily Telegraph*, 2 August 2007.
6.   'Dangerous, draconian, illiberal and unnecessary', *The Independent*, 9 November 2005.
7.   Email from tutor unit sergeant, GMP, 11 October 2005
8.   'Performance Appraisal (Annual)', GMP, 28 November 2005.
9.   Letter from chief superintendent, GMP, 15 December 2005.
10. 'End of an Era', North Manchester division newsletter, GMP, 2006.
11. 'Grievance Form', KM, GMP, 31 August 2006.
12. 'Good Work Minute', divisional commander, GMP, 2006.
13. 'Cheers for the cops', Yakub Qureshi, *Manchester Evening News*, 10 August 2006.

14. 'Prejudice blighted my hopes over job, claims top policeman', *Manchester Evening News*, 8 August 2006.
15. 'Police Federation discriminated against own member, tribunal finds', Vikram Dodd, *The Guardian*, 2 October 2006.
16. Ibid.
17. 'Ex Cleveland PC Sultan Alam awarded £400,000 damages', *BBC News*, 26 January 2012 (https://www.bbc.co.uk/news/uk-england-tees-16733616).
18. 'Police in new race storm', Nicola Dowling, *Manchester Evening News*, 14 November 2003.
19. Email from tutor unit sergeant, GMP, 4 October 2006.
20. Email from career development unit, GMP, 2 October 2006.
21. 'Grievance Report', KM, GMP, 7 February 2007.
22. Letter from chief superintendent, GMP, 22 December 2006.
23. Email from senior assistant HR director, GMP, 16 February 2007.
24. Email from senior assistant HR director, GMP, 22 February 2007.
25. Note from senior assistant HR director, GMP, 14 March 2007.
26. Memo from internal affairs chief inspector, GMP, 8 March 2007.

7. Divide and Rule

1. 'Top black woman cop in deal over bias case', Brian Lashley, *Manchester Evening News*, 20 October 2004.
2. 'WPC wins five-figure payout for sex slurs at college', Stephen Wright, *Daily Mail*, 15 June 2007.
3. Email from detective inspector, GMP, 31 October 2007.
4. 'Certificate of Excellent Attendance', GMP, 31 March 2008.
5. Report from programme tutor, GMP, 21 April 2008.
6. 'Campaigner in police attack claim', *BBC News*, 7 May 2008 (http://news.bbc.co.uk/1/hi/england/manchester/7388620.stm).
7. 'Manchester community reacts with anger as police cleared of violence', Martin Wainwright, *The Guardian*, 2 September 2010.
8. Ibid.

8. Last-Ditch Attempt

1. 'Performance Development Review (Mid Year)', MPS, 31 October 2008.
2. MPS HR record, 27 October 2008.
3. Email from KM, 18 November 2008.

4. Email from SO15 HR manager, MPS, 19 November 2008.
5. Email from SO15 HR manager, MPS, 19 November 2008.
6. '101,248 people stopped . . . but no terror arrests', Martin Bentham, *Evening Standard*, 28 October 2010.
7. 'Code of Practice for Examining Officers under the Terrorism Act 2000', Home Office, 2001.
8. Ibid.
9. 'Examining Officers under the Terrorism Act 2000, Code of Practice', Home Office, 2009 (https://assets.publishing.service. gov.uk/government/uploads/system/uploads/attachment_data/ file/143819/Code-of-Practice-for-Examin1.pdf).
10. 'Darkening of a nation', Nick Cohen, *The Observer*, 26 October 2003.
11. 'Terrorism Act 2000 Code of Practice', Home Office, 2009.
12. 'David Miranda row: what is Schedule 7?', *BBC News*, 19 August 2013 (https://www.bbc.co.uk/news/uk-23757133). See also 'Review of the Operation of Schedule 7: A Public Consultation', Home Office, September 2012 (https://assets.publishing.service. gov.uk/government/uploads/system/uploads/attachment_data/ file/157896/consultation-document.pdf).
13. Email from KM to SO15 recruitment, 21 November 2008.
14. 'Gordon Brown: 75% of UK terror plots originate in Pakistan', Gaby Hinsliff, *The Guardian*, 14 December 2008.
15. 'Performance Development Review (Annual)', MPS, 31 March 2009.
16. Email from Nigel Quantrell, MPS, 27 February 2009.
17. *Line of Fire*, Brian Paddick (London: Simon & Schuster, 2008), p. 58 and viii.
18. 'The numbers in black and white: ethnic disparities in the policing and prosecution of drug offences in England and Wales', Release, 2019 (https://www.release.org.uk/publications/ numbers-black-and-white-ethnic-disparities-policing-and- prosecution-drug-offences). See also 'Police less likely to find drugs on black people during stop and search', Damien Gayle, *The Guardian*, 13 December 2017.

9. Fight or Flight

1. Note in Official Pocket Book, acting superintendent, MPS, 27 July 2009.

2. 'Occupational Health Referral Form', MPS, 5 August 2009.
3. Email from sergeant, MPS, 26 August 2009.
4. Email from Nigel Quantrell, 27 August 2009.
5. 'Attendance Management Standard Operating Procedure', MPS, 20 May 2009.
6. Email from Nigel Quantrell, MPS, 17 September 2009.
7. Contact log entry, Nigel Quantrell, MPS, 21 September 2009.
8. Notes re: meeting from Nigel Quantrell, MPS, 1 October 2009.
9. Email from Nigel Quantrell to GMP, MPS, 20 October 2009.
10. Email from Police Federation representative, 14 October 2009.
11. Minutes re: case conference, MPS, 14 October 2009.
12. Letter from MPS, 14 October 2009.
13. Note from Nigel Quantrell, MPS, 17 September 2009.
14. Contact diary of KM, 23 October 2009.
15. List of telephone numbers, MPS, 27 October 2009.
16. Actions log, Nigel Quantrell, MPS, 20 October 2009.
17. Memo from Nigel Quantrell, MPS, 2 November 2009.
18. Email from SO15 HR manager, MPS, 10 November 2009.
19. Email from Nigel Quantrell, MPS, 6 November 2009.
20. Email from Raffaele D'Orsi, MPS, 6 November 2009.
21. Letter from sergeant, MPS, 19 November 2009.
22. Letter from sergeant, MPS, 20 December 2009.
23. 'Race row policeman Tarique Ghaffur told to "shut up" and get on with his job', Sean O'Neill, *The Times*, 29 August 2008.
24. 'Police played "spot the black officer in the dark", tribunal hears', Vikram Dodd, *The Guardian*, 2 March 2009.
25. Email from Police Federation representative, 19 November 2009.
26. Report, 'Significant People Issues', MPS, 13 November 2009.
27. Email from sergeant, MPS, 8 December 2009.
28. 'Medical Officer/OHA Recommendations Form', Celia Palmer, MPS, 23 November 2009.
29. Occupational Health 'access forms', MPS, 12 November 2009 and 23 November 2009.
30. Letter from sergeant, MPS, 14 December 2009.
31. Letter from Police Federation representative, 16 December 2009.
32. 'Regulation 28, Police Regulations 2003: Consideration of Sick Pay Form', Rose Fitzpatrick, MPS, 9 December 2009.
33. 'Deputy chief constable at centre of expenses controversy set to retire', Chris Marshall, *The Scotsman*, 28 February 2018.

34. Email from KM, 18 December 2009.
35. Email from HR5 [part of People Development] to deputy HR manager, MPS, 25 November 2009.
36. Report from Robert Oxlade, MPS, 20 November 2009.
37. 'Fairness At Work Standard Operating Procedure', MPS, 25 July 2007.
38. 'Attendance Management Standard Operating Procedure', MPS, 20 May 2009.
39. Email from KM, 24 November 2009.
40. Letter from Mayor of London's Office, 18 January 2010.
41. Email from KM, 24 November 2009.
42. Email from IPCC, 24 November 2009.
43. Email from KM, 24 November 2009.
44. Letter from Home Office, 15 December 2009.
45. Letter from KM, 30 October 2009.
46. 'Not so clever, Trevor', Joseph Harker, *The Guardian*, 19 January 2009.
47. 'Race and Faith Inquiry Report', MPA, July 2010.
48. Email from KM, 4 January 2010.
49. Email from detective chief superintendent, MPS, 6 January 2010.
50. Email from Police Federation representative, 6 January 2010.
51. Email from Nathan Crinyion, MPS, 21 January 2010.
52. Email from Nathan Crinyion to police lawyer and head of Special Branch, MPS, 22 January 2010.
53. Memo re: SO15 staff meeting, Dee Caryl, MPS, 5 October 2009.
54. Minutes re: gold group, MPS, 11 November 2009.
55. Minutes re: gold group meeting, MPS, 25 November 2009.
56. 'Ali Dizaei trial witness "betrayed" by deportation ruling', Nick Beake, *BBC News*, 5 April 2016 (https://www.bbc.co.uk/news/uk-england-london-35964057).
57. 'Ali Dizaei "was investigated as though he was an enemy of state"', Vikram Dodd, *The Guardian*, 8 February 2010.
58. 'Scotland Yard pays 14 bosses more than the prime minister', Justin Davenport, Mark Blunden and Anthony Kimber, *Evening Standard*, 25 August 2011.
59. Letter from Eileen Cahill-Canning, MPS, 29 January 2010.
60. Memo from Eileen Cahill-Canning, MPS, 17 June 2010.
61. Minutes re: gold group meeting, MPS, 19 January 2010.
62. Email from KM to Raffaele D'Orsi et al, 4 March 2010.

63. Email from Arpita Dutt, Russell Jones & Walker (RJW), 12 March 2010.
64. Email from KM, 12 March 2010.
65. Letter from Police Federation, 29 March 2010.
66. 'Met faces another claim of racism', Justin Davenport, *Evening Standard*, 7 May 2010.
67. Respectively under Sections 1(1)(a) and 4(2), Race Relations Act 1976; Regulations 3(1)(a) and 6(1), Employment Equality (Sexual Orientation) Regulations 2003; Section 3A, Race Relations Act 1976; Regulation 5, Employment Equality (Sexual Orientation) Regulations 2003; Section 2, Race Relations Act 1976; and Regulation 4, Employment Equality (Sexual Orientation) Regulations 2003.
68. Section 76 of the Race Relations Act 1976 and Regulation 11 of the Employment Equality (Sexual Orientation) Regulations 2003.
69. 'Details of Claim form (ET1)', RJW, 14 May 2010.

10. Dirty Tricks Campaign

1. Letter from ET, 17 May 2010.
2. Email from welfare officer, MPS, 24 May 2010.
3. Email from Nathan Crinyion, MPS, 28 May 2010.
4. Letter from Jacqueline Morris, MPS, 11 June 2010.
5. Letter from Jacqueline Morris, MPS, 17 June 2010.
6. Email from Nathan Crinyion, MPS, 25 June 2010.
7. Email from Nathan Crinyion, MPS, 5 July 2010.
8. Email from Nathan Crinyion, MPS, 19 July 2010.
9. 'Briefing re: DC Kevin Maxwell', detective chief superintendent, MPS, 22 January 2010.
10. Met–GPA Facebook page, posted on 14 September 2009.
11. 'Shocking survey finds racism is endemic among gay men', Benjamin Butterworth, *Pink News*, 23 May 2017.
12. 'Hanged gay WPC left note', Mike Sullivan and Nick Parker, *The Sun*, 17 June 2010.
13. 'Airport's armed police "used radios to rate sexy women"', Caroline Gammell, *Daily Telegraph*, 15 June 2010.
14. Email from KM, 7 July 2010.
15. Email from Arpita Dutt, RJW, 7 July 2010.
16. Email from KM, 7 July 2010.

17. Email from Raffaele D'Orsi, MPS, 14 July 2010.
18. Email from KM, 14 July 2010.
19. Email from Raffaele D'Orsi, MPS, 14 July 2010.
20. Email from Raffaele D'Orsi, MPS, 22 July 2010.
21. Email from Terry O'Connor, MPS, 6 July 2010.
22. Email from Terry O'Connor to Raffaele D'Orsi et al., MPS, 4 July 2010.
23. Letter from KM, 22 July 2010.
24. Email from welfare officer, MPS, 24 July 2010.
25. Email from Raffaele D'Orsi to welfare officer, MPS, 23 July 2010.
26. Email from Alex Fedorcio to Raffaele D'Orsi, MPS, 23 July 2010.
27. Email from Press Bureau officer, MPS, 24 July 2010.
28. Email from Alex Fedorcio, MPS, 23 July 2010.
29. Email from KM, 25 July 2010.
30. Email from KM, 25 July 2010.
31. Email from Police Federation representative, 25 July 2010.
32. Email from IPCC with KM statement, 25 July 2010.
33. Email from Arpita Dutt, RJW, 27 July 2010.
34. Email from acting superintendent, Special Branch, MPS, 23 July 2010.
35. Email from Martin Tiplady, MPS, 27 July 2010.
36. Email from Martin Tiplady, MPS, 6 August 2010.
37. Notes from KM's partner re: details of conversations with Mike Sunman and Chris Le Pere, 27 July 2010.
38. Letter from RJW, 26 July 2010.
39. Letter from RJW, 27 July 2010.
40. Letter from Raffaele D'Orsi, MPS, 10 August 2010.
41. 'How do the UPP/Attendance Regulations work?', Police Federation, 1 December 2008.
42. Letter from Police Federation representative, 13 September 2010.
43. 'Grounds of Resistance', Philip Mead, MPS, 13 August 2010.
44. 'Notice of Pre-Hearing Review', ET, 18 August 2010.
45. Letter from Mike Sunman, MPS, 23 August 2010.
46. Letter from Victoria Wright, IPCC, 11 November 2010.
47. Minutes re: gold group meeting, MPS, 15 September 2010.
48. Letter to KM from Raffaele D'Orsi, MPS, 4 October 2010.

49. Minutes re: meeting with KM, Raffaele D'Orsi, MPS, 3 November 2010.
50. 'Details of Claim Form (ET1)', RJW, 21 October 2010.
51. 'Questionnaire of Person Aggrieved', RJW, 10 November 2010.
52. 'Answers to Questionnaire', MPS, 10 June 2011.
53. 'Being LGB', KM, *Outnorthwest*, no. 100, October–November 2010.
54. Letter from GP, 19 November 2010.
55. 'Medical Report Form', Paul Obiamiwe, Department for Work and Pensions, 27 June 2010.
56. Letter from KM, 6 December 2010.
57. Letter from Emily Thornberry to KM, 15 February 2011.
58. Email from Chris Haan, RJW, 1 December 2010.
59. Report of Charles Hindler, 25 November 2010.
60. 'Summary of Events', St Charles Mental Health Centre, 4 December 2010.
61. See profiles on Priory Group website (https://www.priorygroup.com/consultants/dr-charles-hindler) and LinkedIn (https://uk.linkedin.com/in/charles-hindler-5614a210); his BMI Healthcare page is no longer active, but see his Bupa page https://finder.bupa.co.uk/Consultant/view/24951/dr_charles_hindler.
62. Email from KM, 2 December 2010.
63. Letter from GMC, 5 January 2016.
64. Judgment on Pre-Hearing Review, ET, 7 January 2011.
65. Email from welfare officer, 21 December 2010.

11. War of Attrition

1. Letter from ET, 19 April 2011.
2. Letter from Jacqueline Morris, MPS, 4 May 2011.
3. Letter to KM from Raffaele D'Orsi, MPS, 4 April 2011.
4. Letter from Police Federation representative, 12 April 2011, referring to Eileen Cahill-Canning's conclusion (memo re: KM, 9 February 2011).
5. Fixed Penalty Notice N98406833, MPS, 9 September 2010.
6. Email from Raffaele D'Orsi, MPS, 11 May 2011.
7. 'Asian people 42 times more likely to be held under terror law', Vikram Dodd, *The Guardian*, 23 May 2011.
8. 'Terrorism Act:"They asked me to keep an eye on the Muslim

community"",Vikram Dodd, *The Guardian*, 23 May 2011.

9. 'Business as usual for police racists', Claudia Webbe, *The Guardian*, 9 October 2008.

10. 'The Secret Policeman Returns', *Panorama*, BBC, 6 October 2008.

11. Email from Police Federation representative, 12 June 2011.

12. Letter,'First Stage Unsatisfactory Police Performance and Attendance Procedures (UPP/A) Appeal',Terry O'Connor, MPS, 6 July 2011.

13. Minutes re: appeal against UPP process meeting meeting, MPS, 6 July 2011.

14. Agenda re: gold group meeting, MPS, 1 February 2011.

15. Minutes re: Stage 2 UPP meeting, MPS, 2 September 2011.

16. Email from Police Federation representative, 2 September 2011.

17. 'Those senior Met Police lunches and dinners with News International', *The Guardian*, 13 July 2011.

18. 'Phone hacking: John Yates has no plans to resign', Mark Hughes, *Daily Telegraph*, 12 July 2011 (https://www.telegraph.co.uk/news/uknews/phone-hacking/8633527/Phone-hacking-John-Yates-has-no-plans-to-resign.html).

19. 'The Met commissioner and the Wolfman of Fleet Street', Mark Hughes, *Daily Telegraph*, 15 July 2011.

20. 'IPCC: John Yates showed "poor judgment" in assisting Neil Wallis's daughter', Martin Evans, *Daily Telegraph*, 13 April 2012.

21. 'Met chief faces questions over spa stay', Juliette Garside, *The Guardian*, 17 July 2011.

22. Reported on his Twitter feed @RhonddaBryant, 16 July 2011 (https://twitter.com/RhonddaBryant/status/92348232511918080).

23. 'John Yates quits Met Police amid phone-hacking scandal', *BBC News*, 18 July 2011 (https://www.bbc.co.uk/news/uk-14181344).

24. 'Met's PR chief Dick Fedorcio resigns after force begins disciplinary action', Sandra Laville, *The Guardian*, 29 March 2012.

25. Email from IPCC, 29 July 2011.

26. Email from Special Branch superintendent to commander Shaun Sawyer, MPS, 17 November 2009.

27. *The Ports Monkey Times*, Metropolitan Police (n.d., copies received 21 September 2011).

28. Letter from RJW to Jacqueline Morris, 7 September 2011.
29. Minutes re: gold group meeting, MPS, 5 July 2010.
30. Minutes re: appeal against UPP process meeting, MPS, 6 July 2011.
31. Gold group meeting, 5 July 2010.
32. Contact log, Welfare Officer, MPS, 26 July 2010.
33. Email from Simon Cuthbert, RJW, 27 September 2011.

12. Trial and Retribution

1. 'Terror checks at Heathrow were racist, claims officer', *Daily Telegraph*, 7 October 2011.
2. 'Heathrow counter-terrorism officers "were racist": former detective suing Met says passengers with Arabic names targeted', *Daily Mail*, 8 October 2011.
3. 'Yates of the yard was "racist and homophobic" in dealing with officer off sick with depression, tribunal hears', *Daily Mail*, 27 October 2011.
4. Email from Police Federation representative, 4 October 2011.
5. Email from Arpita Dutt, RJW, 3 June 2011.
6. '"Disgusted" parents reject Met's offer of £15,000 compensation for dead son', Severin Carrell, *The Independent*, 21 August 2005.
7. 'Phone hacking: John Yates "still working for Met Police"', *BBC News*, 3 October 2011.
8. *The Terrorist Hunters*, Andy Hayman with Margaret Gilmore (London: Bantam Press, 2009).
9. Document re: meeting with Nathan Crinyion, Nigel Quantrell, MPS, 2 October 2009.
10. 'Man arrested over alleged police payments named as *Sun* journalist', Lisa O'Carroll, *The Guardian*, 4 November 2011.
11. Email from Tom Symonds, BBC, 17 January 2013.
12. 'Operation Elveden: three arrested in Hertfordshire and Surrey', *BBC News*, 17 January 2013 (https://www.bbc.co.uk/news/uk-21058379).
13. '*Sun* reporter Anthony France was "given" police contact and told: "I've spoken to a lawyer and it's fine"', *Press Gazette*, 19 May 2015.
14. '*Sun* journalist wins challenge over Operation Elveden conviction', Jasper Jackson, *The Guardian*, 27 October 2016.
15. 'Stephen Lawrence verdict: statements from Doreen and Neville Lawrence', *The Guardian*, 3 January 2012.

16. 'So where are all the black police officers?', Richard Stone, *The Guardian*, 4 January 2012.

17. Letter from KM, 1 December 2011.

18. Letter from Terry O'Connor, MPS, 9 December 2011.

19. Memo from Eileen Cahill-Canning, MPS, 3 January 2012.

20. Email from Eileen Cahill-Canning, MPS, 3 January 2012.

21. Minutes re: gold group meeting, MPS, 9 December 2011.

22. Email from Melanie Bailey, MPS, 5 January 2012.

23. Email to Melanie Bailey from Karen Yearley, MPS, 18 December 2009.

24. Minutes re: welcome meeting, MPS, 11 January 2012.

25. Email from Melanie Bailey, MPS, 27 January 2012.

26. Reserved Judgment, ET, 15 February 2012.

27. 'Met officer Kevin Maxwell wins discrimination case', *BBC News*, 20 February 2012 (https://www.bbc.co.uk/news/uk-england-london-17105019).

28. 'Gay black police officer wins discrimination case', Ben Quinn, *The Guardian*, 20 February 2012.

29. 'Met Police leaked gay officer's abuse case to tabloid, rules tribunal', Mark Hughes, *Daily Telegraph*, 21 February 2012.

30. 'Racist, homophobic colleagues "violated Met officer's dignity"', Benedict Moore-Bridger, *Evening Standard*, 21 February 2012.

31. 'Met officer wins discrimination case, *The Voice*, 23 February 2012.

32. 'Gay police officer wins racial and sexual orientation discrimination case against Scotland Yard', Peter Lloyd, *Pink Paper*, 21 February 2012.

33. 'Tribunal win for gay black policeman', Sean O'Neill, *The Times*, 21 February 2012.

34. 'Apologise to Bullied Cop', Andrew Johnson and Pavan Amara, *Islington Tribune*, 24 February 2012.

35. Letter from Claudia Webbe, Islington Council, 21 February 2012.

36. 'Apologise to Bullied Cop', *Islington Tribune*.

37. 'Met officer Kevin Maxwell wins discrimination case', *BBC News*.

38. Email from Arpita Dutt, Stewarts Law, 21 February 2012.

39. Email from KM, 22 February 2012.

40. Email to KM, 22 February 2012.

41. Letter from Larry Smith, MPS, 9 February 2012.

42. 'Notice of Appeal: *Commissioner of Police of the Metropolis v K. Maxwell*', Employment Appeal Tribunal (EAT) to RJW, 4 April 2012.

43. 'Answers to the Appeal re: *Commissioner of Police of the Metropolis v Kevin Maxwell*', RJW to EAT, 16 May 2012.

44. 'The Met is getting to grips with racism', *Evening Standard*, 13 April 2012.

45. 'I pledge to drive out Met racists', Justin Davenport, *Evening Standard*, 13 April 2012.

46. 'In the dock: just 2 cops lose their jobs out of 2,720 complaints of racism by Met officers', Tom Pettifor, *Daily Mirror*, 7 April 2012.

47. Email from Victoria Sill, BBC, 16 July 2012.

48. 'Police officer called black suspect "n★★★★★" during London riots, court hears', *Daily Telegraph*, 15 October 2012.

49. 'What happened to the Met I saw in black-and-white films?', Tom Foot, *West End Extra*, 9 March 2012.

50. 'Risk Assessment Form', Kieran Witherington, MPS, 25 April 2012.

51. 'Occupational Health Referral Form', Kieran Witherington, MPS, 23 April 2012.

52. 'Notice re: Guidelines to Serving and Former Officers and Staff Intending to Publish Memoirs of Their Police Service Experiences', given to KM in 2012 by Kieran Witherington, MPS.

53. Email from Karen Yearley, MPS, 9 May 2012.

54. Email from KM, 14 May 2012.

55. 'Fairness at Work Policy: Notification of Concern', MPS, 16 May 2012.

56. Email from Chris Burgess to KM, MPS, 23 June 2011.

57. Email from John Fisher, MPS, 7 June 2012.

58. Email from Mark Joncs, MPS, 2 July 2012.

59. Email from Kieran Witherington, MPS, 30 May 2012.

60. Agenda re: review, Kieran Witherington, MPS, 31 May 2012.

61. Email to Diana Hills (HR) from Eileen Cahill-Canning, MPS, 14 May 2012.

62. Email from Mark Jones, MPS, 7 June 2012.

63. Email from Eileen Cahill-Canning, MPS, 19 June 2012.

64. Minutes re: case conference, MPS, 12 June 2012.

65. Letter from Occupational Health, MPS, 13 June 2012.
66. Email from Melanie Bailey, MPS, 25 May 2012.
67. Report re: request for suspension, Melanie Bailey, MPS, 16 May 2012.
68. 'Report for Mr Bob Crawley HR5', Melanie Bailey, MPS, 29 May 2012.
69. Email from Pete Ward (Head of Compliance, Standards and Ethics, SO15), MPS, 8 June 2012.
70. Email from Karen Yearley, MPS, 30 May 2012.
71. Email from Diana Hills, MPS, 19 June 2012.
72. 'Report re: DC Kevin Maxwell', David Price, MPS, 22 June 2012.
73. Email from Mark Jones, MPS, 26 June 2012.
74. Email from Mark Jones, MPS, 28 June 2012.
75. Email from Mark Jones, MPS, 3 July 2012.
76. Email from KM to Mark Jones, 4 July 2012.
77. Email from Dr Eileen Cahill-Canning, MPS, 4 July 2012.
78. Letter re: 'Mr Kevin Maxwell', GP, 4 July 2012.
79. Email from Mark Jones, MPS, 5 July 2012.
80. Email from Eileen Cahill-Canning, MPS, 12 July 2012.
81. 'Notice of Alleged Breach of the Standards of Professional Behaviour', MPS, 13 July 2012.
82. Email from Mark Jones, MPS, 18 July 2012.
83. Letter from Kieran Witherington, MPS, 21 July 2012.
84. Email from Simon Cuthbert, RJW, 27 July 2012.
85. Email from KM, 3 August 2012.
86. 'Notice of Alleged Breach of the Standards of Professional Behaviour', MPS, 17 August 2012.
87. Email from Melanie Bailey, MPS, 23 July 2012.
88. Email from Diana Hills, MPS, 31 July 2012.
89. Email from Lesleyanne Ellis, MPS, 31 July 2012.
90. 'Former officer's fight for justice not an easy one', Syma Mohammed, *The Gazette*, 18 July 2013.
91. *My Fight for Justice*, KM, YouTube, 13 August 2012.
92. 'Development and Exclusivity Agreement', Maddy Allen, Keo Films, 22 August 2012.
93. Email re: skeleton argument from KM to EAT, 3 September 2012.
94. 'Order Document', EAT, 17 September 2012.
95. Email from Melanie Bailey, MPS, 19 September 2012.

96. Email from Nigel Foster, MPS, 20 September 2012.
97. Email from Kieran Witherington, MPS, 28 September 2012.
98. Email from KM, 19 October 2012.
99. Letter from Craig Mackey, MPS, 26 October 2012
100. Letter from Richard Walton, MPS, 15 November 2012.
101. Email from Richard Walton, MPS, 27 October 2012.
102. Email from McCue & Partners, 26 November 2012.
103. Report re: misconduct process, Lesleyanne Ellis, MPS, 17 November 2012.
104. Email from Ingrid Cruickshank, MPS, 17 November 2012.
105. Email from Courtenay Barklem, McCue & Partners, 10 December 2012.
106. 'Met sacks police officer who took on discrimination', Sean O'Neill and Fiona Hamilton, *The Times*, 18 December 2012.
107. Email from Richard Walton, MPS, 17 December 2012.
108. Terry McMillan, 'Introduction', in *By Any Means Necessary: Trials and Tribulations of the Making of* Malcolm X, Spike Lee and Ralph Wiley (New York: Hyperion, 1992).

13. Down and Out

1. Letter from Kieran Witherington, MPS, 18 December 2012.
2. Email from Melanie Bailey, MPS, 18 December 2012.
3. Property Receipt 1281849, MPS, 20 December 2012.
4. Email from McCue & Partners, 13 February 2013.
5. Email from Police Federation, 14 February 2013.
6. 'Acknowledgement of Claim', ET, 19 March 2013.
7. Reserved Judgment, ET, 15 February 2012.
8. Email from Kweku Aggrey-Orleans, 12 King's Bench Walk, 3 May 2013.
9. Judgment, EAT, 14 May 2013.
10. 'Yard found guilty of discrimination of gay, black officer', Sean O'Neill, *The Times*, 14 May 2013.
11. 'Gay black police officer was victimised, employment tribunal rules', Pavan Amara, *Islington Tribune*, 14 May 2013.
12. Claims upheld by the ET in 2012 and by the EAT in 2013.
13. Email to KM, 14 May 2013.
14. Email to KM, MPS, 17 May 2013.
15. 'Justice For Kevin – Court Ruling Highlights Police Racism & Homophobia', BPA, 15 May 2013 (https://www.nbpa.co.uk/

home/justice-for-kevin-court-ruling-highlights-police-racism).

16. Email from Charles Crichlow, BPA, 10 July 2013.

17. Email from KM to McCue & Partners including written message from Ruwan Uduwerage-Perera, Liberal Democrats, 17 October 2013.

18. 'Black and gay police officer hounded out "like enemy of state"', Vikram Dodd, *The Guardian*, 17 May 2013.

19. 'I didn't want to be the Met's gay poster boy', Sean O'Neill, *The Times*, 23 May 2013.

20. 'Met Police "tried to destroy" officer', *BBC News*, 22 May 2013.

21. *Upfront*, BBC Radio Merseyside, 26 May 2013.

22. *Victoria Derbyshire*, BBC Radio 5 Live, 28 May 2013.

23. Email to KM from Courtenay Barklem, McCue & Partners, 20 May 2013.

24. 'Summary of the Findings of the Reading Employment Tribunal in the First Claim', ET, 27 November 2014.

25. Statement re: Kevin Maxwell, MPS, 1 July 2013.

26. 'Report on Metropolitan Police Service Handling of Complaints Alleging Race Discrimination', Independent Police Complaints Commission, July 2013.

27. 'Police uphold just 1% of 7,963 public complaints of racism', Rob Evans, *The Guardian*, 15 June 2014.

28. 'Racism and the police: an insider's view', Hugh Muir, *The Guardian*, 29 July 2013.

29. 'Notice of Remedy Hearing', Employment Tribunals, 24 May 2013.

30. 'Written Evidence Submitted by Kevin Maxwell', Home Affairs Committee, House of Commons, July 2013.

31. 'I was meant to be the future. I ticked the diversity boxes', Paul Peachey, *The Independent*, 18 June 2013.

32. 'Notice of Case Management Discussion', ET, 5 June 2013.

33. Email to KM from Courtenay Barklem, McCue & Partners, 19 June 2013.

34. Order postponing the hearing, Employment Tribunals, 19 June 2013.

35. Letter from ET, 1 July 2013.

36. 'Case Management Discussion', ET, 22 July 2013.

37. 'Officer who challenged racism in police cleared of sexual assault charges', Vikram Dodd, *The Guardian*, 31 July 2015.

38. Email from Courtenay Barklem, McCue & Partners, 9 July 2013.
39. 'Independent Medical Report', David Gill, 10 September 2013.
40. 'Medical Records Release Form', KM, 16 August 2013.
41. 'Proving and Disproving Psychiatric Injury', David Gill, Hertfordshire Partnership NHS Foundation Trust, 25 September 2013.
42. Notes of meeting, Alice Kim, 25 September 2013.
43. 'Police under fire over arbitrary terror arrests at UK borders', Paul Peachey, *The Independent*, 24 August 2013.
44. 'David Miranda detention: Labour demands review of anti-terror powers', Rowena Mason, *The Guardian*, 19 August 2013.
45. 'Lord Neuberger: "Quick and dirty justice is better than the risk of no justice at all"', Martin Bentham, *Evening Standard*, 15 November 2013.
46. Letter from ET, 8 October 2013.
47. Letter from Jacqueline Morris, MPS, 1 October 2013.
48. Letter from Alice Kim, 23 October 2013.
49. Letter from Kevin Maxwell, 23 October 2013.
50. Letter from David Gill, 18 November 2013.
51. Email from KM, 19 November 2013.
52. Email from McCue & Partners, 22 November 2013.

14. Darkest Before Dawn

1. Letter from Deborah Glass, IPCC, 1 November 2013.
2. Letter from Commander Allan Gibson, Directorate of Professional Standards, MPS, 30 October 2013.
3. Email from KM, 18 October 2013.
4. Notes of hearing, Alice Kim, 26 November 2013.
5. 'Case Management Order', Employment Tribunals, 26 November 2013.
6. 'Notice of Outcome of Police Misconduct Hearing', MPS, 17 December 2012.
7. Letter from KM, 27 November 2013.
8. Letter from ET, 5 December 2013.
9. 'If we are to be able to trust the police, misconduct hearings must be out in the open', Paul Peachey, *The Independent*, 29 November 2013.
10. Letter from Binder Bansel, Pattinson & Brewer, 29 November 2013.

11. Email from Binder Bansel, Pattinson & Brewer, 11 December 2013.
12. Medical report, GP, 17 December 2013.
13. Letter to ET from Jacqueline Morris, MPS, 18 December 2013.
14. Email to KM from Binder Bansel, Pattinson & Brewer, 15 January 2014.
15. Minutes re: gold group meeting, MPS, 4 July 2012.
16. Report re: request for suspension, Melanie Bailey, MPS, 16 May 2012.
17. 'Schedule 7: New Figures Released by Home Office for 2010/11 Overview', Islamic Human Rights Commission, 17 October 2011 (https://www.ihrc.org.uk/publications/briefings/9897-schedule-7-new-figures-released-by-home-office-for-2010-11-overview).
18. Letter from James Brokenshire to Emily Thornberry, Home Office, 7 May 2014.
19. 'Inpatient Discharge Letter', Guy's and St Thomas's NHS Foundation Trust, 21 January 2014.
20. Letter from South London and Maudsley NHS Foundation Trust, 21 January 2014.
21. Letter from GP, 22 January 2014.
22. Letter from Binder Bansel, Pattinson & Brewer, 27 January 2014.
23. 'Case Management Orders', Employment Tribunals, 22 January 2014.
24. Email from Joanne Cameron, Pattinson & Brewer, 12 May 2014.
25. Notes of meeting, Stephe Meloy, 16 May 2014.
26. Email from Richard Walton, MPS, 17 December 2012.
27. 'Teenage thugs should face "harsher" prison sentences, Met Police chief Cressida Dick suggests', *Daily Telegraph*, 10 November 2017.
28. 'Stop and search in England and Wales', Full Fact, 24 June 2019 (https://fullfact.org/crime/stop-and-search-england-and-wales).
29. 'Do initiatives involving substantial increases in stop and search reduce crime? Assessing the impact of Operation BLUNT 2', Rhydian McCandless, Andy Feist, James Allan and Nick Morgan, Home Office, March 2016.
30. 'Black people "40 times more likely" to be stopped and searched in UK', Mark Townsend, *The Observer*, 4 May 2019.
31. Minutes re: gold group meeting, MPS, 10 January 2013.

32. '"Malicious" Met Must pay poster girl in race case', Justin Davenport, *Evening Standard*, 2 September 2014.

33. 'Former top gun cop Carol Howard quits Met after reaching final settlement in discrimination case', David Churchill and Robin de Peyer, *Evening Standard*, 14 February 2015.

34. Judgment, ET, 10 September 2014.

35. Email from KM to Kieran Witherington et al. re: meeting, 1 June 2012.

36. 'Case Management Orders', ET, 25 June 2014.

37. Judgment, ET, 18 March 2015.

38. 'The Lammy Review', 8 September 2017 (https://assets. publishing.service.gov.uk/government/uploads/system/uploads/ attachment_data/file/643001/lammy-review-final-report.pdf).

39. 'Racial bias in police stop and search getting worse, report reveals', Mark Townsend, *The Observer*, 13 October 2018.

40. 2014 figure; see 'Criminal Justice System Statistics', Institute of Race Relations (http://www.irr.org.uk/research/statistics/ criminal-justice).

41. 'Black people "three times more likely" to be tasered', Danny Shaw, *BBC News*, 13 October 2015 (https://www.bbc.co.uk/ news/uk-34511532).

42. 'Mental Health Act "needs major reform" as black patients four times as likely as whites to be sectioned', Alex Matthews-King, *The Independent*, 5 December 2018.

43. 'BAME deaths in police custody', Inquest (https://www.inquest. org.uk/bame-deaths-in-police-custody).

44. 'No charges for Scottish police over Sheku Bayoh death in custody', Severin Carrell, *The Guardian*, 3 October 2018.

45. 'Structural racism at heart of British society, UN human rights panel says', Damien Gayle, *The Guardian*, 27 April 2018.

46. 'Stop and search: Theresa May announces reform of police stop and search', Home Office, 30 April 2014 (https://www.gov.uk/ government/news/stop-and-search-theresa-may-announces- reform-of-police-stop-and-search).

47. 'Statement from the new Prime Minister Theresa May', Prime Minister's Office, 13 July 2016 (https://www.gov.uk/government/speeches/ statement-from-the-new-prime-minister-theresa-may).

48. 'More than half of children in custody are from ethnic

minorities for first time, probation report reveals',
Charles Hymas, *Daily Telegraph*, 14 October 2019
(https://www.telegraph.co.uk/politics/2019/10/14/
half-children-custody-ethnic-minorities-first-time-probation).

49. 'Scotland Yard chief Cressida Dick insists the Met Police is
no longer riddled with racism 20 years after the Macpherson
Report branded it "institutionally" prejudiced', Rebecca Camber,
Daily Mail, 10 July 2019.

50. 'Huge Rise In Live Terror Investigations Revealed After
Westminster Arrest', Rachel Wearmouth, *Huffington Post*, 14
August 2018.

51. Martin Luther King's letter from Birmingham jail, Alabama,
16 April 1963. *Oxford Essential Quotations*, 6th edition, edited
by Susan Radcliffe, 2018 (https://www.oxfordreference.com/
view/10.1093/acref/9780191866692.001.0001/q-oro-ed6-
00006293)

52. *I Know Why the Caged Bird Sings*, Maya Angelou (New York:
Random House, 1969).